CATULLAN QUESTIONS REVISITED

Catullan Questions Revisited offers a new insight into the brilliant poet who loved an aristocratic girl, attacked Julius Caesar and became a satirical playwright. Insisting on scrupulous use of the primary sources, Peter Wiseman combines textual, historical and even archaeological evidence to explode the orthodox view of Catullus' life and work. 'Lesbia' was not a woman in her thirties, as has been believed for 150 years, but a girl only recently married; Catullus' poems were written for performance, private or public, and it was only in 54 BC, at what he saw as the turning point of his life, that he collected their texts into a sequence of probably seven volumes. His subsequent literary career, equally successful but much less well attested, was as a 'mime'-dramatist. This book is intended for everyone who is interested in poetry and history, and who does not believe that literary texts exist in a vacuum.

T. P. WISEMAN is a professor emeritus in the Department of Classics and Ancient History at the University of Exeter. He has been a leading scholar of the political and social history of republican Rome for more than half a century and has a particular interest in social historical approaches to Catullus. His books include *Catullan Questions* (1969) and *Catullus and His World* (Cambridge, 1985).

CATULLAN QUESTIONS REVISITED

T. P. WISEMAN

University of Exeter

CAMBRIDGE
UNIVERSITY PRESS

CAMBRIDGE
UNIVERSITY PRESS

Shaftesbury Road, Cambridge CB2 8EA, United Kingdom

One Liberty Plaza, 20th Floor, New York, NY 10006, USA

477 Williamstown Road, Port Melbourne, VIC 3207, Australia

314–321, 3rd Floor, Plot 3, Splendor Forum, Jasola District Centre, New Delhi – 110025, India

103 Penang Road, #05–06/07, Visioncrest Commercial, Singapore 238467

Cambridge University Press is part of Cambridge University Press & Assessment, a department of the University of Cambridge.

We share the University's mission to contribute to society through the pursuit of education, learning and research at the highest international levels of excellence.

www.cambridge.org
Information on this title: www.cambridge.org/9781009235747

DOI: 10.1017/9781009235761

© T. P. Wiseman 2023

First published 2023

A catalogue record for this publication is available from the British Library.

Library of Congress Cataloging-in-Publication Data
NAMES: Wiseman, T. P. (Timothy Peter), author.
TITLE: Catullan questions revisited / T. P. Wiseman.
DESCRIPTION: Cambridge, United Kingdom : Cambridge University Press, 2022. | Includes bibliographical references and index.
IDENTIFIERS: LCCN 2022025730 (print) | LCCN 2022025731 (ebook) | ISBN 9781009235747 (hardback) | ISBN 9781009235716 (paperback) | ISBN 9781009235761 (epub)
SUBJECTS: LCSH: Catullus, Gaius Valerius. | Catullus, Gaius Valerius–In literature. | Elegiac poetry, Latin–History and criticism. | Love poetry, Latin–History and criticism.
CLASSIFICATION: LCC PA6276 .W542 2022 (print) | LCC PA6276 (ebook) | DDC 874/.01–dc23/eng/ 20220629
LC record available at https://lccn.loc.gov/2022025730
LC ebook record available at https://lccn.loc.gov/2022025731

ISBN 978-1-009-23574-7 Hardback

For Chris:
a poet for a poet

Contents

Figures

Preface

In 1968, with the youthful confidence appropriate to that year of revolution, I submitted to my local university press a short text entitled *Catullan Questions*. Their reader (Guy Lee, I was told) was gratifyingly generous about it, and the following year they published the book as an elegant 'slim volume'. The argument was in two parts, as explained on the back cover:

> The first half is designed to show that the order of poems in the collection as we have it, far from being the haphazard result of careless editing, is a deliberate and subtle arrangement which can scarcely be due to anyone but Catullus himself. In the second half the author suggests that the traditional chronology of Catullus' life and writings is inadequate and should be revised.

The reviewers were sceptical, but in the longer term the book attracted quite a lot of attention, and some of its conclusions have become, provisionally at least, part of a general consensus in Catullan studies. However, scholarship always moves on, and many subsequent contributions (including several second thoughts of my own) have variously endorsed, adjusted or rejected my ideas of half a century ago.[1]

What has brought me back to the subject now is the appearance in quick succession of two major works, utterly different in style and content, that offer new, elaborately argued and mutually incompatible solutions to the problem I tried to solve all those years ago. John K. Schafer's monograph *Catullus through His Books* proposes that the collection as we have it consists of 'three separate books of poems designed by the poet himself';[2] Ian Du Quesnay's long chapter in *The Cambridge Companion to Catullus* (of which he is co-editor), while agreeing that our collection is 'a compilation of *libelli* originally arranged and "distributed" by Catullus himself', identifies at least ten separate books.[3]

---

[1] The standard works of Catullan reference, through which details and bibliography can be pursued, are Thomson 1997, Skinner 2007, Skinner 2015, Du Quesnay and Woodman 2021. For systematic opposition to *Catullan Questions* and its influence, see Bellandi 2007.63–84.

[2] Schafer 2020.i (and back cover), cf. 3: poems 1–51, 61–64 and 65–116 as 'three authorially designed books'.

[3] Du Quesnay 2021.217–18: four in the polymetric short poems (2–14, 14b–26, 27–48, 49–60), two in the 'epigrams' (69–92, 93–115), with 61–64 consisting of four independent *libelli*. For 65–68b see Du Quesnay 2021.178, suggesting both that poem 68b 'was released to the public separately and

What sort of 'distribution' was involved? The answer in Schafer's book is an elusive one:[4]

> This work proposes, in broadest outline, that we can recover from the poems the overarching design for their mode of circulation on papyrus rolls. As this structural thesis develops, however, the work will also examine a series of related exegetical issues, the sum of whose conclusions amounts to a second global claim. That is, Catullus' design transforms how his poems read, above all by textually privileging their depictions of their own genesis and by inviting us to interrogate these depictions and their relation both to other Catullan texts and to purported extratextual realities.

It is a very stimulating work, coruscating with ideas,[5] and despite the author's disclaimers,[6] it involves empirical hypotheses that may in principle be tested against evidence and argument. I hope that by engaging with Schafer's work as well as Du Quesnay's – and applying neglected evidence from elsewhere – we may be able to gain a more precise historical sense of Catullus as a poet in his time.

The main argument of this book is in Part I, consisting of four Catullan questions to which I think new and interesting answers can now be given. Part II is more miscellaneous: detailed argument is provided on two complex but essential subjects, the ethnography of Catullus' native region and the nature of 'poem 64', followed by a piece from the archives on how the old view of Catullus' life story was told and retold in fiction. Unless otherwise stated, all translations are mine.

The first section of Chapter 1 was originally part of 'Texts and History: Reflections on Catullus, Cicero and Ovid', the Mary White Memorial Lecture given at Trinity College, University of Toronto, on 6 November 2007 (the full text is in *Pegasus* 51 [2008]: 8–20); Chapter 6, with the subtitle '*Liberior iocus* in Catullus 64', was first published in *Paideia* 73 (2018): 1123–65; and Chapter 7 in *Arion* n.s. 2 (1975): 96–115. I have done some minor editing here and there, put in a few extra footnotes, and added a short postscript to the final chapter.

I am very grateful to John Morgan, John Ramsey, Tony Woodman and the anonymous readers at Cambridge University Press for their comments and suggestions; remaining errors are my fault.

---

intended to fulfil its purpose as a separate *libellus*', and that 'Poems 65–68b may have first been gathered into a *libellus* soon after Catullus' death.'

[4] Schafer 2020.2, locating the subject 'at the seam between his poetry and his lived reality'.

[5] Some of them bizarre, and so described by the author (e.g. Schafer 2020.112).

[6] 'Answering this sort of Catullan question is in principle beyond this work's remit' (Schafer 2020.15).

PART I

CHAPTER I

Who Was Lesbia?

The title of *Catullan Questions* was an allusion to Ludwig Schwabe's *Quaestiones Catullianae* of 1862, which I wanted to refute.

It was Schwabe who created the story about Catullus that most classicists believed for most of the twentieth century: that 'Lesbia', the woman he loved and hated, was Clodia, wife of Quintus Metellus Celer; that he met her in Verona in 62 BC, when Metellus was proconsul of Cisalpine Gaul; that their adulterous affair continued in Rome, presumably in 61 and 60; that Clodia then threw him over for Marcus Caelius Rufus, whose relationship with her is dealt with so entertainingly in Cicero's *Pro Caelio*. By the time of Caelius' trial in April 56, that relationship was over; Catullus, meanwhile, had been away on Gaius Memmius' staff in Bithynia during 57, and returned to Italy some time in 56. According to the Schwabe scenario, Catullus attempted a reconciliation with the now disgraced Clodia, but in vain; she descended into utter promiscuity, and his final message of farewell, poem 11, is securely dated to 55 BC.

It's a seductive story, and what makes it so is the apparent compatibility of the two portraits, that of Lesbia in Catullus' poems and that of Clodia Metelli in Cicero's speech. Surely there couldn't be *two* such women in Rome? Well, of course there could. But we are told by Apuleius, who probably had good sources, that Lesbia's real name was Clodia. That would be a knock-down argument, were it not for the fact that Clodia Metelli had two sisters, also with adulterous reputations.[1] It seemed to me a reasonable inference that Lesbia was one of the three Clodiae, but (*pace* Schwabe) there was no way of telling which one.

---

[1] Apuleius *Apologia* 10; Cicero *Ad familiares* 1.9.15, Plutarch *Cicero* 29.4 (sisters); Wiseman 1969.49–55.

1.1 Schwabe Rides Again

My objection to the Schwabe scenario was (and is) that it's inconsistent with what we know about the date of Catullus' poems. There are about 115–120 poems or fragments of poems in the collection, and thirteen of them are internally datable:

poem 4	56 or after	Bithynia
poem 10	56 or after	Bithynia
poem 11	55 or after	Caesar in Britain
poem 28	56 or after	Memmius
poem 29	55 or after	Caesar in Britain
poem 31	56 or after	Bithynia
poem 35	after 59	Novum Comum[2]
poem 45	55 or after	campaigns to Syria and Britain
poem 46	56 or after	Bithynia
poem 52	56 or after	Vatinius 'consul'[3]
poem 53	56 or after	Calvus' speech In Vatinium[4]
poem 55	55 or after	Pompey's portico[5]
poem 113	55	Pompey's second consulship

That's a good proportion, about 11 per cent, and the consistency of the dates is very impressive. The empirical conclusion is inescapable: the poems belong to the middle fifties BC. Of course it is possible that some of the 103 or so undated poems are earlier or later, but positive arguments would be needed to establish an earlier or later date. The default position is 56–55 BC, and the onus of proof is on whoever proposes a different date.[6]

Schwabe's scenario dates the love affair with Lesbia to the late sixties. Lesbia's husband is mentioned in two of the poems, and Metellus Celer died in 59. Remarriage was normal in the Roman aristocracy, but we know from the *Pro Caelio* that his widow Clodia had *not* remarried by April 56.[7] We know nothing about the marital status of the other two sisters in the

---

[2] Founded in 59 BC (Suetonius *Diuus Iulius* 28.3).
[3] Cf. Cicero *In Vatinium* 6 (March 56 BC) for Vatinius' confidence of his future consulship.
[4] Cicero *Ad Q. fratrem* 2.4.1; see Section 2.5 below for the full argument.
[5] Attached to the theatre that was dedicated in 55 (Asconius 1C, Dio Cassius 39.38.1).
[6] Cf. Skinner 2011.133: 'if we assume, just for the sake of argument, that Wiseman's chronological premise is correct . . .' But the dates of the poems are not just a hypothesis you can take or leave.
[7] Cicero *Pro Caelio* 38 (*uidua*).

fifties BC, but the negative evidence we happen to have for Clodia Metelli makes her the *least* likely of the three to be 'Lesbia'.

One new argument I was able to offer in *Catullan Questions* concerned poem 36:[8]

> Volusius' *Annals*, shat-on pages, discharge a vow on my girl's behalf. For she vowed to holy Venus and to Cupid that if I were restored to her and stopped hurling fierce iambics, she'd give the choicest writings of the worst of poets to the lame-footed god, to be burned on ill-omened wood. Bad girl! She saw herself making this vow to the gods as an elegant joke.
>
> So now, o goddess born from the sky-blue sea, you who dwell in holy Idalium and open Urii and Ancona and reedy Cnidos and Amathus and Golgi and Dyrrachium, tavern of the Adriatic, make it that the vow is paid and received, if it's not lacking in elegance and charm. As for you, meanwhile, into the fire with you, full of clodhopping clumsiness, Volusius' *Annals*, shat-on pages.

The poem presupposes the love affair; we may infer a quarrel from line 4, but there is none of the bitterness and contempt found in the poems attributed to the late stages of the affair. When was it written? I suggested that the odd list of Venus's addresses in lines 12–15 might provide a *terminus post quem*.[9] Idalium, Amathus, Golgi and Cnidos were all known cult centres of Aphrodite; Dyrrachium, Urii and Ancona, on the other hand, were the three necessary ports of call for a ship sailing from Greece to Sirmio, as poems 4 and 31 show Catullus' vessel doing in the summer or autumn of 56 BC. I concluded that the poem was written after that date.

One of the supposed arguments in favour of the Schwabe scenario is the fact that two poems are addressed to a Caelius, and another two to a Rufus. But the combination of the two into the Marcus Caelius Rufus of the *Pro Caelio* won't work, because the Rufus poems (69 and 77) are hostile and the Caelius poems (58 and 100) are friendly. It remains possible that *either* the Rufus of the poems *or* the Caelius of the poems could be Caelius Rufus, but neither of those hypotheses is at all plausible.

---

[8] *Annales Volusi, cacata charta, | uotum soluite pro mea puella. | nam sanctae Veneri Cupidinique | uouit, si sibi restitutus essem, | electissima pessimi poetae | scripta tardipedi deo daturam | infelicibus ustulanda lignis. | et hoc pessima se puella uidit | iocose lepide uouere diuis. | nunc o caeruleo creata ponto, | quae sanctum Idalium Vriosque apertos | quaeque Ancona Cnidumque harundinosam | colis quaeque Amathunta quaeque Golgos | quaeque Durrachium Hadriae tabernam, | acceptum face redditumque uotum, | si non illepidum neque inuenustum est. | at uos interea uenite in ignem, | pleni ruris et inficetiarum | annales Volusi, cacata charta.*

[9] Wiseman 1969.42–5.

'Rufus' is a very common *cognomen*, and the man Catullus addresses by that name could be anyone; even with our limited information, we can immediately point to Caecilius Rufus, Egnatius Rufus, Herennius Rufus, Marcius Rufus, Mescinius Rufus, Messalla Rufus, Minucius Rufus, Numerius Rufus, Paquius Rufus, Pompeius Rufus, Pomponius Rufus, Quinctius Rufus, Sempronius Rufus, Sextilius Rufus, Titius Rufus, Tullius Rufus and Vibullius Rufus – and that's just counting senators.[10]

What about Caelius? Here are the two poems in which he features:[11]

> Caelius: my Lesbia, yes *Lesbia*, that Lesbia whom alone Catullus loved more than himself and all his kin, now on street-corners and down alleys peels the descendants of great-hearted Remus.
>
> Caelius and Quintius, the flower of Veronese youth, are dying for (respectively) Aufillenus and Aufillena, one for the brother, one for the sister. That really is what they call sweet fraternal comradeship. Whose side should I be on? Yours, Caelius; for your friendship alone was tried by fire at the time when the mad flame was burning my marrow. Be lucky, Caelius, and potent in love.

In poem 58, *Lesbia nostra* in line 1 is often translated '*our* Lesbia', as if it meant 'the woman we have both loved'. I find it implausible that Catullus would have used that tone of fellow-feeling to an ex-rival, but there is no need to rely on subjective impressions. We know from poem 100 that Caelius was Veronese (Caelius Rufus came from Interamnia Praetuttiorum),[12] and at the time Catullus was crazy about Lesbia he was a loyal friend. The identification just doesn't work.

These matters haven't much concerned Catullan scholars in recent years. Fashions change, and academics became more excited by the erotics of domination, the language of social performance and the poetics of Roman manhood.[13] But ordinary readers are still interested in real lives, and the translators who make Catullus available to them still have to grapple with these traditional questions. When two really excellent Catullus translations appeared in 2002 (David Mulroy) and 2005

---

[10] See the index to Broughton 1952.
[11] Catullus 58: *Caeli, Lesbia nostra, Lesbia illa,* | *illa Lesbia, quam Catullus unam* | *plus quam se atque suos amauit omnes,* | *nunc in quadriuiis et angiportis* | *glubit magnanimi Remi nepotes.* Catullus 100: *Caelius Aufillenum et Quintius Aufillenam* | *flos Veronensum depereunt iuuenum,* | *hic fratrem, ille sororem. hoc est, quod dicitur, illud* | *fraternum uere dulce sodalicium.* | *cui faueam potius? Caeli, tibi:* *nam tua nobis* | *perspecta est igni tum unica amicitia,* | *cum uesana meas torreret flamma medullas.* | *sis felix, Caeli, sis in amore potens.*
[12] Cicero *Pro Caelio* 5.   [13] Greene 1999, Krostenko 2001, Wray 2001.

(Peter Green), it turned out that *Catullan Questions* had to be argued about all over again – and I regret to report that the standards of empirical enquiry seem to be in sharp decline.[14]

David Mulroy begins his argument with a firm statement that 'the identification of Lesbia with Clodia Metelli . . . is certainly the most likely of possible scenarios'. He then goes on to address the chronology question with the assertion that 'Clodia Metelli became a widow in 59 BC and is not known to have remarried.'[15] The relative order of two little words may seem a minor matter, but in fact it is crucial. What he should have said was '. . . and is known not to have remarried', at least by 56 BC. What the widow Clodia's marital status was at the time to which Catullus' poems are datable is not the open question that he implies.

Mulroy then addresses poem 36. Accepting that the poem must be dated after Catullus' return from Bithynia, he argues as follows:[16]

> If Lesbia prayed for Catullus' safe return from Bithynia, she must have had a relationship with him before he went to Bithynia. Furthermore, if her prayer was connected with the hope that he would 'stop brandishing fierce iambs', it is obvious that their relationship had run into stormy weather before Catullus set sail.

That is, we assume without argument that line 4 ('if I were restored to her') refers to Catullus' return from abroad rather than to making up a quarrel, and that line 5 ('and stopped hurling fierce iambics') refers to attacks on Lesbia herself rather than political invectives like the iambic poem 29 on Caesar and Mamurra, which the reader of the collection has just read. And even if the inference were sound, it would take the affair back only to 58 BC, and not to the period when Clodia Metelli was a married woman. For Mulroy, however, it's enough. 'The identification of Lesbia with Clodia Metelli', he concludes, 'thus seems to me to acquire the status of high probability.'[17]

As for Peter Green, he assumes from the start that Apuleius' statement that Lesbia's real name was Clodia means that Lesbia was Clodia Metelli. He declares that 'the Clodia painted by Cicero in his speech in defence of Caelius is Lesbia to the life', and he knows without arguing that poem 58 is addressed to Caelius Rufus, and that Catullus 'speaks of "*our* Lesbia" (*Lesbia nostra*), the woman who by then had been the lover of both, abandoning one only to be herself discarded by the other'.[18] He explicitly

---

[14] Mulroy 2002.xiii–xvi, Green 2005.6–7.   [15] Mulroy 2002.xiii, xiv.   [16] Mulroy 2002.xv.
[17] Mulroy 2002.xvi.   [18] Green 2005.5; 'Lesbia to the life' is borrowed from Quinn 1972.135.

endorses the whole Schwabe scenario, right down to the meeting in
Verona in 62 BC,[19] and he adds an absurdity, borrowed from Mulroy,
that goes beyond even Schwabe's inventions: he announces, without
evidence, that Caelius Rufus suffered from gout, and can therefore be
identified as the gouty Rufus of the poems.[20]

In a forty-one-page introduction, Green allows himself one sentence on
the datable poems, and sweeps away, with a casual reference to Mulroy on
poem 36, any idea that they count against his identification of Lesbia.[21]
He makes a novel contribution to the complex debate about the dates of
Catullus' birth and death, citing Cornelius Nepos' *Life of Atticus* as proof
that the poet was dead by the age of thirty-two.[22] What the Nepos passage
actually shows is that he was dead by 32 BC – not quite the same thing.

However, Green's translation is brilliant, a book that will surely *be*
Catullus for at least a generation of English-speaking readers. And riding
on its success will go the unlikely figure of Ludwig Schwabe, a ghost from
the age of the kings of Prussia, his fallacies still flourishing after more than
a century and a half.

1.2   A Better Idea

The article on Clodia Metelli in the standard modern work of classical
reference duly reports her traditional identification as 'Lesbia'.[23] Marilyn
Skinner's *Companion to Catullus* regards it as 'probably correct', and in her
monograph on Clodia Metelli the chapter entitled 'Lesbia' gives the reader
no cause to doubt the identification.[24] The students who use Julia Dyson
Hejduk's sourcebook are invited to take it as read.[25] So too are the mass-
market readers of Daisy Dunn's biography of Catullus.[26] Even the new

---

[19] Green 2005.6 ('they probably met for the first time in 62/1'), 22 ('in essence Schwabe was right')
[20] Green 2005.5, 255–6 (cf. Mulroy 2002.xiii–xiv).   [21] Green 2005.6 (cf. Mulroy 2002.xiv–xvii).
[22] Green 2005.2, citing Nepos *Atticus* 12.4.
[23] Stegmann 2003.463–4: 'the plausible identification of C[lodia] with Lesbia, the mistress of the
      poet Catullus'.
[24] Skinner 2007.3 ('the identification of Clodia Metelli as Catullus' mistress is not wholly certain, but
      there is a reasonable probability that it is correct'), referring to Dyson 2007.254 ('it is most probable
      that the commonly accepted equation of Lesbia with Clodia Metelli ... is correct'); Skinner
      2011.126–36.
[25] Hejduk 2008.4: 'In her promiscuity, her intelligence, her charm, and her status as the poet's equal
      or even superior, the poetic fiction called "Lesbia" would appear to have much in common with the
      femme fatale of Cicero's speech.' The next three pages try to explain away the arguments against.
[26] Dunn 2016.272 (an unobtrusive endnote): 'Clodius had three sisters. Scholars have therefore
      disputed the precise identity of Catullus' "Lesbia".... The eldest Clodia was married to a
      politician called Quintus Caecilius Metellus Celer until 59 BC, and contemporary descriptions of
      her involvement in the politics of Clodius, and her interests as a poet herself, seem to chime with

Cambridge Companion to Catullus finds 'a measure of broad but not complete consensus focused on the patrician Clodia Metelli'.[27] It is all very unsatisfactory, and in retrospect I blame myself.

In *Catullan Questions*, assuming that 'Pulcher' in poem 79 was Publius Clodius, I made two over-confident assertions:[28]

> Whichever one of the sisters Lesbia was, she was the daughter of Ap. Claudius Pulcher [consul 79 BC] and Metella.... No woman of the family is known to have spelt her name in this way except the three sisters.

I did at least concede, in a footnote to the latter sentence, that Clodia the wife of D. Brutus Callaicus (consul in 138 BC) evidently belonged to the Claudii Marcelli,[29] but I offered no reason why the Claudii Pulchri should have been more strict – or strict at all – about using the spelling 'Clodius/ Clodia'. On the strength of this argument from silence I took the identi-fication of Lesbia to be merely a 'one-in-three chance', one or other of the sisters of Clodius,[30] and forty years later that was still what set the terms of the debate, as in Julia Haig Gaisser's excellent general introduction to Catullus:[31]

> The spelling of her name (Clodia, not Claudia) tells us that she was a sister of the infamous demagogue Publius Clodius Pulcher, who used the 'pop-ular' spelling. But it is not clear which sister she was. Clodius had three sisters, all named Clodia, the feminine form of their *nomen*.

Since the sisters had been married to the consuls of 74, 68 and 60 BC, any of the available choices would make Lesbia older than the poet.

Now at last that unnecessary assumption has been queried. In the *Cambridge Companion* Ian Du Quesnay and Tony Woodman point out what should have been obvious to everyone, including me: 'Catullus very frequently refers to his beloved as his *puella*, a word which implies youth rather than middle age.'[32] They note a recent suggestion, unpublished

---

Catullus' portrait.' (For Clodia as a poet, see Cicero *Pro Caelio* 64: *fabella ueteris et plurimarum fabularum poetriae*.)

[27] Gibson 2021.93: e.g. Harrison 2021.358 on 'Lesbia's likely alternative lover Caelius Rufus (cf. poem 58)'.

[28] Wiseman 1969.57, 59.

[29] Cicero *Ad Atticum* 12.22.2 (Cicero was collecting precedents for enduring the loss of a child): *scribes ad me cum scies ... num Clodia D. Bruto consulari filio suo mortuo uixerit. id de Marcello ... sciri potest.* Note also Cn. Lentulus Clodianus, praetor in 59 BC (Cicero *In Vatinium* 27, *Ad Atticum* 1.19.3), evidently a Clodius before adoption; what would his sister or daughter have been called?

[30] Wiseman 1969.60, repeated in Wiseman 1985.136.

[31] Gaisser 2009.3, citing Wiseman 1969.50–60.

[32] Du Quesnay and Woodman 2021.3: Catullus 2.1, 3.3–4, 3.17, 8.4, 8.7, 8.12, 11.15, 13.11, 36.2, 36.9, 37.11. Note too the mini-biography of Catullus by Gerolamo Squarzafico in the first printed

except for a brief reference at second hand, that she might be a daughter of Appius Claudius Pulcher (consul in 54 BC).[33] Appius had two daughters, married, respectively, to Marcus Brutus, the later assassin, and Gnaeus Pompeius Magnus, Pompey's elder son.[34] Did either or both of them spell the family name as 'Clodia'? We don't know, but it's possible.

As John Ramsey has noted, Catullus' poem 83 may be an argument for Gnaeus Pompeius as Lesbia's husband:[35]

> Lesbia constantly insults me in her husband's presence. He's an idiot, and this gives him great delight. Aren't you aware of anything, you mule? If she forgot about me and said nothing, *then* she'd be well.

Of course, a lover's view of a husband shouldn't be taken too literally, but even so, there is a striking parallel in a letter of Gaius Cassius to Cicero early in 45 BC, when Gnaeus Pompeius was leading a rebellion against Caesar in Spain:[36]

> I'd rather have the mild old master than try a cruel new one. You know what an idiot Gnaeus is, how he thinks cruelty is bravery, how he thinks we're always mocking him. My fear is that like a lout he may want to sneer back at us with his sword.

Perhaps Catullus' poem was an example of that mockery; on the other hand, for all we know he could have said the same about Marcus Brutus.

A further argument for Lesbia being one or other of Appius' daughters is provided by poem 79, which begins *Lesbius est pulcher*.[37] Appius had no

---

edition (Venice, 1472), which may have used material from Suetonius' *De poetis* (evidently still extant in 1460): *amauit hic puellam primariam Clodiam, quam Lesbiam suo appellat in carmine.* See Wiseman 1985.189–90, 207–8; Gaisser 1993.26 and Kiss 2021.293 assume without argument that Squarzafico's only sources were Jerome and the fifteenth-century biographer Sicco Polenton, but this sentence does not come from either of those texts.

[33] Hutchinson 2012.56 n. 16 (cited by Du Quesnay and Woodman 2021.3 n. 12): 'In a lecture in Oxford in 2010 Professor J. D. Morgan argued that Lesbia was not a mature *materfamilias* but a young bride (cf. Poems 2, 3 and 72). She was rather to be identified with the daughter (*RE* no. 388) of Ap. Claudius Pulcher (*cos.* 54 BC), as Professor J. T. Ramsey had suggested to him in 2007.'

[34] Cicero *Ad familiares* 3.4.2 (51 BC). The marriages are not datable; cf. Tatum 1991, who argues for 56 BC in the case of Cn. Pompeius.

[35] Catullus 83.1–4: *Lesbia mi praesente uiro mala plurima dicit:* | *haec illi fatuo maxima laetitia est.* | *mule, nihil sentis? si nostri oblita taceret,* | *sana esset.*

[36] Cassius in Cicero *Ad familiares* 15.19.2, pointed out by Ramsey to Morgan (n. 33 above) in 2007: *malo ueterem et clementem dominum habere quam nouum et crudelem experiri. scis Gnaeum quam sit fatuus, scis quo modo crudelitatem uirtutem putet, scis quam se semper a nobis derisum putet; uereor ne nos rustice gladio uelit* ἀντιμυκτηρίσαι. The letter is (mis)quoted by the elder Seneca (*Suasoriae* 1.5) as referring to Pompeius' *stultitia*.

[37] This point too has evidently been current but unpublished since 2010 (n. 33 above). John Morgan confirms it was his idea (email to author, 10 February 2021); I first heard of it from Armand D'Angour in 2019.

sons of his own, but his brother Gaius had two; Appius adopted his elder nephew, whose name thus changed from C. Claudius C.f. to Ap. Claudius Ap.f.; but since Gaius' younger son was called Appius,[38] the two young men, brothers by birth and cousins by adoption, now both had the same distinctive *praenomen*.[39] They could be distinguished as *Appius maior* and *Appius minor*,[40] but it seems clear that the elder also used 'Pulcher' as a *praenomen* to differentiate himself from his brother.[41] So if Lesbia were his adoptive sister, as one of the daughters of the consul of 54, *Lesbius est Pulcher* would be precisely true, and not just a general reference to the family name.

A young Lesbia changes the dynamic of the story – and a story is always what people want.[42] This one belongs, as the evidence shows, in 56–54 BC. Imagine her as seventeen or eighteen, three or four years into marriage,[43] heiress to generations of pride and privilege, beautiful, lively and intelligent, perhaps with little formal education. Imagine Catullus six or seven years older, brought up in a quite different Roman tradition,[44] well-off but family 'in trade', funny, quarrelsome and brilliantly talented. Her world, in particular, was one of casual arrogance and hedonism that requires an imaginative effort to understand.[45]

The *beau monde* of Lesbia and her lovers was on the brink in the mid-fifties BC. So too was that of Lady Diana Cooper (*née* Manners) in the Edwardian age, whose memoirs offer a useful parallel. These lines echo in them like a *Leitmotiv*:[46]

---

[38] Ap. Claudius C.f. Pulcher, consul in 38 BC (*CIL* 10.1423–4).

[39] Asconius 34C (*duo adulescentuli qui Appii Claudii ambo appellabantur*), 38C (*a duobus Appiis Claudiis adulescentibus*); both were active in the prosecution of Milo in 52 BC.

[40] Asconius 39, 41C (*Appius maior*); Caelius in Cicero *Ad familiares* 8.8.2 (*Appius minor*).

[41] Suetonius *De grammaticis* 10.3 (*Appio quoque et Pulchro Claudiis fratribus*), cf. *CIL* 1².775 = *ILLRP* 401 ([*Pulcher Clau*]*dius et Rex Mar*[*cius*], heirs of Appius the consul of 54). I no longer believe, as I did fifty years ago (Wiseman 1970.210–13 = 1987.45–8), that the Pulcher Claudius in Suetonius was the son of P. Clodius named as 'Pulcher' at Valerius Maximus 3.5.3; that hypothesis, based on the convenient assumption that when Suetonius said 'brothers' he meant 'cousins' (*fratres patrueles*), was refuted by Kaster 1995.143–5.

[42] Holzberg 2002.19–23 ('The Catullus Novel'), Gaisser 2009.201–3, 212–14 ('Story Telling'); even now, literary analysis is happy to morph into rom-com mode (e.g. Schafer 2020.127, 194). See Chapter 7 below for fictional elaborations of the Schwabe version.

[43] See Shaw 1987 for the evidence on the usual age of Roman girls at marriage.

[44] See Section 5.3 below on the *Transpadani*, Wiseman 1985.92–115 on the contrasting attitudes.

[45] For repeated attempts, see Wiseman 1979.122–5, 1985.38–53, 2009.201–5; Cicero *Pro Caelio* 21–2 is a key text.

[46] Cooper 1958 (born 1892, youngest daughter of the eighth Duke of Rutland); the lines were taken from Thomas Gray's poem *The Bard* (1757) and illustrated in a famous painting by William Etty (1832).

Fair laughs the morn, and soft the zephyr blows,
While proudly riding o'er the azure realm,
In gallant trim, the gilded vessel goes,
Youth on the prow and Pleasure at the helm,
Unmindful of the sweeping whirlwind's sway,
That, hushed in grim repose, expects his evening prey.

Over to you, novelists!

CHAPTER 2

How Many Books?

Catullan Questions was concerned with 'the collection as we have it', which contains about 2,300 lines of poetry. I wanted to justify Wilamowitz' *ex cathedra* statement that Catullus 'arranged his book of poems with the most careful reflection'.[1] I didn't ask myself why such a substantial corpus of work was introduced in the first poem as a 'little book' (*libellus*).[2] Wilamowitz had a footnote that seemed to deal with that:[3]

> For [the ordering of the poems] it is a matter of complete indifference whether the bookseller had it written on to one roll or sold it in one box containing several rolls; at that time the book trade in Rome was only starting, and didn't suffice for Cicero, for example. A generation later Catullus would have divided his collection into books; if he had done that, the citations would give book numbers. Catullus might have considered it modest to call his whole book 'trifles' after the first part of it, but that is not what he did: he merely said that Nepos valued his 'trifles',[4] and that was why he dedicated to him the elegantly produced dedication copy of his works, for which Nepos prophesied a long life.

His works, plural; perhaps a box (*capsula*) containing several rolls. So what *was* the supposed 'book of poems' that Catullus arranged so carefully? One work in several parts, or several works combined? If so, how many, and combined on what criterion?

---

[1] Wiseman 1969.1–2, citing Wilamowitz 1913.292 ('Sein Gedichtbuch hat er mit sorgsamster Überlegung geordnet').

[2] Catullus 1.1: *cui dono lepidum nouum libellum . . .?* Not that the diminutive necessarily means small size: Horace *Satires* 1.92 (*i, puer, atque meo citus haec subscribe libello*) closes a book of 1,030 lines.

[3] Wilamowitz 1913.292–3 n. 2: 'Dafür ist ganz gleichgültig, ob der Buchhändler es auf eine Rolle schreiben ließ oder in einer Kapsel mit mehreren Rollen verkaufte; das Buchgewerbe kam damals in Rom eben erst auf und genügte z.B. dem Cicero nicht. Ein Menschenalter später würde Catull die Sammlung in Bücher Geteilt haben; hätte er's getan, würden die Citate Bücher zählen. Catull konnte es bescheiden finden, sein ganz Buch nach dem ersten Hauptteil *nugae* zu nennen; aber er hat es nicht getan, sondern nur gesagt, daß Nepos seinem *nugae* Wert beilegte und er ihm daher das elegant ausgestattete Dedicationsexemplar seiner Werke widmete, denen er lange Leben prophezeit.'

[4] Catullus 1.3–4: *namque tu solebas | meas aliquid putare nugas.*

The collection as we have it evidently derives, at several removes, from a parchment *codex* edition that was probably already in existence by about AD 200.[5] What is not known is how many papyrus book-rolls (*uolumina*) were copied to create it, nor how they were chosen and put in order.

2.1 Internal Evidence

Five other poetry collections survive that were certainly put together within twenty years of Catullus' time: Virgil's *Eclogues* (829 lines), Horace's *Epodes* (625 lines), two books of Horace's *Satires* (1,030 and 1,083 lines), and Propertius' first book (706 lines). Compare those figures with c. 848 lines for Catullus' 'polymetric' short poems (1–60) and c. 646 lines for his poems in elegiacs (65–116); the four long poems in other metres (61–64) total about 802 lines.

There is an obvious prima facie case for seeing the surviving collection as a combination of three constituent parts.[6] The most careful and thorough account of the subject is that of Gregory Hutchinson, who concludes that 'the Catullan corpus offers us, in at least somewhat distorted form, two books that we can have reasonable confidence were designed by the author: 1–60 and 65–116'.[7] He labels them, respectively, *a* and *c*, the latter subdivided as *c1* (65–68b) and *c2* (69–116), with the implied *b* (61–4) consisting of four longer works that would originally have circulated independently.[8]

That formulation has now been adopted and extended by Schafer, who uses it to draw a different conclusion:[9]

> The Catullan corpus, I claim, consists in three authorially designed books: at the close of one of these is found a short, heterogeneous run of poems, whose status is uniquely problematic. The books and their parts, which will be referred to throughout this work by the accompanying shorthand, are:

---

[5] Du Quesnay 2021.169–70, inferred from Terentianus Maurus 2560–4 (poem 1 already the introduction?) and 2899 (*ipse liber*, citing 63.1); at that time it evidently included at least one poem subsequently lost from it, the dedication of a grove to Priapus that modern editors call 'fr. 1' (Terentianus Maurus 2754–60). For the general transition from book-roll to *codex*, see Harris 1991, Oakley 2021.263.

[6] 'That is now, broadly speaking, the orthodox position' (Du Quesnay and Woodman 2012.265); e.g. Wiseman 1979.265–6.

[7] Hutchinson 2003.206–14, quotation from 212. Some scholars prefer to attach 65–68b to the other long poems (61–4) rather than to the epigrams (69–116), but that ignores the Callimachean cross-reference (*carmina Battiadae*) from 116.2 to 65.16: 'this forms a ring so palpable and significant as to indicate both that 116 is the end of the book and that 65 is the beginning' (Hutchinson 2003.212).

[8] Hutchinson 2003.210–11 (poems 61–4), 212–13 (*a* and *c*).   [9] Schafer 2020.3.

A: poems 1–51, consisting of a bipartite first half and a (unitary?) second half:

    1–14 and 14b–26

    27–51

    [**Ax:** 52–60]

B: 61–64

C: 65–116, consisting of halves:

    C1: 65–68b, itself consisting of halves:

        65–67 to Ortalus

        68a and 68b to Mallius

    C2: 69–116, itself consisting of halves:

        69–92

        93–116

The problematic run, **Ax**, are genuine Catullan poems, but they are also generically distinct from what precedes (and follows) them, frequently obscure, and apparently ill-fitting.

That is more complicated than is strictly necessary, and one aspect of it seems to me very vulnerable (the 'two halves' of **C1**, which depend on assumptions that are unproven or downright invalid).[10] But Schafer's paradigm is a very helpful basis for argument, and I shall use his 'short-hand' in what follows.

His **Ax** category rightly focuses attention on something that has troubled many scholars (though not, alas, my own younger self), and that is the failure of the last eight to ten poems of the 1–60 collection to offer any sort of convincing closing sequence. 'Very little can be made of 54; 55 reads like a failed metrical experiment; 58b must be unfinished; and 60 is a scrap. Would Catullus end his pretty book of poems with such?' That was Wendell Clausen in 1976, and many others since then have agreed with him.[11] Clausen thought the book as designed by the poet originally ended with poem 50, but Schafer, following David Wray, believes that

---

[10] Namely, (1) the far-fetched notion that poem 67, a dramatic dialogue on the subject of scandal and adultery in Verona, 'is partially translated from Callimachus' (Schafer 2020.158, Section 4.2 below), and (2) the arbitrary decision to take Allius in poem 68b as a pseudonym for Mallius in poem 68a (Schafer 2020.12, Section 4.4 below).

[11] Clausen 1976.40. See, for instance, Skinner 1981.74 ('a jumble of unrelated and curiously unfinished verses'), Hubbard 1983.220 ('a rather embarrassing grab-bag of doggerel and fragments'), Thomson 1997.8 ('short effusions that are clearly unfinished, experimental, or rejected drafts'), Hutchinson 2003.207 (59 and 60 'seem unlikely to be complete poems, as they lack a point'), Hutchinson 2012.49 ('*a* in particular has suffered some accretions (notably 52, 59 and 60)'), Schafer 2020.51 ('the text of poem 54 is utterly hopeless; 55 and 58b are quite troubled, and 59 and 60 may be fragmentary'). Contra Wiseman 1985.155–7, which I find much less convincing now than I did then.

50 and 51 belong together,[12] and detects a 'discontinuity', 'formal break' or 'disjunction' between poems 51 and 52.[13] I don't think that can be demonstrated,[14] but the general point about this sequence of poems and fragments is still valid. Wherever it starts, it is still a problem that has to be explained.

The sequence is a problem even for those who don't accept the Hutchinson-Schafer tripartite model. Thomas Hubbard, for instance, detects two separate *libelli* in the polymetric collection, 1–14 and 14b–51.[15] But the poems after 51 (Schafer's **Ax**) can't be fitted into his scheme:[16]

> The artistic totality [in 14b–51] is simply too rich not to have been the author's original arrangement. The case is quite different with regard to *C.* 52–60. Although pieces like *C.* 56 and 57 are not without some merit, these poems are on the whole rather slighter efforts than most of what one finds among the earlier polymetra.... I cannot help but hold to my original view that these epigrammatic squibs were felt by the poet himself to be too insignificant or ephemeral to make the cut.

Hubbard assumes that 'the miscellaneous *C.* 52–60 found their way into the codex when Catullus' work was being gathered together',[17] but offers no suggestion about when or how. He also accepts 65–116 (Schafer's **C**) as a coherent elegiac *libellus* ordered by the poet himself.[18]

Ian Du Quesnay has now gone even further than Hubbard, identifying no fewer than four 'Catullan *libelli*' in the polymetric collection, as well as two more in the 'epigrams' 69–116. Helpfully, he ends his long chapter in the *Cambridge Companion* with a very clear synopsis:[19]

> This chapter seeks to set out the arguments for understanding the *Catulli Veronensis Liber* as a compilation of *libelli* originally arranged and 'distributed' by Catullus himself.

---

[12] Schafer 2020.7–9 (after Wray 2001.91–9), 107–16; Wray's suggestion is exploited also by Hubbard 2005.260–2, but like Du Quesnay (2021.198 n. 145) I see no good reason to believe that *hoc ... poema feci* (50.16) must refer to poem 51.

[13] Schafer 2020.3, 41, 42; cf. 43 on 'textual intrusion', 'transmission accident' or 'textual corruption' (unspecified) as the reason for it.

[14] A case will be made below (Section 2.5) for 53 as the original closing poem.

[15] Hubbard 2005.259–69, esp. 260–2 (following Wray, n. 12 above) for the supposed closure.

[16] Hubbard 2005.269, referring back to Hubbard 1983.220.

[17] Hubbard 2005.269, cf. Hubbard 1983.220 ('One can well understand a posthumous editor's motivation to preserve these poems out of a desire for completeness').

[18] Hubbard 2005.269–75 (revising Hubbard 1983.219–21); like Hutchinson (n. 8 above), he regards the long poems 61–4 as 'probably separate publications in their own right' (2005.269).

[19] Du Quesnay 2021.217–18; the paragraphing and the footnotes are mine.

It is assumed that Catullus is most likely to have followed the practices of his contemporaries in first trying out his works in readings or performances at *conuiuia* and by circulating to close friends written copies for comment, reactions and suggestions.[20] They will then have been released for wider circulation through networks of social contacts and further refinement and revision would no longer be possible.[21] Readers will make (or have made for them) copies which they can and did collate, annotate, reorder and perform as they thought appropriate.

The non-elegiac long poems (61–64) circulated as individual *libelli*, each to be read on its own terms.[22] Similarly, the longer elegies (65–68B) are, with the exception of the paired 65 and 66, individual pieces that are best understood as separate poems.[23] The situation for the short poems (1–60 and 69–116) is the reverse. Some (such as 17, 34, 101) may have had separate formal 'release' prior to inclusion in a *libellus*. Generally however it seems more likely that they were distributed as *libelli* by Catullus rather than as either single pieces or even very limited 'cycles' of poems on such themes as 'Iuventius' or 'Gellius'.[24]

The *libelli* are here (tentatively) identified as: 2–14 (for Calvus?); 14B–26 (for Quintilius Varus?); 27–48, prefaced by poem 1 (for Cornelius Nepos); 49–60 (for Calvus?); 69–92, prefaced by 116; and 93–115. Neither of the books of epigrams has an obvious (potential) dedicatee. Each of these *libelli* has its own distinctive character and its own principles of organisation.[25]

The *libelli* were not assembled in chronological order, which is difficult to determine because the range of datable references is so narrow. It is possible that there was some overlap between the collections. The most likely order for the polymetric books seems to be, to judge by the *termini post quos*,

[20] As Caecilius sent his *Magna Mater* to Catullus (poem 35)?

[21] Cf. Wiseman 2015.5–6: 'The nearest modern parallel is not a published edition but an author's complimentary copies.... Probably each separate scroll would have a personalised dedication.' I think that should be remembered when considering poem 1 (Section 2.3 below).

[22] Cf. Du Quesnay 2021.174: 'The scant evidence that we have suggests that these poems circulated as independent pieces until the end of the first century AD. If the poems of Catullus were not transferred to the codex form until the second century AD [n. 5 above], then the arrangement in which we now read them derives from the aesthetics of the editor who compiled the collection.' The chronology is dictated by Quintilian 9.3.16, where a line from poem 62 is ascribed to 'Catullus in the *Epithalamium*', implying an individual *uolumen*.

[23] Schafer's C collection is ruled out: 'There is no compelling reason to see Poem 65 as dedicating to Hortalus all the longer elegies (65–68B), much less all the poems in elegiacs (65–116)'; 'The verbal similarity [of 65.16 and 116.2] is not, in itself, conclusive. Such a combination of elegies and epigrams seems to be without parallel' (Du Quesnay 2021.175 and n. 43). Contrast Hutchinson 2003.212 (n. 7 above), Hubbard 2005.269–70, Schafer 2020.34–5.

[24] On what grounds should we distinguish between a short independent *libellus* and a 'cycle' of poems within a larger one?

[25] It is hard to detect any distinctive character and principle of organization in the supposed 49–60 *libellus* (which includes the problematic **Ax** of Schafer's paradigm), given that 'the group neither opens nor closes with clearly programmatic material' (Du Quesnay 2021.194).

27–48 (+ 1); 49–60; 14B–26; 2–14. For the elegiac epigrams, the books are
69–92 and 93–115, with the latter group possibly the earlier of the two.

This adventurous hypothesis presupposes a very particular definition of the
'Catullan *libellus*'. The six proposed short-poem collections are constituted
as follows:[26]

1. poems 2–14: c. 230 lines
2. poems 14b–26: c. 151 lines
3. poems 1, 27–48: c. 331 lines
4. poems 49–60: c. 124 lines
5. poems 116, 69–92: c. 180 lines
6. poems 93–115: c. 140 lines

How much does it matter that these line counts are so poor a match for
those of the known near-contemporary book collections of Virgil, Horace
and Propertius?

The fact is that we know nothing for certain about what a *libellus* of
Catullus' time would look like;[27] apart from his gift to Nepos in poem 1
(whatever that originally introduced), the only *libellus* mentioned by
Catullus is Calvus' gift to him in poem 14, which was evidently an
anthology of poems by various authors. Nevertheless, for one part of Du
Quesnay's scheme, and for Hubbard's as well, there exists a very strong
piece of positive evidence.

2.2 'Poem 14b'

> si qui forte mearum ineptiarum
> lectores eritis manusque uestras
> non horrebitis admouere nobis . . .

If by chance any of you are going to be readers of my absurdities, and won't
hesitate to apply your hands to us . . .

Nothing more of the poem survives. Since we cannot know how the
sentence ended, we must do our best with what there is.

---

[26] Exact totals are impossible because of missing lines and/or textual damage at 2b, 14b, 54, 58b, 78b
and 95b.

[27] See Bellandi 2007.27–32 on Catullus' use of *libellus* and *liber*. 'Note that there was no "standard" or
"average" length to which bookrolls tended, as some earlier researchers supposed. Since the roll end
was determined by the stroke of a knife, there was no incentive to fill out the contents' (Johnson
2009.265). It was entirely the author's choice how many poems he wanted to include.

The first thing is to take note of the plural address.[28] Since a book can be read by only one person at a time, authors naturally address that person in the singular, as in the preface to *The Golden Ass* or the last chapter of *Jane Eyre*.[29] Here, on the other hand, Catullus (or his book) is talking to an unspecified group of people who may or may not be readers of his work, may or may not lay hands on it.

Next, it is important to bear in mind that when Romans thought about reading books, they thought about hands. The Latin for 'to publish' is *dare in manus hominum*;[30] 'to become generally available' is *(per)uenire in manus*;[31] 'to be widely read' is *in manibus esse*[32] or *inter manus uersari*;[33] 'to take to read' is *in manus sumere*;[34] and even just 'reading' can be *in manibus habere*.[35] In a library, when you asked for a book it was delivered 'into your hands' (*in manus*).[36] A *uolumen* was a substantial physical object, anything up to thirty feet of rolled-up papyrus,[37] and it took both hands to read it (Fig. 2.1), the right unrolling and the left rolling up again as the successive columns of script (*paginae*) were revealed in order. Physically grasping it in two hands was fundamental to the very concept of reading.[38]

In 'poem 14b' there are people who may perhaps do that with Catullus' poetry. But who are they, and where are they? We may find an answer if we look a few lines back. The previous poem (14) is Catullus' good-humoured protest to Calvus about his Saturnalia present, an anthology

---

[28] As I failed to do in *Catullan Questions* (Wiseman 1969.7, 'a warning to the reader').

[29] *Lector intende, laetaberis*; 'Reader, I married him.' So too (for instance) Ovid *Tristia* 4.1.2 and 4.10.132.

[30] E.g. Pliny *Letters* 7.17.15, 8.19.2; cf. Seneca *De uita patris* fr. 5 Haase = *FRHist* 74 T1 (*in manus populi edere*).

[31] E.g. Cicero *De oratore* 1.94, *Ad Atticum* 7.17.2, *Topica* 72, Quintilian 12.10.50.

[32] E.g. Cicero *In Verrem* 1.17, *Brutus* 125, *De senectute* 12, *De amicitia* 96, Horace *Epistles* 2.1.53, Pliny *Letters* 1.2.6, Suetonius *Gaius* 16.1. Not to be confused with *in manibus esse* = 'being worked on (by the author)': Cicero *De senectute* 38, *Ad Atticum* 13.20.4, cf. Tacitus *Dialogus* 3.1 (*inter manus*).

[33] E.g. Caelius in Cicero *Ad familiares* 8.3.3, Pomponius in *Digest* 1.2.2.42 and 47; cf. Tacitus *Dialogus* 21.2, Apuleius *Apologia* 55.11 (*manibus uersari*).

[34] E.g. Cicero *De oratore* 3.15, *Tusculan Disputations* 2.8, Asconius 61C, Quintilian 10.1.22 and 58, Pliny *Letters* 1.16.3, 9.22.2. Cf. Ovid *Tristia* 3.1.82: *sumite plebeiae carmina nostra manus!*

[35] E.g. Porphyrio on Horace *Epistles* 2.1.90; cf. Lucian *Apologia* 3 (διὰ χειρὸς ἔχειν).

[36] E.g. Aulus Gellius 6.3.55, 11.17.1.

[37] See Kenyon 1951.53–5 for typical lengths of surviving literary book-rolls; Johnson 2009.264 suggests 'a normative range of 3–15 meters' (c. 9–49 feet).

[38] As implied by, e.g., Horace *Epistles* 1.19.34 (*manibusque teneri*), Phaedrus 3.prol.6 (*manibus tangi tuis*), Tacitus *Annals* 3.16.1 (*uisum saepius inter manus Pisonis libellum*).

Fig. 2.1   Reading with the hands. Detail of a marble sarcophagus in the Metropolitan
Museum of Art, New York (inv. 48.76.1, 'gift of Mrs Joseph Brummer and
Ernest Brummer, in memory of Joseph Brummer, 1948'), Ostia, early fourth
century AD. © 2021: image copyright The Metropolitan Museum of Art/Art Resource/
Scala, Florence.

of dreadful poems designed to 'destroy' him.[39] But Calvus won't get away
with it:[40]

> As soon as morning comes I'll hurry down to the booksellers' stock-boxes
> and collect Caesiuses, Aquinuses, Suffenus, all the poisons, and I'll make
> these punishments my return gift to you.

---

[39] Catullus 14.4-5 (*quid feci ... cur me tot male perderes poetis?*); as Schafer argues (2020.92–3), the
point is probably that they were hostile attacks, not just bad verse.

[40] 14.17–20: *nam, si luxerit, ad librariorum | curram scrinia, Caesios, Aquinos, | Suffenum, omnia
colligam uenena | ac te his suppliciis remunerabor.*

Bookshops were places where people gathered to read and talk,[41] and one of them, I suggest, was where Catullus presents himself (or his book) in 'poem 14b', talking to the browsers.

Two other poets may provide confirmation of this idea. First, look at the end of Horace *Epistles* I. In his early days as Maecenas' protégé Horace had boasted that *his* poems would not be found in a shop or displayed on a pillar, to be sweat-stained by the hands of the public.[42] But he still wanted his work to be widely read, and in 20 BC his book of *Epistles* is on sale at Sosius Bros. Casual readers in a bookshop wouldn't take the trouble to roll a *uolumen* back to the beginning,[43] so the author presents his artful self-portrait at the end of the roll, where the browsers will see it and be tempted.[44] The book is prettily made up, looking for custom, and naturally gets 'pawed and dirtied by the hands of the crowd'.[45] Catullus' phrase *manusque uestras ... admouere nobis* seems to imply a similar scenario.

Now consider the final three poems in Martial's eleventh book of epigrams, set at the Saturnalia in AD 96:[46]

> Vibius Maximus, if you have time for a greeting just read these four lines: for you are busy, and not over-industrious either. You're skipping these four lines too? How sensible!

> Septicianus, you give me back my book unwound right to its horns as if you had read it all the way through. And you have read it all the way through, of course. I believe you, I know it, I'm pleased, it's true! I read your five books through in precisely the same way.

> Although you could be satisfied by such a long book, reader, you still want a few distichs more from me. But Lupus wants his loan back and my slaves want their rations. Reader, pay up! You pretend you can't hear? Goodbye then.

Again the scene is a bookshop, perhaps that of Atrectus in the Argiletum,[47] and again, thanks to Septicianus, the book-roll is open at the end. One

---

[41] Aulus Gellius 5.4.1–2, 13.31.1–7, 18.4.1; Galen *De libris propriis* 19.8 Kühn. See in general White 2009, and Wiseman 1980.8–10 = 1987.178–80 on Catullus 55.4 (looking for Camerius *in omnibus libellis*).

[42] Horace *Satires* 1.4.71–2 (*quis manus insudet uolgi*).

[43] Kenyon 1951.61: 'When a roll had been read it was left with its end outside.... Hence a newcomer would only have to look at the exposed end of the roll to ascertain its contents.'

[44] Horace *Epistles* 1.20.19–24 (cf. 1–2 for the Sosii); compare Propertius 1.21–2, a decade earlier.

[45] Horace *Epistles* 1.20.2 (*ut prostes ... pumice mundus*), 11–12 (*contrectatus ubi manibus sordescere uolgi | coeperis*).

[46] Martial 11.106–8 (trans. Kay 1985.284–6); cf. 11.2.5, 11.6.1–5, 11.15.2 for the Saturnalia, and Kay 1985.1 for the year.

[47] Where you could buy a book of Martial for five *denarii* (Martial 1.117.11–17).

rather grand person can't be bothered to stop and read,[48] and someone else (*lector*, unnamed) is reading it but thinks it's a bit short. Martial just wants one of them to fork out twenty sesterces and buy it.

We shall return to Martial in the next section. For the moment, it's enough to note that the future tenses in 'poem 14b' imply material still to come that some people might hesitate to pick up, and that in the collection as we have it some of Catullus' most brutally explicit obscenities occur in the poems that follow. The question is whether the poem was a programmatic piece within a large collection, indicating to a reader already well into the book that a change of subject would follow,[49] or whether it referred to a separate *libellus* that was going to contain such material. The physical detail of *manus uestras admouere* strongly suggests the latter, and the bookshop seems a likely setting for the poem.

Hubbard has made a strong case for 14b being part of the introduction of a second book of short poems,[50] and Du Quesnay, who infers three subsequent *libelli* instead of Hubbard's one, takes the same view.[51] In that case the link between poems 14 and 14b (Catullus at the bookshop) will be a link between one *libellus* and the next, signing off the first with a threat of what's to come and opening the second with a warning about it. Books in the ancient world did sometimes end with an indication of what the next one would be,[52] and that may be what Catullus was doing here.

A *libellus* consisting of 1–14 (Hubbard) or 2–14 (Du Quesnay), about 230 or 240 lines of poetry, would be comfortably accommodated on a small roll, say, six inches wide and four feet long.[53] As it happens, such a roll is depicted in Catullus' hands in a fragmentary wall painting from the great villa of the Valerii Catulli at Sirmione (Fig. 2.2).[54]

---

[48] Vibius Maximus may have been the *praefectus uigilum* (Syme 1979.355); he later rose to be Prefect of Egypt.
[49] Wiseman 1969.7–8, developed by Schafer 2020.94–100; for doubts, see Hubbard 1983.232–3, Thomson 1997.8–9, 247, Bellandi 2007.70–3.
[50] Hubbard 1983.223, 232–3; cf. Thomson 1997.247 ('a fragment of an introductory poem').
[51] Du Quesnay 2021.178 (14b 'probably introductory'), 181 ('may have been part of a formal prologue').
[52] See, for instance, Callimachus *Aetia* 112.9 (αὐτὰρ ἐγὼ Μουσέων πεζὸν [ἔ]πειμι νομόν); I think Catullus 116 is another example (Wiseman 1985.183–9).
[53] Missing lines at 2b make an exact count impossible. See Pliny *Natural History* 13.78 (with Kenyon 1951.49–52) on various widths of roll, and Johnson 2009.257–9 on typical sizes of *paginae* and margins; the poems from 1 (or 2) to 14 would fit into ten columns of script.
[54] Roffia 2018.89–90, fig. 104; Wiseman 2007.65–7; Dunn 2016, plate 1. See Roffia 2018.45–6 for the date of the villa (late Augustan), Wiseman 2007.59–65 for the history of the family (consulships in AD 31, 73 and 85).

Fig. 2.2   The young poet. Fragmentary wall painting from the Roman villa at Sirmione, late first century BC or early first century AD: Roffia 2018.89–90, fig. 104. The narrow stripe and gold ring denote equestrian rank, the bare feet perhaps a 'heroized' ancestor.

2.3   *Passer Catulli*

If poem 14 ended a short poetry book, which poem began it? The obvious answer would be 'poem 1',[55] but that seems to be ruled out by the development of Catullus' metrical practice in hendecasyllables. David Butterfield provides a helpful summary:[56]

> Catullus retained the freedom of deploying all three possibilities in the so-called 'aeolic base' (x x, the two opening syllables, one of which must be long), namely a spondee (———), trochee (—u) or iamb (u—). However, ... Poems 2–26 (263 lines) have spondaic bases throughout, with only three (1.1%) exceptions (all iambic); Poems 27–60, by contrast, have 63 (22.6%) non-spondaic bases (33 iambic, 30 trochaic), i.e. exceptions are over 20 times more common.

These statistics imply 'distinct phases of composition', as Catullus came to allow himself greater freedom, and the natural conclusion is that the poems were arranged in roughly chronological order, with the latter group mainly composed later:[57]

> It fits neatly with this theory that Poem 1, the ten introductory verses to the collection, follows the practice of Poems 27–60, with four (40%) lines exhibiting non-spondaic basis (one iambic, three trochaic).

That is, poem 1 was evidently not written at the same time as poems 2–14, and is thus not likely to be the introduction to a *libellus* containing those poems alone.[58] One possible explanation of its position in the surviving collection is that it was placed there by whoever put together the codex edition.

If Du Quesnay is right that the codex edition was created some time in the second century AD,[59] it was at a time when Catullus and his contemporaries were still widely read and their late-republican background still well understood.[60] We should imagine the codex-compiler as a learned person quite capable of transcribing the poet's various *libelli* in the correct order, and there is no good reason to impute to him or her any rearrangement of individual poems. On the strength of the metrical data, however,

---

[55] As assumed by Hubbard 1983.221–3 and 2005.259; *contra* Du Quesnay 2021.178–9.
[56] Butterfield 2021.145 and 146, after Skutsch 1969.   [57] Butterfield 2021.146.
[58] Du Quesnay 2021.178, 185–6.   [59] See above, n. 5.
[60] See, for instance, Suetonius *Diuus Iulius* 49.1, 73, *De grammaticis et rhetoribus* 4–18, 26–30; Tacitus *Annals* 4.34.5, Juvenal 8.186, 13.111; Aulus Gellius 6.20.6, 7.16.2, 12.12, 19.9.7, 19.13.5; Apuleius *Apologia* 6, 10, 11. The historians Appian and Dio Cassius were clearly well informed about the late republic: see especially Dio Cassius 53.19.2 on the availability of evidence.

Du Quesnay assumes that poem 1 *was* relocated: he sees it as a dedication poem moved from its original context to serve the same purpose for the whole combined edition.[61]

But the metrical data need not imply a lengthy passage of time between the composition of poems before and after Catullus changed his practice; his decision to modify the scansion rule seems to have been taken in the middle of the composition of a single poem, the wedding song for Manlius Torquatus (poem 61).[62] All we need to assume is that shortly after putting this small collection together Catullus made a presentation copy for Cornelius Nepos, adding a personal gift-dedication poem,[63] and that that copy happened to be the one used by the compiler of the codex edition.

If that is the case, two important consequences follow. First, there is now no evidence that any of the *libelli* (much less the whole collection) was dedicated to an individual.[64] Catullus didn't have, or need, a patron,[65] and the bookshop scene in 'poem 14b', addressing potential readers in the plural, implies that each book-roll was conceived as the poet's direct offering to the general book-buying public. He had more subtle ways of honouring particular friends.[66]

The second consequence is that the little book that ended with poem 14 began with the words *passer, deliciae meae puellae* (2.1). Since poetry books were often known by their opening words (for instance, Propertius' first book as '*Cynthia*'),[67] was '*Passer*' the title of this one? Four passages of Martial suggest that it was.

Martial introduces his first collection with an announcement of Catullan freedom of speech,[68] and five of the first six poems in it are

---

[61] Du Quesnay 2021.186, 217; he suggests it was written to introduce a *libellus* starting with poem 27.

[62] Skutsch 1969.38 ('It looks as though in the process of composing the poet had relaxed his technique'), followed by Butterfield 2021.145–6 (whose arbitrary dating of poem 61 to 60 BC is an unnecessary complication).

[63] See above, n. 21. The first two and last three lines of poem 1 could have been used for several such gift-dedications, with appropriate particulars inserted between.

[64] *Pace* Du Quesnay 2021.168, 186, 194 (Cornelius Nepos), 217 (Calvus? Quintilius Varus?).

[65] The idea is still current: see most recently Newlands 2021.254.

[66] Like Veranius, *omnibus e meis amicis | antistans mihi milibus trecentis* (9.1–2), a tribute placed exactly halfway through the 2–14 *libellus* (so far as we can tell, given the loss of some lines at 2b).

[67] Propertius 2.42.2, Martial 14.189; cf. Ovid *Tristia* 2.261 for Lucretius' '*Aeneadum genetrix*'. On 'citation by opening words' in general, see Schröder 1999.16–20.

[68] Martial 1.pref.: *sic scribit Catullus, ... sic quicumque perlegitur.* The date was probably AD 86 (Howell 1980.5), the year after the second consulship of L. Valerius Catullus Messallinus; see Wiseman 2007.66–8 on the social prominence of the poet's family at this time.

about books – writing them, reading them, buying them, selling them.[69]
Then we get this, on the poetry of the senator L. Arruntius Stella:[70]

> My Stella's pet, Maximus, his Dove (I may say it, though Verona hear), has
> surpassed Catullus' Sparrow. My Stella is greater than your Catullus by as
> much as a dove is greater than a sparrow.

In the context, it is a reasonable inference that 'Stella's Dove' and
'Catullus' Sparrow' refer not just to poems but to *libelli* that were named
after them. The matter is put beyond doubt by our second Martial passage,
from book 4 a couple of years later. The third poem in the book to talk
about *libelli*,[71] it presents Martial's work to Silius Italicus as a gift for the
Saturnalia, when anything is allowed:[72]

> Be your brow not grim but relaxed as you read my little books, all steeped
> in wanton jests. Thus, it may be, did tender Catullus venture to send his
> Sparrow to great Maro.

Saturnalia gifts were precisely the subject of Catullus' poem 14, at the end
of the putative *libellus* that began with the *passer*.

Saturnalia was also the setting of Martial's eleventh book, the one
that ends with the bookshop scene used in the previous section as an
analogy for Catullus' 'poem 14b'. Now we can take a further step in
that direction.

The opening poem is addressed to the book itself. Do you want to be
read by the imperial chamberlain Parthenius? No chance: he doesn't read
books, he reads petitions (*libelli* in a different sense). Will you be happy if
lesser mortals get their hands on you?[73] Try the idlers in the public
porticos, like the one at the temple of Quirinus, just round the corner
from Martial's house:[74]

---

[69] 1.1.3 (*libellis*), 1.4 (*lector*), 2.1 (*libellos*), 2.4 (*scrinia*), 3.2 (*liber, scrinia*), 4.1 (*libellos*), 5.2 (*libro*).

[70] Martial 1.7, trans. D. R. Shackleton Bailey (Loeb): *Stellae delicium mei Columba, | Veronae licet audiente dicam, | uicit, Maxime, Passerem Catulli. | tanto Stella meus tuo Catullo | quanto passere maior est columba.* For Stella (consul in AD 101) and his family (from Patavium), see Syme 1988.384–6. 'Maximus' is unidentified, but could be the Vibius Maximus who was too busy to dawdle at the bookshop (Martial 11.106, cf. Section 2.2 above).

[71] After 4.6 (on the presumptuousness of reciting in the house of Stella) and 4.10 (on Martial's own book, sent to his patron Faustinus).

[72] Martial 4.14.10–14, trans. D. R. Shackleton Bailey (Loeb): *nec torua lege fronte, sed remissa | lasciuis madidos iocis libellos. | sic forsan tener ausus est Catullus | magno mittere Passerem Maroni.*

[73] Martial 11.1.8 (*contingunt tibi si manus minores*); cf. nn. 37 and 44 above.

[74] Martial 11.1.13–16: *sunt illic duo tresue qui reuoluant | nostrarum tineas ineptiarum, | sed cum sponsio fabulaeque lassae | de Scorpo fuerint et Incitato.*

There are two or three there who might unroll the bookworms of my absurdities, but only when they're tired of betting and telling stories about [the charioteers] Scorpus and Incitatus.

The distinctive phrase 'my absurdities',[75] coming so soon after those unknown hands touching the book, looks like a deliberate allusion to Catullus 14b.

Five poems later, the Saturnalia is celebrated again, and here too there is a Catullan echo.[76] In a scene now notorious in Catullan scholarship, Martial addresses the wine-servant:[77]

> Mix half measures, boy, like the ones Pythagoras gave to Nero, mix them, Dindymus, but make them more frequent: I can't do anything when I'm sober; dozens of poets will help me if I'm drunk. Give me kisses now, Catullan kisses: if they are as many as he said, I will give you Catullus' *passer*.

What leaps out immediately is the homage not just to Catullus but to one particular sequence of Catullan poems: 2 and 3 (the '*passer*-poems') and 5 and 7 (the 'kiss-poems'), which form a substantial part of the *libellus* that ended with poem 14. It seems highly likely that that *libellus* was known in Martial's time as '*Passer Catulli*'.

Martial was not, of course, hoping to give the boy a book. Shackleton Bailey's note on the last line says all that needs saying: 'Clearly with an obscene double sense here, but that is M.'s contribution. Catullus meant no such thing, nor is M. likely to have thought he did.'[78] But since recent scholarship has become obsessed by the notion that Catullus' *passer* meant 'penis', I offer a reluctant paragraph on the subject.[79]

Taken for granted by Giovanni Pontano in 1449, the obscene meaning was explicitly asserted by Angelo Poliziano in 1489; both men were poets

---

[75] As in *si qui forte mearum ineptiarum*.... There is only one other use of *ineptiae* in Martial (2.86.10).

[76] In fact a multiple one: with Martial 11.6.6 (*pallentes procul hinc abite curae*) compare Catullus 14.21 (*uos hinc interea ualete abite*) and 27.5 (*at uos quo lubet hinc abite, lymphae*), the latter addressed to a wine-pouring *puer*.

[77] Martial 11.6.9–16, trans. Kay 1985.71: *misce dimidios, puer, trientes, | quales Pythagoras dabat Neroni, | misce, Dindyme, sed frequentiores: | possum nil ego sobrius; bibenti | succurrent mihi quindecim poetae. | da nunc basia, sed Catulliana: | quae si tot fuerint quot ille dixit, | donabo tibi passerem Catulli.* Cf. Catullus 5.7 (*da mi basia mille, deinde centum*).

[78] Shackleton Bailey 1993.3.9. So too Gaisser 1993.240: 'Martial surely felt free to pretend what he liked about the meaning of ... Catullus' poetry, and it would be quite characteristic if he had replaced a sentimental image in his source with a crude one of his own.' In a book where obscenity was to be expected (cf. 11.2 and this very poem, 11.6.1–8), a one-off usage would be immediately intelligible; it does not, of course, mean that the word always had that sense.

[79] Partly borrowed from *Hermathena* 155 (1993) 78–80 (reviewing Gaisser 1993).

and Catullan interpreters whose judgement demands respect.[80] On the other hand, Jacopo Sannazaro rightly objected that *passer Catulli* can't mean that at Martial 4.14.14,[81] and in 1522 the poet and professor Pierio Valeriano produced an eloquent refutation of the whole idea.[82] Poliziano seems to have been influenced by his study in 1485 of the much-damaged Farnese manuscript of Pompeius Festus,[83] which includes the following item:[84]

> In mimes particularly they call the obscene male member *strutheum*, evidently from the salaciousness of the sparrow, which in Greek is called στρουθός.

What is missing from Festus' explanation – so conspicuously as to provide a compelling argument from silence – is any hint that *passer* in Latin meant the same.[85] If it did, what would that mean for poems 2 and 3 in the Catullan collection as we have it, or for the 2–14 *libellus* that we have argued formed the first part of it? We would have to believe that these opening items depended on a double entendre that characterized the collection's main love interest as merely and trivially physical.[86] I don't like that idea, but as Julia Haig Gaisser wisely observes, 'it is in the end a matter of taste'.[87] Let's leave it at that.

The Martial passages fit very well with the inference that poem 14 concluded a short book of poems that began with poem 2, and that 'poem 14b' warned potential readers that the next one was rather different. There were no serious obscenities in the *Passer Catulli* book,[88] and no political invective either – but plenty of both would feature in the book that followed.

---

[80] Pontano: Gaisser 1993.76, 242–3. Poliziano: Gaisser 1993.75–8 and 2007.305–7.

[81] Gaisser 1993.243–5 and 2007.308–10.

[82] Gaisser 1993.134–6 and 2007.311–13; Gaisser deserves the gratitude of all readers for her detailed account of this 'dynamic and charismatic teacher', of whose lectures on Catullus a fragmentary transcript was rescued after the sack of Rome in 1527 (Gaisser 1993.109–45).

[83] Gaisser 1993.74–6 and 2007.306.

[84] Festus 410L: *strutheum in mimis praecipue uocant obscenam partem uirilem, <a> salacitate uidelicet passeris, qui Graece* στρουθός *dicitur.*

[85] So too Thomson 1997.202–3.

[86] To mention nothing else, it would contradict what the poet says at 72.3.

[87] Gaisser 1993.240, going on to note that 'sustained allegory is not a technique used elsewhere in Catullus; if it is present in his sparrow poems it is so skilfully integrated as to hide its presence'. Contrast Schafer 2020.238 on the allegorical reading ('there is simply too much there for there to be nothing to it') and 2020.241–3 for his own elaboration of it ('what if the *passer* is not Catullus' penis, but Lesbia's clitoris?').

[88] The joky description of Flavius at 6.13 (*non tam latera ecfututa pandas*) and the characterisation of an unnamed provincial governor at 10.12–13 (*irrumator praetor*) hardly count; and *ilia* at 11.20 is a respectable anatomical term, not an obscenity.

2.4 Abuse and Invective

What *was* the book that followed? Two hypotheses are currently on offer (Section 2.1 above): Du Quesnay identifies it as poems 15–26, the second of four *libelli* that he believes were combined into the 1–60 polymetric collection; Hubbard, on the other hand, argues that it was poems 15–51, the whole of the rest of that collection minus the items (Schafer's **Ax** sequence) that many believe were subsequently added at the end.[89]

To make progress now we must look beyond the poems themselves and ask how Catullus and his work were described by other authors. The argument is a complex one, and it begins with a much neglected item, one of the first attested citations of Catullus.

The seventh book of Varro's *De lingua Latina*, written about 45 BC and dedicated to Cicero, was concerned with words used by poets.[90] One of his examples of words for stars ran as follows:[91]

> 'Vesperugo' is the star which rises in the evening, which is why Opillius writes it as 'Vesper'. Thus Valerius says 'Vesper is come' of the star the Greeks call 'Diesperios'.

'Vesper is come' (*Vesper adest*) is the opening phrase of Catullus 62, which makes 'Valerius says' the preferable reading in the corrupt Florentine manuscript: *dicitualerius* for the practically meaningless *dicituralterum*.[92]

Catullus as 'Valerius' is also attested in a work by his contemporary Asinius Pollio, as quoted by the fourth-century grammarian Charisius:[93]

> You should say '*hi pugillares*', masculine gender and always plural, as Asinius does in *Against Valerius*, because *pugillus* is what contains several writing-tablets sewn together in order. However, the same Catullus in his hendecasyllables [or: in *Hendecasyllables*] frequently says '*pugillaria*', neuter, and similarly Laberius in *The Fisherman* says *hoc pugillar*, singular.

---

[89] See above, n. 11.

[90] Varro *De lingua Latina* 6.97 (*in proximo de poeticis uerborum originibus scribere in<cipiam>*), 7.5 (*dicam in hoc libro de uerbis quae a poetis sunt posita*).

[91] Varro *De lingua Latina* 7.50 (de Melo 2019.450): *Vesperugo stella quae uespere oritur, a quo eam Opillius scribit uesperum. itaque dicit Valerius 'Vesper adest', quem Graeci dicunt* διεσπέριον.

[92] Schwabe 1870.351, briefly noted by Wiseman 1985.260; cf. Baehrens 1878.17, who prefers *diciturapualerium* (i.e. *dicitur apud Valerium*) since the words are those of the boys' chorus, not the poet himself.

[93] Charisius 124B (Panayotakis 2010.331): *hos pugillares et masculino genere et semper pluraliter dicas, sicut Asinius in Valerium, quia pugillus est qui plures tabellas continent in seriem sutas. at pugillaria saepius neutraliter dicit idem Catullus in hendecasyllabis. item Laberius in Piscatore singulariter hoc pugillar dicit.* The 'correct' spelling *pugillares* would not fit in a hendecasyllable line.

'The same Catullus' makes it clear who the Valerius was whose usage Pollio was criticizing, and it is likely that the two examples of what Pollio didn't like (the neuter *pugillar* or *pugillaria*) came from Pollio's own text. In the extant poems *pugillaria* occurs only once,[94] so if Pollio said 'frequently' (*saepius*) it may be because he had heard hendecasyllable poems by Catullus that did not become part of a *libellus*.

Was Pollio using 'hendecasyllables' as a description or '*Hendecasyllables*' as a title? The elder Seneca used the same citation formula in his entertaining digression on Licinius Calvus in the seventh *Controuersia*. Having just told a story about Calvus' famous prosecution of Vatinius (who stood up and shouted at the jury 'I ask you – do *I* have to be condemned just because *he*'s eloquent?'), Seneca went on with another anecdote from the same year, 54 BC:[95]

> Later, when he saw Asinius Pollio in the Forum being surrounded and beaten by the clients of Cato, whom Calvus was defending, he got someone to put him up on a pillar (because he was short of stature, which is why Catullus in his hendecasyllables [or: in *Hendecasyllables*] calls him an 'eloquent manikin') and swore on oath that if Cato did any injury to his accuser Asinius Pollio, he would take legal action against him. After that Pollio was never attacked by Cato and his supporters in either word or deed.

What Seneca wanted to emphasise was Calvus' energy and boldness, the *ingens animus* apparent also in his poetry:[96]

> This is what he says about Pompey: 'He scratches his head with one finger. What would you say he wants? A man.'

Calvus and Catullus were both famous for abusive political poems, and it took all of Caesar's famous diplomacy to get them to ease off even a little.[97] When Seneca first came to Rome eight or nine years later,[98] that uninhibited freedom of speech must have been still vivid in people's

---

[94] Catullus 42.4–5: *negat mihi nostra reddituram* | *pugillaria*.

[95] Seneca *Controuersiae* 7.4.7 (quoting Catullus 53.5): *idem postea, cum uideret a clientibus Catonis rei sui Pollionem Asinium circumuentum in foro caedi, inponi se supra cippum iussit – erat enim paruolus statura, propter quod etiam Catullus in hendecasyllabis uocat illum salaputium disertum – et iurauit si quam iniuriam Cato Pollioni Asinio accusatori suo fecisset, se in eum iuratum calumniam.* The accused was C. Cato, who had been tribune in 56 BC; he was acquitted on 4 July 54 (Cicero *Ad Atticum* 4.15.4, 16.5).

[96] Seneca *Controuersiae* 7.4.7 quoting Calvus fr. 18 Courtney = 39 Hollis; the full version is given by the scholiast on Juvenal 9.133 ('Magnus, whom everyone's afraid of, scratches his head . . .').

[97] Suetonius *Diuus Iulius* 73 (Calvus' *famosa epigrammata* and Catullus' *uersiculi de Mamurra*); for other Calvan examples, see Asconius 93C (citing *hendecasyllabus Calui*), Suetonius *Diuus Iulius* 49.1, Porphyrio on Horace *Satires* 1.3.1.

[98] Date inferred from Seneca *Controuersiae* 1.pref.11 (after the civil wars, so not before 36 BC).

memories, but a lot had happened in the meantime. Caesar had fought a civil war 'to free the Roman People from the domination of an oligarchy',[99] treating his defeated opponents with conspicuous generosity;[100] the *optimates* had murdered him nonetheless, and those responsible, condemned by judicial process,[101] had been executed or defeated in war by the People's elected agents, of whom the most prominent, in Rome in the mid-thirties, was Caesar's son and heir. Caesar himself was now *diuus Iulius*, honoured and worshipped in public cult.

Catullus and Calvus had both died young.[102] Soon they would be celebrated by Propertius and Ovid as the great forerunners of Roman love poetry,[103] but in 35 BC Horace was a lot less enthusiastic. In an argument about satire, whether one should admire Lucilius, he insisted on classical Greek precedent:[104]

> Humour is often better and more effective than ferocity in cutting through great affairs. It's in this way that those great men whose writings were Old Comedy succeeded, it's for this that they should be imitated. But handsome Hermogenes has never read them, nor has that ape who's trained to sing nothing but Calvus and Catullus.

We don't know who the ape was,[105] but it's clear from the context that what he liked about Catullus and Calvus was their ferocity in attacking the great men of the time – their *ingens animus*, as Seneca put it. Understandably, Maecenas' protégé took a different view.

By the late years of Augustus, and even more under Tiberius, that traditional freedom of slanderous speech was no longer acceptable: another *ingens animus* described by the elder Seneca had his books burned by decree of the Senate.[106] The shift in attitude may account for an odd

---

99 Caesar *De bello ciuili* 1.22.5.

100 As Cicero acknowledged at the time (*Ad familiares* 6.6.10), and denied later (*De officiis* 2.27, 3.84).

101 Augustus *Res gestae* 2.1 (*iudiciis legitimis*); cf. Livy *Epitome* 120 (*C. Caesar consul legem tulit de quaestione habenda*), Velleius Paterculus 2.69.5, Suetonius *Nero* 3.1, *Galba* 3.2 (*lege Pedia*); Appian *Civil Wars* 3.95.392 (νόμῳ), Dio 46.48.2 (νόμον).

102 Ovid *Amores* 3.9.61–2.   103 Propertius 2.25.3–4, 2.34.87–90, Ovid *Tristia* 2.427–32.

104 Horace *Satires* 1.10.14–19: *ridiculum acri | fortius et melius magnas plerumque secat res. | illi scripta quibus comoedia prisca uiris est | hoc stabant, hoc sunt imitandi: quos neque pulcher | Hermogenes umquam legit neque simius iste | nil praeter Caluum et doctus cantare Catullum.* Cf. *Satires* 1.4.1–7 on Eupolis, Cratinus and Aristophanes as Lucilius' models in everything but metre.

105 Porphyrio (*ad loc.*) assumes he is the Demetrius mentioned with Hermogenes at lines 90–1, where they are evidently teachers of literature; for the problem of Hermogenes' identity (cf. *Satires* 1.2.1–4, 1.3.1–19 and 129–30, 1.4.72, 1.10.80), see Rudd 1966.292–3.

106 The orator and historian T. Labienus (Seneca *Controuersiae* 10.pref.4–8, esp. 5 *animus inter uitia ingens*); the occasion may have been the crackdown on libellous writings in AD 12 (Dio Cassius 56.27.1).

phrase in Velleius Paterculus' list of the *eminentia ingenia* of Roman literature in the late republic. He names twelve orators, one historian and three poets:[107]

> Who doesn't know that the following authors, separated by differences in age, flourished at this time? Cicero and Hortensius; before them Crassus, Cotta and Sulpicius and after them Brutus, Calidius, Caelius, Calvus and (second only to Cicero) Caesar; then their pupils, as it were, Corvinus and Asinius Pollio; Sallust, the rival of Thucydides; and the poetic authors Varro and Lucretius, and Catullus, not inferior [to them] in any poem of his admired work.

That implies Catullan work that was *not* admired, which was surely his political invective, particularly against Caesar. Velleius was writing only a few years after the trial for treason of Cremutius Cordus, who pleaded in vain that Caesar and Augustus had ignored the insults written about them by Catullus and Furius Bibaculus.[108]

Catullus called his invective poems *iambi*, but that was a generic term, not a metrical description.[109] One poem in which he threatened an attack, evidently lost in the transmission of our collection,[110] was quoted by Pomponius Porphyrio in his third-century commentary on Horace's *Odes*. Noting Horace's reference to the 'swift iambics' he had written as an angry young man, Porphyrio explained:[111]

> Iambics are held to be the most appropriate verses for invective. In fact Catullus too, when threatening abuse, says this: 'But you won't escape my iambics.'

This is a hendecasyllable line, and since all Catullus' extant references to iambic invective, and some of his most savage attacks, come in hendeca-syllabic poems,[112] they could easily have been part of a miscellaneous

---

[107] Velleius Paterculus 2.36.2: *quis enim ignorat diremptos gradibus aetatis floruisse hoc tempore Ciceronem Hortensium, anteque Crassum Cottam Sulpicium, moxque Brutum Calidium Caelium et proximum Ciceroni Caesarem eorumque uelut alumnos Coruinum ac Pollionem Asinium, aemulumque Thucydidis Sallustium auctoresque carminum Varronem ac Lucretium neque ullo in suspecti operis sui carmine minorem Catullum?* The underlined phrase is the transmitted text as printed and defended by Kritz 1840.224; I am very grateful to Tony Woodman for this information and discussion of the passage. Most editors follow Lipsius in changing *suspecti* to *suscepti*; but what would be the point of specifying 'the work he undertook'?

[108] Tacitus *Annals* 4.34.5 (AD 25) .

[109] There are only three poems in the collection (4, 29 and 53) that were composed in iambic trimeter.

[110] For another such loss see above, n. 5; it's unlikely that Porphyrio knew the poem independently of the *codex* edition.

[111] Porphyrio on Horace *Odes* 1.16.22: *iambi autem uersus aptissimi habentur ad maledicendum. denique et Catullus cum maledicta minaretur sic ait: 'at non effugies meos iambos'.*

[112] References: also Catullus 36.5, 40.2, 54.6. Attacks: e.g. poems 15, 16, 21, 33.

collection entitled '*Hendecasyllables*', if we choose to infer that title from the Pollio and Seneca citations.

Quintilian seems to make that very point in his famous list of recommended reading in book 10 of the *Institutio oratoria*:[113]

> Iambic has not been much used by the Romans as a work in its own right, but mixed up with other [metres]; its bitterness will be found in Catullus, Bibaculus and Horace (though in Horace the short line intervenes).

Quintilian knew Catullus well, citing him by name on subjects as various as Transpadane vocabulary, aspirated consonants, the definition of wit and the figure of *heteroiosis* (altered idiom).[114] When it came to attacks on Caesar, however, the holder of a public chair had to be cautious:[115]

> Harsh invectives, however, as I have said, make their attack in iambics: 'Who can witness this, who can endure it, except a pervert, a glutton and a gambler?'
>
> One of the poets says he doesn't much care whether Caesar is a black man or a white. Madness!

These items belonged to Catullus' non-admired work (to adapt Velleius' phrase), so Quintilian didn't attribute them.

It evidently didn't matter when the victim of the lampoon wasn't Caesar. The elder Pliny, another admirer of Catullus, quotes him twice in the *Natural History* when discussing luxury materials:[116]

> Cornelius Nepos reports that the first man in Rome to cover entire walls with marble veneer was Mamurra, who did so at his house on the Caelian

---

[113] Quintilian 10.1.96: *iambus non sane a Romanis celebratus est ut proprium opus, sed aliis quibusdam interpositus; cuius acerbitas in Catullo Bibaculo Horatio, quamquam illi epodos interueniat, reperietur.*

[114] Respectively, 1.5.8 (*sicut Catullus*), quoting 97.6; 1.5.20 (*Catulli nobile epigramma*), referring to poem 81; 6.3.18 (*Catullus, cum dicit*), quoting 86.4; 9.3.16 (*Catullus in epithalamio*), quoting 62.45.

[115] 9.4.141 (quoting Catullus 29.1–2): *aspera et maledicta, ut dixi, etiam in carmine iambis grassantur: quis hoc potest uidere, quis potest pati,| nisi impudicus et uorax et aleo?* 11.1.38 (referring to poem 93): *negat se magni facere aliquis poetarum, utrum Caesar ater an albus homo sit, insania.* Public chair: Jerome *Chronica* on Ol. 216.4 (AD 88, *primus Romae publicam scholam et salarium e fisco accepit et claruit*).

[116] Pliny *Natural History* 36.48 (paraphrasing Catullus 29.2–3): *primum Romae parietes crusta marmoris operuisse totos domus suae in Caelio monte Cornelius Nepos tradit Mamurram, Formiis natum equitem Romanum, praefectum fabrum C. Caesaris in Gallia, ne quid indignitati desit, tali auctore inuenta re. hic namque est Mamurra Catulli Veroniensis carminibus proscissus, quem, ut res est, domus ipsius clarius quam Catullus dixit habere quidquid habuisset comata Gallia.* Ibid. 37.81 (referring to Catullus 52.1–2): *insignis etiam apud nos historia, siquidem exstat hodieque huius generis gemma, propter quam ab Antonio proscriptus est Nonius senator, filius Strumae Noni eius quem Catullus poeta in sella curuli uisum indigne tulit, auusque Seruili Noniani quem consulem uidimus.*

hill; he was a Roman knight born at Formiae who served as Gaius Caesar's prefect of engineers, and it completes the outrageousness of the thing that such a man should be the inventor of it. For this Mamurra is the man cut to pieces in the poems of Catullus of Verona, though in fact his house stated more clearly than Catullus did that Mamurra possessed whatever long-haired Gaul had once had.

The history [of opals] is famous among us as well, in as much as even today there exists the jewel of this type for which Antony put a senator on the proscription list; he was Nonius, son of the Nonius Struma whom the poet Catullus was indignant at seeing in a curule chair, and grandfather of Servilius Nonianus, whom we have seen as consul [in AD 35].

Here the attacks are seen as justified, or at least neutral. Pliny has enrolled his fellow-Transpadane 'Catullus of Verona', celebrated at the very start of the great work,[117] as part of his criticism of rampant extravagance.

Pliny's nephew shared his pride in the region[118] and was himself a keen imitator of Catullus.[119] So were his friends, for instance, the orator and historian Pompeius Saturninus:[120]

He also writes verses like Catullus and Calvus – yes, really like Catullus and Calvus. How much charm, sweetness, bitterness and love they contain!

Or Sentius Augurinus, later a distinguished senator:[121]

He calls them 'little poems'. Many are simple, many grand, many charming, many tender, many sweet, many angry. [A quotation:] 'I sing my songs in tiny verses, the same ones my Catullus used long ago, and Calvus and the men of old.'

The bitterness (*amaritudo*) and anger (*cum bile*) show that the association with Calvus was not just for love poetry, as in Propertius and Ovid, but for invective as well, as in Horace.[122]

Those early references and these much later imitations equally presuppose a widely accessible text of Catullus in which the invective attacks – including those dangerously directed at the first of the Caesars – were

---

[117] Pliny *Natural History* pref. 1 (*Catullum conterraneum meum*); see Section 5.3 below on the moral standards of the *Transpadani*.
[118] Pliny *Letters* 1.14.4 (*illa nostra Italia*), 7.22.2 (*regio mea*); Syme 1979.694–8.
[119] Pliny *Letters* 4.14.2 (quoting Catullus 16.5–8); cf. 5.10.1–2, 7.4.8 (his book of hendecasyllables).
[120] Pliny *Letters* 1.16.5: *praetera facit uersus qualis Catullus aut Caluus, re uera qualis Catullus aut Caluus. quantum illis leporis dulcedinis amaritudinis amoris!*
[121] Pliny *Letters* 4.27.1 and 4: *poematia appellat. multa tenuiter, multa sublimiter, multa uenuste, multa tenere, multa dulciter, multa cum bile*.... *'canto carmina uersibus minutis,* | *his olim quibus et meus Catullus* | *et Caluus ueteresque.'* Sentius also used the Catullan metre, hendecasyllables.
[122] See above, nn. 102 and 103.

mixed in with poems of a very different character. That sounds just like the surviving polymetric collection. If the *Passer Catulli* was originally an entity in itself, the rest could have been a single longer book, possibly called '*Hendecasyllables*' after the metre of the majority of its contents.[123]

2.5 Chronological Consequences

That conclusion helps a little with the problem of the misfit poems at the end of the 1–60 collection (Schafer's **Ax** sequence).[124] Since poem 52 was quoted by the elder Pliny and poem 53 by the elder Seneca, I think we can safely rule out the proposal of Hubbard and Schafer that the *libellus* ended with poem 51.[125] A better possibility is available: that 52 and 53 closed this *libellus* in just the same way that poem 14 closed the first one, with a reminder of Calvus' famous feud with Vatinius.[126] That has useful consequences for the chronology of the books, but before exploring them it is worth thinking about the rest of the **Ax** sequence (54–60). How did they come to be there?

Schafer's answer is 'textual intrusion', 'transmission accident' or 'textual corruption',[127] later refined with the more helpful suggestion of 'ad hoc private "suppletions" of an authorial book'.[128] But he then abandons this insight for a proposal he rightly calls 'speculative'.[129] It is this:[130]

> The poems of **Ax** present themselves, within their dramatic conceit, as instances of the Catullo-Calvan exchange described in poem 50 . . . (depicted as) the improvised verses Catullus and Calvus wrote together "yesterday". . . . My proposal from the beginning is to take **Ax** as the *Appendix Catulliana*. By framing them like this, as meta-doggerel, Catullus himself would have marginalized them, appendicized them.

He imagines the poets competing in a 'call and response' scenario,[131] which is hardly compatible with the fact that seven of the relevant poems

---

[123] Pliny's own book entitled *Hendecasyllabi* (n. 119 above) is no help here, since it evidently consisted entirely of poems in that metre.

[124] See above, n. 11.   [125] See above, nn. 12 (Hubbard and Schafer), 92 (Seneca), 113 (Pliny).

[126] Catullus 14.2–3 (*iucundissime Calue, munere isto* | *odissem te odio Vatiniano*), 52.3 (*per consulatum peierat Vatinius*), 53.2–3 (*cum mirifice Vatiniana* | *meus crimina Caluus explicasset*).

[127] Schafer 2020.43, cf. 46, 51.

[128] Schafer 2020.46, citing Barchiesi 2005. Cf. Hutchinson 2003.207: 'The papyri suggest that collections of epigrams were easily modified. In principle, authors, later editors and readers could omit from or add to an existing collection.'

[129] Schafer 2020.127–33, cf. 61: 'a speculative proposal for how it might have fit in and been legible at (or as) the authorial ending of **A**.'

[130] Schafer 2020.128, 133.   [131] Schafer 2020.129–31, based on Catullus 50.1–6.

(54, 55, 56, 58, 58b, 59, 60) are addressed to people other than Calvus. This arbitrary and unnecessary complication is better left out of the argument.

Schafer's first idea, too soon abandoned, is much more promising. If we were right to see poem 1 as a personalized dedication poem for a single copy rather than the opening poem of the *libellus* as publicly available,[132] then 'ad hoc private "suppletions" of an authorial book' do indeed become available as an explanation. Let's suppose, as suggested above, that the authorial text of the second book concluded at poem 53. Now let's assume that someone who owned a copy added at the end of the scroll some uncollected Catullan pieces they happened to know, or as much as they could remember of them, and that their copy, obtained on the market or preserved in some library, happened to be one used by the compiler of the codex edition. If the compiler got all the required Catullan *libelli* from the same source, there's a good chance that poems 54–60 were added at the end of the second *libellus* by the man who was given a personal copy of the first: the historian and biographer Cornelius Nepos.

From now on, therefore, I shall take it as the default position that the surviving 1–60 polymetric collection consisted of two papyrus book-rolls, 2–14 and 14b–53, with poem 1 added to the first by the author and poems 54–60 added to the second by the owner of the book.

At this point we must look at the one independently attested piece of Catullan biography that has come down to us, in Suetonius' very well-informed life of Julius Caesar:[133]

> [Caesar] did not conceal the fact that Valerius Catullus had inflicted everlasting marks of infamy on his name with his verses about Mamurra; but when he apologised he invited him to dinner the same day, and continued to use the hospitality of Catullus' father, as was his custom.

The poem concerned must be 57, which openly calls Caesar a *cinaedus*.[134] Given the apology, it is inconceivable that the poem featured in a written collection circulated to the public. Such slanderous attacks were designed

---

[132] Thus explaining the metrical anomaly (Section 2.3 above).

[133] Suetonius *Diuus Iulius* 73: *Valerium Catullum, a quo sibi uersiculis de Mamurra perpetua stigmata imposita non dissimulauerat, satis facientem eadem die adhibuit cenae hospitioque patris eius, sicut consuerat, uti perseuerauit.* See Wallace-Hadrill 1983.61–4 on the quality and variety of Suetonius' late-republican sources.

[134] Caesar's reference to *perpetua stigmata* must echo 57.3–5 (*maculae ... impressae resident nec eluentur*). Cf. Schafer 2020.51: 'The frank accusation of pathic homosexuality by Caesar in 57 is harsher in several respects than anything in poem 29', which in any case did not refer to Caesar by name.

to be repeated *in ore uulgi*,[135] and Caesar will certainly have heard this one by word of mouth.

The first of the two published *libelli* (2–14), probably also composed first since all its hendecasyllables have the 'spondaic base' (Section 2.3 above), contained in poem 11 a handsome tribute to 'great Caesar' and his campaigns across the Rhine and the Channel in 55 BC. The inevitable conclusion is that the book was put together after the poet had made his apology. The second *libellus* contained the attack on Mamurra's profiteering from Gaul and Britain (poem 29); but since it didn't quite *name* Mamurra's two deplorable protectors, the poet may have felt he could get away with that one. If we are right, the owner of the second book has preserved the text of the attack that caused the trouble in the first place (poem 57), and part of another attack on Caesar that wasn't included in the published collection: 'Commander One-and-only, you're going to be angry again with my blameless iambics.'[136]

The apology and the dinner invitation must have taken place in the Transpadana, as Caesar was on his way from Gaul to Illyricum in the early months of 54 BC.[137] That provides a firm *terminus post quem* for the composition of the two polymetric *libelli* that were transcribed as the first part (1–60) of the codex edition. As it happens, the early months of 54 BC were just the time when the long-running feud between Calvus and Vatinius, which Catullus celebrated in both those books,[138] was at a particularly critical point.

Publius Vatinius was the tribune of 59 BC who had forced through the popular vote for Caesar's Gallic command against furious optimate opposition. Three years later, he was the main prosecution witness in a politically motivated trial where Calvus appeared for the defence. Cicero reported the outcome in a letter to his brother:[139]

---

[135] See, for instance, Terence *Adelphoe* 91–3 (*clamant omnes indignissume factum esse . . . in ore est omni populo*), Cicero *In Verrem* 2.1.121 (*istius nequitiam et iniquitatem tum in ore uulgi atque in communibus prouerbiis esse uersatam*), *Ad Q. fratrem* 2.3.2 (*cum omnia maledicta, uersus denique obscenissimi in Clodium et Clodiam dicerentur*, February 56 BC). The wretched Ravidus knew what to expect (Catullus 40.5, *an ut peruenias in ora uulgi?*).

[136] Catullus 54.6–7 (quoting 29.11): *irascere iterum meis iambis | immerentibus, unice imperator*.

[137] Caesar *De bello Gallico* 5.1.1–5, with Wiseman 2015.104–5.   [138] See above, n. 126.

[139] Cicero *Ad Q. fratrem* 2.4.1: *Sestius noster absolutus est a.d. II Id. Mart. . . . Vatinium, a quo palam oppugnabatur, arbitratu nostro concidimus dis hominibusque plaudentibus. quin etiam Paulus noster, cum testis productus esset in Sestium, confirmauit se nomen Vatini delaturum si Macer Licinius cunctaretur, et Macer ab Sesti subselliis surrexit ac se illi non defuturum adfirmauit.* For some unknown reason Cicero here calls Calvus by his late father's *cognomen*, but his identity is confirmed by the scholiast (*Scholia Bobiensia* 125 Stangl).

Our friend Sestius was acquitted on 14 March [56 BC].... Vatinius, whose
attack on him was undisguised, I cut to pieces just as I chose, to the applause
of gods and men. Not only that, but our friend Paulus, even though he'd
been called as witness against Sestius, formally announced that he would
prosecute Vatinius if Licinius Macer [i.e. Calvus] didn't get on with it. Macer
got up from the Sestius benches and declared that he wouldn't let him down.

At this point the *optimates* were in the ascendancy, but a month or so later
Caesar came as far south as he could and conferred with his allies at
Luca.[140] The rest of the year, and beyond, was taken up by a power
struggle to get Pompey and Crassus elected to the consulship, and Vatinius
to the praetorship, of 55 BC. Calvus must have found it hard to proceed
against such newly invigorated opposition, and once in office Vatinius was
safe from prosecution till the end of the year. Meanwhile Pompey and
Caesar exerted diplomatic pressure on Cicero to get him to give up his
hostility and defend Vatinius when Calvus eventually got his chance.[141]

It isn't surprising that the prosecution was on Catullus' mind when he
was composing those two *libelli*. At the time of his own conversation with
Caesar, Vatinius had been out of office for only a matter of weeks, but it
seems Catullus had already heard Calvus in action against him at one of
the preliminary hearings to get the case started.[142] It is surely also significant that in his poem of thanks to Cicero (for what, he doesn't say)
Catullus describes him with studied ambiguity as 'the best advocate of all'
or 'the best advocate of *everyone*' – even Vatinius!'[143]

The suggestion is that Caesar's generous approach to Catullus resulted in
the poet making a collection of polymetric short poems, in two quite
different *libelli* for public distribution, which deliberately did *not* contain
the attack Caesar had resented.[144] But at the end of each *libellus* he put in a
reminder of the ongoing Vatinius saga, cheering Calvus on in his efforts.[145]

[140] While all this was going on Catullus was still in Bithynia, or on his way back via 'the famous cities
of Asia' (poem 46).

[141] Cicero *Ad familiares* 1.9.19. Cf. *Ad Q. fratrem* 2.8.3 (February 55 BC): 'They're in total control
and they want everyone to know it.'

[142] Catullus 53.3 (*meus crimina Caluus explicasset*) makes it likely that the occasion was the *criminis
delatio*, to get the charges legally defined (cf. Cicero *De inuentione* 2.58, *Pro Sex. Roscio* 28,
Diuinatio in Caecilium 10, *Pro Ligario* 1).

[143] Catullus 49.7: *optimus omnium patronus*.

[144] No doubt plenty of people remembered it, like the reader (Nepos?) who we have suggested added
it to his personal copy.

[145] It didn't work: when Vatinius was eventually put on trial later in the year Calvus' prosecution
speeches became oratorical classics (Tacitus *Dialogus* 21.2), but Cicero got him off anyway, and
agonized about it afterwards (*Ad Q. fratrem* 3.5.4, October 54 BC).

So far as we can tell, all the poems collected in those two *libelli* had been written in the previous two years,[146] beginning with the leisurely return from Bithynia in the spring and summer of 56 BC that is a conspicuous theme in both of them.[147] But is that also true of the other book-rolls that were used to make the codex edition? Does *all* the collection as we have it consist of work made public at that time?

2.6 Goodbye to All That

In one case there is an easy answer. Poem 61, the wedding hymn for Manlius Torquatus and Vibia (?) Aurunculeia, shows the same development in Catullus' metrical technique as the hendecasyllables in the polymetric *libelli*, and was therefore being composed about the same time that they were. Recognition of this has been complicated by the unnecessary assumption that poem 61 is a 'probably early composition'.[148] That is based entirely on the assumption that the bridegroom was the L. Manlius Torquatus who was praetor in 49 BC, one of the interlocutors in Cicero's *De finibus*.[149] Of course he is a possibility, but the patrician Manlii Torquati were a quite extensive family in the late republic,[150] and there is no reason to identify the bridegroom with that one in particular. I think we must accept the metrical evidence as dating Catullus' commission for this high-society wedding to late 56 or more probably 55.[151]

There is no way of dating poems 62–4, but poem 65 records another commission, this time from Atticus' friend Hortalus.[152] What he had

---

[146] See Section 1.1 above for the datable poems, though 55 no longer counts for dating the authorial collection.

[147] Poems 4, 31, 34, 46 and fr. 1, attesting a route that included Lampsacus (where the poet dedicated a grove to Priapus), 'noble Rhodes' and Delos (the likely setting for his hymn to Diana); on poem 34, see the rival views of Zetzel 1992.47–50 and Wiseman 1992.61–3. Cf. Du Quesnay 2021.181: 'On the assumption that he took his time visiting the cities of Asia (46.6) and then spent some time on family affairs in Verona, he may not have been much if at all in Rome before the winter of 56/55.'

[148] Butterfield 2021.146, citing Neudling 1955.119, who 'suggests an approximate date of 60 BC'.

[149] Caesar *De bello ciuili* 1.24.3, Cicero *De finibus* 1.13. Schafer and Du Quesnay both take the identification for granted, and both build adventurous speculations on it: Schafer 2020.12, with 181–94; Du Quesnay 2021.172, with 173–4 and 189.

[150] See Mitchell 1966, with a stemma at 30–1. More than one of them had literary interests similar to Catullus' (Pliny *Letters* 5.3.5, *Torquatum, immo Torquatos*); Horace's friend Torquatus (*Epistles* 1.5, *Odes* 4.7) is one we happen to know.

[151] June, after the Ides, was an auspicious time for weddings (Ovid *Fasti* 6.219–25).

[152] Catullus 65.2 and 15; cf. Cicero *Ad Atticum* 2.25.1, 4.15.4. Usually identified as the famous orator Q. Hortensius, to whom however no *cognomen* is ever attributed in the very numerous contemporary sources that mention him; the only evidence for the identification is Tacitus *Annals* 2.37.1 (*preces Marci Hortali nobilis iuuenis ... nepos erat oratoris Hortensii*), but it is now

asked for we don't know, but Catullus sent him a substantial Callimachus translation (poem 66) as the only thing possible in his grief for his dead brother. It must have been at about the same time that he wrote poem 68a, an elaborate letter to Mallius apologizing for not being able to provide the 'gifts of the Muses and Venus' that Mallius had asked for.[153] Two items of evidence may help us with the chronology of these poems.

The first, discovered only in 2012, is an inference from Catullus' apology to Hortalus. 'I send you this translation', he said, 'lest you should think that your words were entrusted in vain to the wandering winds, and had happened to slip from my mind.'[154] This has always been taken as a variant on the traditional metaphor of empty words 'scattered by the wind', as used of the Phaeacians in the *Odyssey* and of Alfenus, Theseus and the poet's mistress in Catullus.[155] But that's not good enough, as Tony Woodman has shown:[156]

> The fact is that the phrase *credere (aliquid) uentis* occurs in no other example of the proverbial 'words on the wind'. On the contrary, the phrase is used exclusively of sailing the seas.... In the light of this evidence it seems most unlikely that Catullus would use the phrase *credere uentis* of anything other than a sea-voyage.... If that is the case, he is not referring to the proverbial motif of 'words on the wind' at all but is referring to the hazards of the long-distance postal service.... Hortalus and Catullus are separated from each other and can communicate only by sea-borne letters.

Woodman goes on to suggest that perhaps Catullus 'is in the middle of his journey to Troy to visit his brother's grave, to which he famously refers in Poem 101'. Certainly, the context in poem 65 makes that a natural inference.

Our second item of evidence is what Catullus said to Mallius about the effect of his brother's death. It put an end to everything he enjoyed, meaning love and poetry (*totum hoc studium | abstulit*), and so he banished

---

clear that this refers to Marcius Hortalus, praetor in AD 25 (*AE* 1987.163, cf. *IGRR* 3.944; I am very grateful to John Morgan for alerting me to this).

[153] Catullus 68.10 (*muneraque et Musarum hinc petis et Veneris*). See Thomson 1997.473 on the transmission of the name of the addressee in line 11 and 30; *pace* Schafer (2020.12, 182), there is absolutely no reason to identify him as the bridegroom Manlius of poem 61.

[154] Catullus 65.17–18: *ne tua dicta uagis nequiquam credita uentis | effluxisse meo forte putes animo.*

[155] Homer *Odyssey* 8.409 (ἄφαρ τὸ φέροιεν ἀναρπάξασαι ἄελλαι); Catullus 30.9–10 (*tua dicta omnia factaque | uentos irrita ferre ac nebulas aereas sinis*), 64.59 (*irrita uentosae linquens promissa procellae*), 64.142 (*quae cuncta aerii discerpunt irrita uenti*), 70.4 (*in uento et rapida scribere oportet aqua*).

[156] Woodman 2012.148, citing Tibullus 1.7.20, Germanicus *Aratea* 14, Seneca *Agamemnon* 443, *Hercules Furens* 152, Quintilian 12.pref.3, Virgil *Aeneid* 5.850, Seneca *Medea* 304, Manilius 1.77–8, Catullus 64.212–13.

all such activity from his mind (*tota de mente fugaui | haec studia*).[157] That rules out, I think, the widely held assumption that the brother's death predated the poet's service in Bithynia in 57–56 BC;[158] it makes sense only if the poems in the surviving collection had almost all been written *before* Catullus heard of his brother's death. Now, 'all such activity' was over.

We have to accept what he says: it was a devastating event. All he could do now was write his brother's epitaph (poem 101), put together an apology for Mallius (poem 68a), and give Hortalus, whose request may have caught up with him when he was already on his way to the grave in the Troad, something that had already been written (poem 66). The only available time is the early spring of 54 BC – after he had had his conversation with Caesar, and before he collected the poetry he had written so far into carefully composed *libelli* for public circulation. Perhaps the collection itself was a signal that he had finished with that kind of poetry.

Now we must take account of poem 68b, Catullus' most ambitious achievement in the *studia* of poetry and love, which contains at lines 91–100 a lament for his brother. The scenario we have suggested is clearly impossible if poem 68b was written after the brother's death, and even exploited it as the centre of its construction.[159] That is indeed the modern consensus, but it ignores a substantial body of opinion that sees lines 91–100 as a later insertion into an essentially completed poem.[160] It seems to me that the elaborately perfect symmetry created at lines 73–130, the long passage comparing the poet's mistress with Laodamia, makes it overwhelmingly likely that lines 91–100, which disrupt it, were indeed a later addition. I made the case in 1974, and I still think it's compelling:[161]

> One thing must be made clear: it is *not* suggested that Catullus created a careful symmetry and then botched it for no good reason, but rather that before he included 68b in his published collection, he had decided that his brother's death was a theme important enough to include even at the expense of disturbing the original structure.

---

[157] Catullus 68.19–20, 25–6.
[158] A date of 58 BC for the brother's death is assumed without argument by Du Quesnay and Woodman 2021.4 and Du Quesnay 2021.177, 191 n. 106, 202.
[159] See, for instance, Gaisser 2009.121 ('This central panel is the emotional heart of the poem'), Gale 2012.186–7 ('the centre of the poem').
[160] Wohlberg 1955.44–5, Copley 1957.31–2, Vretska 1966.323–5, Wiseman 1974.73–6; allowed as a possibility by Thomson 1997.472.
[161] Wiseman 1974.74: omitting lines 91–100, the structure is marked by *se intulit* (70–1), *coniugis* (73), *coniugium* (84), *coniugium* (107), *sed tuus* (117), *sed tu* (129) and *se contulit* (132).

It was a new and urgent theme,[162] and there was little time to act on it as the collection was being put together.

The two polymetric *libelli* we have detected, 2–14 and 14b–53 (perhaps *Passer* and *Hendecasyllables*, if the poet gave them titles at all), roughly correspond to **A** in Schafer's scheme (Section 2.1 above). Poems 61–4 are his **B**, described as an 'authorially designed book',[163] though perhaps we should imagine the four poems as separate book-rolls that owe their position to the compiler of the codex edition. The poems in elegiac couplets, both the long ones (65–68b) and the 'epigrams' (69–116), are Schafer's **C**, held together as a unit by the *carmina Battiadae* cross-reference at 116.2 and 65.16.[164]

Since **C** shares many names and themes with **A**,[165] and one of its poems is specifically dated to 55 BC,[166] this *libellus* too no doubt consisted of poems written in the period from spring 56 to winter 55–54 BC. But it alone mentions Catullus' brother, in just those four places,[167] and that is why I think the news of his death probably came while the 'collected poems' were being set in order. By the time the poet had returned from his journey to the grave on the Trojan shore,[168] those tributes had been composed and could take their place in the last of the *libelli*.

Giving up personal poetry, whether of love or hate, did not entail giving up being a poet. On the contrary, the last poem in the whole collection promised more to come,[169] and may have indicated by its metrical peculiarities what sort of writing Catullus would be doing next.[170] The books in our collection were not the only ones that would bear his name.

2.7   Scriptwriter

Again, as in Section 2.4 above, we must look for quotations in other texts, and again the argument is not a simple one.

[162] Catullus 65.12: *semper maesta tua carmina morte canam.*
[163] Schafer 2020.3, cf. 135: 'It makes sense ... for four long poems with deep thematic resonances to offer themselves to readers synoptically, implicitly offering themselves as a whole greater than the sum of its parts.' So too, though now I doubt it, Wiseman 1985.180 ('Book Two'), cf. 265–6 ('a three-volume collection').
[164] See above, n. 7 (*pace* Du Quesnay, n. 23 above).
[165] Besides Lesbia (68b, 70, 72, 75–6, 79, 83, 85–7, 91–2, 104, 107, 109) and Juventius (81, 99), note also Cinna (95, 113, cf. 10.30), Calvus (96) and 'Mentula' (105, 114–15, identified as Mamurra by 29.13).
[166] 113.1–2: *consule Pompeio ... nunc iterum.*   [167] 65.5–14, 68.19–26, 68.91–100, 101.
[168] 65.7 (*Rhoeteo litore*), 68.99–100.   [169] 116.7–8 (future tenses); see above, n. 52.
[170] 116.3 (wholly spondaic) and 8 (elided *s*), with Wiseman 1985.184–6; for varied reactions to my interpretation here, see Fowler 1986.89, Syndikus 1987.249, Townend 1987.14–15, Zetzel 1988.82–4.

First, a citation by the anonymous commentator whose work is preserved on the ninth-century Bern manuscript of Lucan's epic on the civil war:[171]

> Because of his wife Aerope's adultery, Atreus slew the sons of his brother Thyestes at the altar in a pretended sacrifice. It is said that at a banquet he served Thyestes with wine mixed with blood and the entrails of his sons. The sun hid himself in clouds so as not to see this horror – that is, the sun was eclipsed, and there was night at Mycenae. But I have found in a book of Catullus entitled *On Mime-Performances* that this is a legend. He says that Atreus was the first to explain to his fellow-citizens the true and hitherto unfamiliar courses of the sun, and convince them that it rises opposite the signs [of the Zodiac], and what the other planets are said to do, and that becoming famous through this expertise he supplanted his brother and became king. Later tragedians turned this into a prodigy.

This passage is baffling if one assumes, as many Latinists do,[172] that mime-performances were nothing but trivial mass entertainment.

We do indeed know from Cicero that mime was characterized by physical clowning and obscene language,[173] and that its plots might be improvised;[174] but we also know that the two leading mime-dramatists of the time were masters of the witty word-play Cicero himself used,[175] and wrote scripts that he referred to as *poemata*.[176] Two generations later, when 'mime' still implied obscenity of both word and deed,[177] the mimographer Publilius was proverbial for morally improving observations, and his *sententiae* were collected for teaching ethics.[178]

---

[171] *Commenta Bernensia* on Lucan 1.543–4 (*qualem fugiente per ortus | sole Thyesteae noctem duxere Mycenae*): *Atreus Thyestis fratris sui filios ob adulterium Aeropae uxoris suae ad aram mactauit simulato sacrificio. uinum sanguine mixtum uisceraque filiorum eius pro epulis Thyesti adposuisse dicitur. quod nefas ne sol aspiceret, nubibus se abscondit, hoc est eclipsin passus est, Mycenisque nox fuit. sed hoc fabulosum inueni in libro Catulli qui inscribitur* περὶ μιμολογιῶν. *qui ait <Atreum> primum ciuibus suis solis cursus ueros et ante inauditos ostendisse ac persuasisse illum contrarium signis omnibus ascendere et quod ceterae uagae stellae facere dicuntur: et ob hanc scientiam inclitum summoto fratre regnum accepisse. quod in prodigium minores tragoedi conuerterunt.* The phrase underlined is Mueller's correction (1869.622) of the transmitted text *quis cribitur permimologiarum*.

[172] E.g. Syndikus 1987.249: 'it is hard to believe that a critic of trivial literature, committed to Callimachus' strict concept of art, would suddenly want to entertain a mass audience with the most trivial of popular amusements'.

[173] Cicero *De oratore* 2.242 (*obscenitas*), 251 (*ore uultu uoce denique corpore ridetur*), *Orator* 88 (*subobsceno*).

[174] Cicero *Pro Caelio* 65 (*cum clausula non inuenitur, fugit aliquis e manibus, dein scabilla concrepant, aulaeum tollitur*); cf. Macrobius *Saturnalia* 2.7.7 for a contest of extemporary performance.

[175] Seneca *Controuersiae* 7.3.8–9 (quoting Cassius Severus) on Publilius, Laberius and Cicero.

[176] Cicero *Ad familiares* 12.18.2 (September 46 BC): *equidem sic iam obdurui ut ludis Caesaris nostri animo aequissimo . . . audirem Laberi et Publili poemata.*

[177] Ovid *Tristia* 2.497 and 515, Valerius Maximus 2.6.7.

[178] Petronius *Satyrica* 55.5 (*quid enim his melius dici potest?*), Aulus Gellius 17.14.3–4. *Sententiae*: Duff and Duff 1934.14–111 (text and translation), Giancotti 1967.277–462.

It's clear there was constant variety, and interplay with other genres. Caecilius, who wrote comedies of the same sort as Plautus and Terence, is said to have incorporated mime material,[179] and according to Nicolaus of Damascus the pleasure Sulla took in 'mimes and clowns' was demonstrated by 'the satyric comedies he himself wrote in his native language'.[180] Virgil's sixth *Eclogue* was sung in the theatre – and surely danced as well – by the *mima* Cytheris.[181] When her younger contemporary Pylades introduced the new 'Italian dance' or 'all-mime' (*pantomimus*), in which the dancer was silent and wore a mask with closed lips, it was in order to avoid the difficulty of the same performer having to sing and dance at the same time.[182] Innovations were happening already in Catullus' time: Alexandrian mime-plots were a novelty in 54 BC, and the description of the Syrian Publilius, newly arrived in Rome, as 'the founder of the *mimus* stage' certainly suggests the start of something new.[183]

Publilius' rival was Decimus Laberius, famous for his outspokenness about public affairs:[184] as Horace rather sourly put it, if excoriating the city were all that mattered, the mimes of Laberius would be admired as splendid poems.[185] We can see what it meant in practice from a letter of Cicero to the young lawyer Trebatius, who was on Caesar's staff in Gaul, written a few months after the second campaign in Britain:[186]

> If you come back soon there won't be any talk, but if you're away too long with no result I'm terrified not just of Laberius but of our friend Valerius too. A legal expert from Britain would be a wonderful character to bring on stage!

---

[179] Aulus Gellius 2.23.12: *alia nescio quae mimica inculcauit.*

[180] Athenaeus 6.261c (*FGrH* 90 F75): Σύλλαν φησὶ τὸν Ῥωμαίων στρατηγὸν οὕτω χαίρειν μίμοις καὶ γελωτοποιοῖς φιλόγελων γενόμενον, ὡς καὶ πολλὰ γῆς μέτρα αὐτοῖς χαρίζεσθαι τῆς δημοσίας. ἐμφανίζουσι δ' αὐτοῦ τὸ περὶ ταῦτα ἱλαρὸν αἱ ὑπ' αὐτοῦ γραφεῖσαι σατυρικαὶ κωμῳδίαι τῇ πατρίῳ φωνῇ.

[181] Servius on *Eclogues* 6.11 (*cum eam postea Cytheris cantasset in theatro*); for dancers see Section 6.3 below.

[182] Details at Section 6.4 below and Wiseman 2014, esp. 264–6; Athenaeus 1.20e (τὴν Ἰταλικὴν ὄρχησιν).

[183] Cicero *Pro Rabirio Postumo* 35 (*nunc cognoscimus . . . mimorum argumenta*), Pliny *Natural History* 35.199 (*Publilium Antiochium, mimicae scaenae conditorem*).

[184] Aulus Gellius 17.14.2, Macrobius *Saturnalia* 2.6.6, 2.7.4, cf. 2.7.7–9 for the rivalry.

[185] Horace *Satires* 1.10.5–6 (*nam sic | et Laberi mimos ut pulchra poemata mirer*); so the ape that could sing only Catullus and Calvus (n. 104 above) would presumably approve of them.

[186] Cicero *Ad familiares* 7.11.2 (January 53 BC?): *denique si cito te rettuleris, sermo nullus erit; si diutius frustra afueris, non modo Laberium sed etiam sodalem nostrum Valerium pertimesco. mira enim persona induci potest Britannici iureconsulti.*

What they offered was not just low-level entertainment, but satirical comment on people in the news. At the first theatre games after the murder of Caesar, what the *mimi* had to say about it mattered urgently to people like Cicero and Atticus.[187]

'Our friend Valerius' was clearly a playwright too. Some idea of his place in the literary world of the late republic can be got from two passages of Priscian on early grammatical usages:[188]

> Neuter nouns ending in *–a* are Greek, and make the genitive by adding *–tis*, like *hoc peripetasma, huius peripetasmatis*, or *hoc poema, huius poematis*. However, the very early writers often presented these as first declension feminine, e.g. Plautus in *Amphitruo* [117] *cum seruili schema* instead of *schemate*.

The further examples he gives, where *schema, syrma, diadema, dogma* and *glaucoma* were treated as first-declension feminine nouns, are two more from Plautus and then 'Valerius in *Phormio*, Caecilius in *Hypobolimaeus*, Pomponius in *Satura*, Laberius in *Cancer*'. Later, where Priscian discusses fourth-declension nouns treated as second-declension (*ornati, tumulti, fructi, quaesti, aduenti, senati, uersorum, uersis, uersi*),[189] the examples are four from Terence, one from Sallust, and then 'Laberius in *Lake Avernus*, Valerius in *Phormio*, Laevius in *Polymetra*'. The two lists are like a roll-call of the lost literature of Roman theatre.

Both the *Phormio* citations use the same line: 'What are you doing here with your tragic verses and trailing robe?'[190] Clearly, one of those 'wonderful characters' Cicero knew has just been 'brought on stage'. The identity of this playwright who ranked with Laberius is not certain, but there is one obvious candidate: Varro and Pollio both referred to Catullus as 'Valerius',[191] and the mimes of a Catullus were known to later authors.[192] Add the book *On Mime-Performances* referred to by the Bern

---

[187] Cicero *Ad Atticum* 14.2.1 (*theatrum Publiliumque cognoui*), 14.3.2 (*populi* ἐπισημασίαν *et mimorum dicta perscribito*), written on 8 and 10 April 44 BC during the *ludi Megalenses*.

[188] Priscian 6.7 = *Grammatici Latini* 2.199–200K: *neutra eiusdem terminationis Graeca sunt et addita 'tis' faciunt genetiuum, ut 'hoc peripetasma huius peripetasmatis', 'hoc poema huius poematis'. haec tamen antiquissimi secundum primae declinationis saepe protulerunt et generis feminini, ut Plautus in Amphitrione 'cum seruili schema' pro 'schemate'*.

[189] Priscian 6.73 = *Grammatici Latini* 2.257–8K: *inueniuntur tamen antiquissimi multa ex supra dictis in genetiuo etiam i terminasse*.

[190] Bonaria 1965.79: *quid hic cum tragicis uersis et syrma facis?*

[191] See above, nn. 91–3. It may not be totally accidental that Pollio's two citations on *pugillaria* were to Catullus and Laberius, and that Laberius wrote plays named after the signs of the Zodiac (*Cancer, Gemelli, Taurus, Virgo*), a subject touched on by Catullus in his περὶ μιμολογιῶν (n. 171 above).

[192] Martial 5.30.3–4, 12.83.3–4; Juvenal 8.185–8, 13.110–11; Tertullian *Aduersus Valentinianos* 14.

commentator, and the case for Catullus as a writer for the stage is surely proved.

Martial and Juvenal attest his *Phasma* and *Laureolus* as part of an enduring performance repertoire;[193] a Theocritean sorceress mime is known from the elder Pliny and Servius;[194] and one more title can be elicited from a corrupt citation in Nonius Marcellus' dictionary:[195]

> *Ligurrire*, 'to taste', whence *abligurrire*, 'to gulp down greedily'. Horace [*Satires* 1.3.81]: 'he'd tasted the half-eaten fish and lukewarm sauce'. Catullus in *Priapus* [?]: 'It's my fancy to taste at my own expense.'

The evidence is fragmentary, as is normal in ancient history, but despite the determination of distinguished Latinists to discount it a priori,[196] there is enough of it to build a confident hypothesis: when, in the spring of 54 BC, his brother's death caused him to draw a line under all he had written before, Catullus turned to a different kind of writing in a new and more popular milieu.[197]

And he was good at it: his plays were performed, their texts were preserved. They just didn't survive to be copied, as his other works did.

* * *

All this is a very long way from my innocent appeal in 1969 to the authority of Wilamowitz. At that time I simply had an uninstructed sense that 'the collection as we have it' hung together as an artistic unity. That feeling is now the basis of Schafer's incomparably more sophisticated literary analysis:[198]

---

[193] *Phasma*: Juvenal 8.185–6. *Laureolus*: Martial *De spectaculis* 9 (7), Juvenal 8.187–8 and the scholiast *ad loc.*; see Coleman 2006.83–4.

[194] Pliny *Natural History* 28.19 (*hinc Theocriti apud Graecos, Catulli apud nos proximeque Vergilii incantamentorum amatoria imitatio*), Servius on Virgil *Aeneid* 7.378 (*Catullus 'hoc turben' dicit*); Wiseman 2015.112.

[195] Nonius Marcellus 195L: *Ligurrire, degustare: unde abligurrire, multa auide consumere. Horatius: semessos pisces tepidumque ligurrierat ius. Catullus †priopo†: de meo ligurrire libido est.* Lachmann emended to *Priapeo*, but Nonius cites by title, not metre.

[196] Shackleton Bailey 1977.338 ('can hardly be taken seriously'), 1991.45 ('is properly scouted'); Skinner 2015.117 ('has generally been dismissed'); *contra* Wiseman 1985.188–9, 2015.92. Zetzel's scepticism (1988.83–4) depends on an unexamined concept, 'the immense gap between the literal and the literary', leading to an arbitrary limitation: 'Catullus . . . knew and used the theatre, but he did not write for the stage.'

[197] With a change of style for a different audience (n. 170 above); the effectively bilingual Catullus of the surviving collection (Sheets 2007.197–8) would hardly have treated Greek neuter nouns as Latin feminine ones (n. 188 above).

[198] Schafer 2020.37 n. 34 (Section 2.1 above for the *sigla*); cf. 39 ('the three coherent poetic unities bespeak three books of poems').

In my view, Catullus represents himself as working on a future work, **B**, as his present work, **A**, is coming together. After these, he produces **C**, whose structure chiastically reprises those of his first two books. I do not say that this self-presentation reflects historical fact, but I do not see why it could not. My Catullus need not have started his *oeuvre* with a master plan; he need only have intended that any book he produced should have a nice structure, and then, with two books produced, hit upon the idea that his third should mirror the first two jointly.

Although I no longer believe that poems 61–4 were composed in order to be an authorial book (Schafer's **B**), it does seem to me very likely that they were placed together between the short-poem collections (**A** and **C**) at the time when those collections were created.

The best hypothesis, I think, is that the whole sequence of *libelli*,[199] as used centuries later to make up the codex edition, was designed as a coherent unity. It was Catullus' self-chosen body of work, from the start of his poetic career up to the point when the trauma of his brother's death, itself memorialized in the final *libellus*, caused him to rethink his life and turn to writing for the general public.

---

[199] Seven of them, I suggest (Section 2.6 above): (1) poems 2–14, (2) poems 14b–53, (3) poem 61, (4) poem 62, (5) poem 63, (6) poem 64, (7) poems 65–116.

CHAPTER 3

Where Was the Audience?

After so much concentration on books and collections, papyrus rolls and individual readers, it is time to take a step back and focus on the moment when a poem first reached its public. It ought to be self-evident that short poems, especially punchy or malicious epigrams, were composed in the first instance for *uiua uoce* delivery to an appreciative audience. Collection into a *libellus*, to be read in columns of ink, was later business; the primary purpose of these poems was to be spoken and heard.

Where, when and by whom are questions of social history, not literary criticism. But there is one feature of the text that may be helpful: the neglected phenomenon of plural addressees.

3.1 *In ioco atque uino*

Poem 59, the penultimate item in the surviving polymetrics collection, is a five-line squib that starts like this:[1]

> Rufa from Bononia sucks Rufulus – she's Menenius' wife, the one you've often seen in the cemeteries snatching the grave-meats off the pyre itself . . .

What English translation cannot show is that the 'you' is plural. I think it is significant that this comes in Schafer's **Ax** sequence, poems we have suggested were added to the *libellus* from a particular reader's memory; it would surely have been inartistic to include in the authorized collection an item 'addressing itself to unnamed, unhinted-at parties'.[2] For our purpose it usefully focuses the question: Who was being addressed, and where?

---

[1] Catullus 59.1–3: *Bononiensis Rufa Rufulum fellat, | uxor Meneni, saepe quam in sepulcretis | uidistis ipso rapere de rogo cenam.*
[2] Schafer 2020.50; see Section 2.5 above.

One obvious answer is 'fellow-guests at a dinner party'.[3] That was where wit, eloquence, flattery and malice competed for attention and applause;[4] *in ioco atque uino* was precisely where Catullus and his friends were most at home.[5] Some poems have a seemingly purposeless single addressee,[6] and the reason is surely that he was the host, and the poem had found its cue at an appropriate point in the conversation. Martial provides plenty of evidence for poets reciting at dinner parties, whether it's the host himself, one endless roll after another,[7] or one of the guests, knowing that some of those taking down his words may one day produce them as their own.[8]

We may imagine the sort of company Catullus' obscene invectives were meant to entertain. At the other extreme of respectability were the dinner parties at the house of Atticus, where a slave or freedman would provide literary readings.[9] Something new from Cicero, for example:[10]

> I am sending you *De Gloria*, so you will keep it safe as usual. Make a note of the two excerpts for Salvius to read to a suitable audience at dinner – nothing more.

'Nothing more' (*dumtaxat*) because otherwise Atticus might have organized a more formal reading to publicize it. That sort of occasion (*acroasis*), appropriate to a substantial work, will concern us in the next chapter (Section 4.4 below). For the moment, still focusing on the short poems, we can register the *conuiuium* as a likely context for plural addressees. Unfortunately, however, the most explicit piece of evidence has been obscured by the scholarly tradition that should have illuminated it.

---

[3] See Du Quesnay 2021.217 ('first trying out his works in readings or performances at *conuiuia*'), with Schafer 2020.56 on 'scholars sympathetic to a performance model of the poems' composition, whereby poems well-received at convivia or the like would subsequently make it into later authorial collections'. Note the tacit assumption that such readings were merely preparatory to 'real' publication.

[4] The *locus classicus* for such applause is Martial 2.27.3–4: *'effecte! grauiter! cito! nequiter! euge! beate!* | *hoc uolui!' facta est iam tibi cena: tace.*

[5] Catullus 12.2, 50.6; cf. Cicero *Pro Caelio* 67 on the *lauti iuuenes* surrounding a patrician lady: *quam uolent in conuiuiis faceti, dicaces, non numquam etiam ad uinum diserti sint...*

[6] Catullus 22.1 (*Suffenus iste, Vare, quem probe nosti*...), 56.1 (*o rem ridiculam, Cato, et iocosam*...), 113.1–2 (*consule Pompeio primum duo, Cinna, solebat* | *Maeciliam*). Similarly, Furius Bibaculus *FPR* 85.1–2 Hollis (Suetonius *De grammaticis* 11.3): *Catonis modo, Galle, Tusculanum* | *tota creditor urbe uenditabat.*

[7] Martial 3.45, 3.50, 5.78.25.   [8] Martial 2.6.5–6, 7.51.13–14, 11.52.16–18.

[9] Nepos *Atticus* 14.1: *nemo in conuiuio eius aliud acroama audiuit quam anagnosten ... neque umquam sine aliqua lectione apud eum cenatum est.* Cf. Cicero *Ad familiares* 7.1.2–3 for M. Marius' *anagnostes* Protogenes (Wiseman 2015.87–8).

[10] Cicero *Ad Atticum* 16.2.6 (trans. D. R. Shackleton Bailey): *'de gloria' misi tibi. custodies igitur ut soles, sed notentur eclogae duae quas Saluius bonos auditors nactus in conuiuio dumtaxat legat.*

3.2 The Guests and the Lake

Phaselus ille, quem uidetis, hospites . . . What could be clearer? The guests are at dinner in the summer *triclinium* that overlooks the lake.[11] (Of course, the poet doesn't *say* that the scene is Sirmio and the lake is Garda, but that is the default position;[12] the onus of proof is on whoever wants to deny it.) Sirmio was, and is, one of the finest villa sites in Italy, and although the surviving ruins date from a hugely extended reconstruction two or three generations after the poet's time, there is good evidence that the original house was at the same position.[13] The setting of poem 4 is known to within a matter of metres.

The great late-Augustan villa (Figs. 3.1 and 3.2) consisted of two separate groups of rooms with a large peristyle garden between them, flanked by long outward-facing colonnades on either side.[14] The southern nucleus, the only part built on the natural rock, was evidently the site of the original house, now reconstructed with an enormous new entrance hall; the rest of the complex was built out on an artificial platform, the substructures of which at the northern end still stand 18 metres high. That was where the new panoramic dining room must have been, surrounded by a terrace equipped with poles (some anchoring blocks survive) from which awnings could be hung for shade (Fig. 3.3).[15]

The equivalent in the poet's time was at the south-east corner of the complex, at the same height but looking north and east over what was then still the rocky slope down to the shore.[16] Somewhere down there, no doubt moored at a jetty, was the battered old boat the guests could see.

For generations of literary scholarship, however, that has not been good enough. The problem started when Latinists took up the New Criticism's disapproval of specific reference to real conditions. The following is by Frank Copley in 1958:[17]

---

[11] Catullus 4.1; for *triclinia aestiua* (which should face north), see Varro *De lingua Latina* 8.29, Vitruvius 6.4.2.

[12] Cf. Catullus 31.1–10, 35.1–4, 68.27–30; he was known as *Catullus Veronensis* (Pliny *Natural History* 36.48, Nonius 876L, Priscian *Grammatici Latini* 2.16 Keil, Verona scholiast on Virgil *Eclogues* 6.1).

[13] See Roffia 2018.25–6 ('a building that preceded the great villa, situated below it and completely obliterated by the new construction'), 29 fig. 18d ('vano 88').

[14] Full details in Wiseman 1987.350–9; for up-to-date plans of the different levels, see Roffia 2018.28–9 figs. 18a–d.

[15] Wiseman 1987.354–5, with Roffia 2018.29 fig. 18d (where 'D2' is the terrace, 'D3' the putative dining room).

[16] See Roffia 2018.27 fig. 17 for the natural contours.

[17] Copley 1958.9; 'a return by land' presumably refers to 46.8 and 11 (*iam laeti studio pedes uigescunt . . . diuersae uarie uiae reportant*).

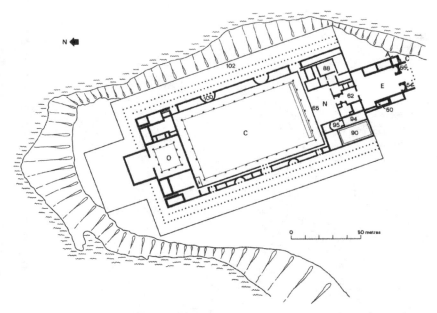

Fig. 3.1 Hypothetical ground-floor plan of the Sirmio villa: Wiseman 1987.351. The spacious room north of the smaller peristyle (O) is the proposed summer *triclinium* (see Fig. 3.2); the equivalent in the original house would have been at or near room 88.

Editors and students of Catullus have found in the *phaselus*-poem a host of puzzling, unanswered, and unanswerable questions. What kind of ship was a *phaselus*? How big? If big enough for a sea-voyage, how did Catullus get it up the Po and the Mincio to Lake Garda? Is the *limpidus lacus* indeed Lake Garda, or is it some other lake; and if so, what lake? Was the *phaselus* not an actual ship but only a model or picture or carving? Whose ship was it? Did Catullus come back from Bithynia in it? If so, then why in *c.* 46 does he seem to be talking about a return by land? How many trees is a *silua*? Was the ship built of one tree or many? If we are to believe the commentaries, these and many similar questions must be answered before we may be sure of having grasped the meaning and intent of the poem.

But a poem is itself. It presents its own world to its readers and demands that they accept it as true for the purposes of the poem and not for anything else.

Ten years later – and more conspicuously, in Gordon Williams' *magnum opus* on Roman poetry – the same questions were being asked, with the same insistency:[18]

---

[18] Williams 1968.192.

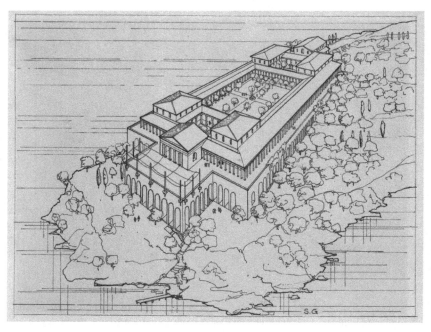

Fig. 3.2   Hypothetical reconstruction of the Sirmio villa by Sheila Gibson, 1978.

Fig. 3.3   Sirmio villa, two of the blocks used for anchoring the poles for the terrace awning
(author's photograph, 1978): Roffia 2018.145–6.

There are endless difficulties: (*a*) How could a large sea-going yacht be worked up to the Lago di Garda? (*b*) Even if it could, what sense would there be in doing it? (*c*) Why waste a sea-going yacht on a lake, retiring it shortly after a long and successful voyage? (*d*) Why does Catullus describe the ship's other voyages but not this – the most extraordinary – from sea to lake? (*e*) Why is everywhere else that is mentioned given a name, but not the lake? The questions must be asked because it cannot be supposed that Catullus wishes his reader to imagine all this, yet at the same time realize that it did not happen.

Williams was using the poem as an example in the chapter he subtitled 'The Demand on the Reader'. The unspoken premise, so obvious it didn't have to be mentioned, was that 'poem 4' was composed in order to be read in a book by unknown persons whose understanding was defined by what the poem told them.

That assumption seems to be hardwired into Latinists' thinking. Three decades on, Ted Courtney was playing the same game by the same rules:[19]

> Anyone who seeks to understand the *phaselus*-poem (4) of Catullus has to start by asking what situation the poem presents within itself to the reader. When that has been done, and not before, it is a matter of legitimate interest to enquire whether the poem relates in any way to the biographical facts of the author's life.

So now, another three decades on, John Schafer can confidently appeal to past authority:[20]

> The previously credible itinerary of a fictional speaker ends dubiously, with the yacht making its way up first the Po, then the Mincius. As scholarship on the poem has repeatedly seen, this claim deeply taxes our credence.... Even if such a route was possible – or if a costly overland hauling can be imagined – it seems like a deeply unmotivated and implausible thing actually to do.

It's understandable: Schafer's subject is 'Catullus through his books', and the section heading at this point, 'Construals and Credence', indicates clearly enough the argument's uneasy relationship with what he is careful to call 'purported extratextual realities' and 'putative biographical information'.[21]

Even on its own terms, however, this literary-critical fuss is paradoxical. If the poem really does present its own world and demand that readers accept it as true, then the seagoing boat now growing old on the lake is

---

[19] Courtney 1996.113, cf. 122 on 'the oddity of going to the trouble and expense of bringing the boat from the sea to Lake Garda'.
[20] Schafer 2020.14 and n. 28.   [21] Schafer 2020.12, 2, 14.

simply a datum. Catullus expected his readers to accept it, and we are in no position to decide otherwise. The hydrography of the Peschiera-Mantova area has been so thoroughly adapted and re-managed in the last two thousand years that the non-navigability of the present-day Mincio cannot be used as an argument;[22] on the other hand, having a vessel of seagoing size available for use on a lake as big as Garda is an aim we might easily attribute to the owner of the Sirmio villa, a local grandee who habitually hosted the proconsul of the province.[23]

One might expect serious critics to remember that host-guest relationship (*hospitium*) when interpreting the vocative plural *hospites* in the first line of poem 4. But no, the commentators just toe the party line:[24]

> *Hospes* represents the common ὦ ξεῖνε of Greek epigrams, especially sepulchral epigrams which address the passer-by.

> The addressee of a grave-epigram, including literary amplifications of the form (e.g. Propertius 4.1) is normally singular; the plural here is a hint of an actual dramatic setting.

> The address to the casual visitor (ξεῖνε) belongs to the genre of sepulchral, rather than dedicatory, inscriptions.

But sepulchral epigrams have nothing to do with this poem. Nor have dedicatory ones, unless we take the *phaselus* to be a model of a ship, or a painting of a ship, or anything rather than the ship itself afloat in the lake.[25]

Forget the New Critics' dogma, use what little external information there is, accept that a poem has a life and purpose before being read in a book, and the scene is totally intelligible. Catullus senior had some distinguished guests – Caesar perhaps among them – and expected his talented son to help entertain them. Which he did with a gem of a poem,

---

[22] The main interventions have been (1) the system of dams and weirs constructed by the city of Mantova in the late twelfth and thirteenth centuries, to control the level of water and limit flooding, and (2) the nineteenth-century canal from Peschiera to just downstream of Mantova, which now takes most of the water that would have flowed down the Mincio. For the extensive navigability of the Padus (Po) in Roman times, see Polybius 2.16.10, Strabo 5.1.11 (C217), Pliny *Natural History* 3.123.

[23] Suetonius *Diuus Iulius* 73 (*hospitioque patris eius, sicut consuerat, uti perseuerauit*); see Section 2.5 above.

[24] Fordyce 1961.100; Quinn 1970.103; Thomson 1997.215. Cf. Williams 1968.193: 'The poem uses the form of a dedication-epigram but, unlike any example of the form in the *Palatine Anthology*, it is addressed to "passers-by" or "strangers" or "guests" (*hospites*); that is one clue, for, though the plural is metrically convenient, it is still unique and it would have a reasonable point of reference if it were used in a private house to address all who happened to look at a painting on the wall.'

[25] 'Options, at this point, are multiple' (Schafer 2020.14).

full of wit and verbal music, designed for delivery in that summer dining room above the lake shore. Everyone present knew who he was, where he'd been, how the vessel had been brought up to the lake. The poem wasn't written for unknown readers; it was written for the people it addressed on that occasion. *Phaselus ille, quem uidetis, hospites . . .*

3.3 Nine Columns from Castor and Pollux

A third poem featuring plural addressees evokes a scene of a very different sort:[26]

> Randy pub and you messmate drinkers, ninth column from the brothers in caps, do you think you're the only ones with pricks, the only ones allowed to fuck all the girls there are and think the rest of us just goats? Because you're sitting there stupid, a hundred or two hundred all in a row, do you think I won't dare to stuff all two hundred sitters at once? Well, think on – because I'll write the pub's face with phalluses.

He probably means that this poem itself will be the graffiti that deface the pub's reputation. What riles him is that his girl – no name given, but it must be Lesbia – 'has sat down there',[27] lusted after not just by 'all you great and good' (*boni beatique*) but even by 'all you small-time sidewalk studs', and in particular you, Spanish Egnatius, with your long hair, your dense stubble and your piss-polished teeth.[28]

Why the emphasis on *sitting*? Two very disparate items of evidence may help. The first is a passage in Cicero's *De finibus* discussing the natural instinct for action:[29]

> We see that even the most idle of men, those given over to some depravity or other, are still constantly in action in both body and mind, and when not hindered by necessary business they ask for a gaming board or look for some

---

[26] Catullus 37.1–10: *salax taberna uosque contubernales, | a pilleatis nona fratribus pila, | solis putatis esse mentulas uobis, | solis licere quicquid est puellarum | confutuere et putare ceteros hircos? | an, continenter quod sedetis insulsi | centum an ducenti, non putatis ausurum | me una ducentos irrumare sessores? | atqui putate: namque totius uobis | frontem tabernae sopionibus scribam.*

[27] 37.11–14: *puella nam mi . . . consedit istic.* There is no need to suppose that she 'has set up as a whore available to all and sundry' (Du Quesnay 2021.190, with footnote references to Messallina).

[28] 37.14–20: *hanc boni beatique | omnes amatis, et quidem, quod indignum est, | omnes pusilli et semitarii moechi; | tu praeter omnes une de capillatis, | cuniculosae Celtiberiae fili, | Egnati, opaca quem bonum facit barba | et dens Hibera defricatus urina.*

[29] Cicero *De finibus* 5.56: *quin etiam inertissimos homines, nescio qua singulari nequitia praeditos, uidemus tamen et corpore et animo moueri semper et, cum re nulla impediantur necessaria, aut alueolum poscere aut quaerere quempiam ludum aut sermonem aliquem requirere, cumque non habeant ingenuas ex doctrina oblectationes, circulos aliquos et sessiunculas consectari.*

entertainment or seek some conversation; because they have no liberal intellectual pursuits, they go in search of *circuli* and *sessiunculae*.

A *circulus* was a group of people standing and talking together,[30] whether in the Forum or elsewhere;[31] such informal gatherings were notorious for malicious gossip and political criticism, the open-air equivalent of dinner-table conversations.[32] That much is straightforward, but what were *sessiunculae*? The word ought to mean 'sittings' or 'benches'.

Once again the help is archaeological, this time from Pompeii and Herculaneum, where 'streetside benches' were a familiar phenomenon.[33] Sometimes they were outside grand houses, useful perhaps for those waiting to be admitted to a morning *salutatio*, but other types of site are more relevant to Catullus' poem 37:[34]

> Of the fifty bench-fronted properties to which we can with some degree of confidence assign a primary purpose, twenty-one were commercially or industrially oriented to judge from their broad doorways and other diagnostic features such as masonry countertops, amphorae, or industry-specific equipment. Of these, nine were bars/taverns.

What was true of the Campanian towns in AD 79 was probably also true of Rome in the late republic. At the bar, you sat outside to enjoy your drink.

Since the surviving benches are on raised sidewalks (*semitae*),[35] Catullus' contemptuous crack about 'sidewalk studs' (*semitarii moechi*) seems to make a perfect fit. But his 'randy pub' wasn't in a street; it was in a piazza, in fact *the* piazza, the Roman Forum, at the ninth column from the temple of Castor and Pollux ('the brothers in caps'). Once again, we can place the setting of the poem to a matter of metres.

---

[30] *Sermo(nes) in circulis*: Cicero *Ad Atticum* 2.18.2, *De officiis* 1.132; Livy 3.17.10, 28.25.5, 34.61.5. Standing: Aulus Gellius 15.9.2 (*adsistens*), Apuleius *Metamorphoses* 2.13 (*circumstantium*), Porphyrio on Horace *Satires* 1.6.114 (*in his uulgi circulis stare*).

[31] Forum: Cicero *Ad Q. fratrem* 3.4.1 (*Cato ... de circulo se subduxit*), Quintilian 2.12.10 (a histrionic orator *mire ad pullatum circulum facit*), 12.10.74 (*illi per fora atque aggerem circuli*). At the baths: Petronius *Satyrica* 27.1 (*immo iocari magis et circulis accedere*). On the Palatine: Aulus Gellius 4.1.1 (*in uestibulo aedium Palatinarum ... in circulo doctorum hominum*).

[32] Cicero *Pro Balbo* 57 (*in circulis uellicant*), Tiberius in Tacitus *Annals* 3.54.1 (*nec ignoro in conuiuiis et circulis incusari ista*); full details in O'Neill 2003.

[33] Full details in Hartnett 2017.195–223.

[34] Hartnett 2017.202–3, cf. 197 fig. 60 and 203 fig. 63 for benches outside taverns.

[35] See, for instance, Plautus *Curculio* 287 (*in uia de semita*), *Mercator* 115 (*plenis semitis qui aduorsum eunt*). Often mentioned in building inscriptions: *ILLRP* 116.3–4 (*semitam de s.p.f.c.*), 528.3–4 (*facienda coerauit semitas in oppido omnis*), *CIL* 10.5055 = *ILS* 5349 (*uiam semitas faciundum, clouacam reficiundam d.s.p.c.*).

The republican Forum had shops and colonnades around it, a config-
uration supposedly dating back to the time of Tarquinius Priscus.[36] Those
on the shady south side, the 'old shops', were traditionally high-class
premises for bankers and money changers,[37] still called *tabernae argentariae*
even when the occupancy became more varied.[38] Vitruvius gives us an
architect's view of what it was like:[39]

> In the cities of Italy we must work to a different plan [i.e., not like a Greek
> *agora* with close-set columns all round], because of the custom handed
> down from our ancestors of holding gladiatorial shows in the Forum. For
> that reason wider intercolumniations should be arranged round the shows,
> and *tabernae argentariae* should be provided in the porticos round about,
> with balconies on joists above, which will be appropriately placed for
> usefulness and public revenue.

By his time, and indeed very soon after Catullus' poem was written, the
tabernae along the south side of the Roman Forum had been redeveloped
as part of the monumental *basilica Iulia*; extending from the temple of
Castor across to the temple of Saturn, its portico consisted of eighteen
columns.[40] Although we cannot know how precisely it reproduced the
previous layout,[41] the middle of the row at the ninth column must be the
approximate address of the establishment where Lesbia sat in the shade
with the great and the good (and all those other deplorable chancers).

3.4   Reaching the Public

It's not enough just to point out plural addressees;[42] to understand how
short poems might find their first audience, we need external evidence.
Two poems of Martial and one of Horace may be helpful here.

---

[36] Livy 1.35.10 (*circa forum ... porticus tabernaeque factae*), Dionysius of Halicarnassus *Roman
Antiquities* 3.67.4 (τὴν τε ἀγοράν ... ἐκόσμησεν ἐργαστηρίοις τε καὶ παστάσι περιλαβών); Papi
1999.12–13.

[37] Plautus *Curculio* 480 (*sub ueteribus ibi sunt qui dant quique accipiunt faenore*), cf. Pliny *Natural
History* 35.25 and 113 (*sub ueteribus*), Livy 44.16.10–11 (*pone ueteres*); Cicero *Academica*
2.70 (shade).

[38] E.g. Varro *De uita populi Romani* fr. 76 Pittà (Nonius 853L), Livy 9.40.16, 26.11.7; Papi
1999.10–12.

[39] Vitruvius 5.1.1–2: *Italiae uero urbibus non eadem est ratione faciendum, ideo quod a maioribus
consuetudo tradita est gladiatoria munera in foro dari. igitur circum spectacula spatiosiora intercolumnia
distribuantur circaque in porticibus argentariae tabernae maenianaque superioribus coaxationibus
conlocentur, quae et ad usum et ad uectigalia publica recta erunt disposita.*

[40] Augustus *Res gestae* 20.4 (*basilicam quae fuit inter aedem Castoris et aedem Saturni*); Giuliani and
Verduchi 1993, Gorski and Packer 2015.239–60.

[41] For a conjectural sketch of the republican Forum, see Gorski and Packer 2015.4, fig. 1.1.

[42] Poems 59, 4 and 37 in this chapter, 'poem 14b' at Section 2.2 above.

Martial's friend Severus was evidently a fellow poet, someone he trusted to read and comment on his own work.[43] Severus yawned when he read the published Book Two, because, as Martial explains, he'd seen nearly all of it before:[44]

> These are the ones you used to catch while I was reading them and copy out, on Vitellian tablets too; these are the ones each of which you'd carry in the fold of your toga to all the dinner parties and all the theatres.

Another friend, Caesius Sabinus, took Book Seven to his home town in Umbria. That was good news for the book:[45]

> What great publicity you've got coming, what glory, what a crowd of enthusiasts! You'll be heard at dinner parties and in the Forum, at temples, cross-roads (compita), porticos and taverns. You're sent to one person, but you'll be 'read' by all.

What Severus and Caesius did was take their Martial with them to wherever there would be appreciative audiences – fellow guests at dinner, fellow spectators in the theatre, fellow idlers in *circuli* in public places,[46] fellow drinkers sitting outside bars – and their likely opening gambit would be 'Have you heard Martial's latest?' One text reached many 'readers', because those who heard the poems could memorize them or transcribe them and read them out again at another such gathering. That was how a poet got his work known.[47]

When someone approached your group with a book-roll in hand or in the fold of the toga, you might say, 'What have you got there? Read it out for us!'[48] But that was only safe for those with a clear conscience; if you had a guilty secret, Horace tells us, you'd be outed by 'fierce Sulcius and Caprius', walking about with their *libelli* and hoarse from constant recitation.[49]

---

[43] Martial 5.80.1–3, 11.57.

[44] Martial 2.6.5–9: *haec sunt quae relegente me solebas | rapta exscribere, sed Vitellianis, | haec sunt singula quae sinu ferebas | per conuiuia cuncta, per theatra.*

[45] Martial 7.97.9–13: *o quantum tibi nominis paratur, | o quae gloria, quam frequens amator! | te conuiuia, te forum sonabit, | aedes, compita, porticus, tabernae. | uni mitteris, omnibus legeris.*

[46] The *aedes* in line 12 are more probably 'temples' than 'houses' (as in Shackleton Bailey's Loeb translation): for possible audiences in temples and their colonnades, see Martial 3.20.10 (*porticum templi*), 11.1.9 (*porticum Quirini*).

[47] See Martial 7.51.5–14, 7.52.1–2 for Pompeius Auctus as another of Martial's publicists.

[48] As Favorinus did in the courtyard at Titus' Baths: Aulus Gellius 3.1.1 (*Catilina Sallustii, quem in manu amici conspectum legi iusserat*). In hand or in fold of toga: Martial 6.60.1–2 (*laudat amat cantat nostros mea Roma libellos, | meque sinus omnes, me manus omnis habet*).

[49] Horace *Satires* 1.4.65–6 (*Sulcius acer | ambulat et Caprius, rauci male cumque libellis*); identified as satirical poets by Ullman 1917.117–19.

Horace didn't read his poems in public because those with something to hide would treat him like a dangerous bull:[50]

> They all fear verses and hate poets. 'Keep well away, he's got hay on his horns! As long as he gets a laugh, he won't spare either himself or any of his friends. Whatever he's once smeared on to his pages, he'll be dying for all the people coming back from the bakehouse and the water-fountain to know about it, even the boys and the old ladies.'

The water-fountain tells us where we are. As the source of running water for the whole neighbourhood, the marble basin was normally placed at the neighbourhood's main cross-roads, the *compitum*.[51] Naturally, people gathered there. The *compita* were one of Caesius Sabinus' venues for publicizing Martial, and notorious throughout Latin literature as sites of gossip and slander.[52] They were ideal places for a poet to find an audience.[53]

Another of Caesius' venues was the Forum, capacious enough to accommodate various gatherings of bystanders in various favoured spots. The *locus classicus* is the famous speech by the property manager in Plautus' *Curculio*:[54]

> I'll just give you an easy guide to which places you can find which people in, so if you want to set up a meeting with anyone, good or no good, honest or crooked, you won't trouble yourself with too much trouble.
> You want to meet a perjurer? Go to the Comitium. A boastful liar? Shrine of Cloacina. For rich spendthrift husbands, look near the Basilica – and there'll be worn-out tarts there too, and people who like to do deals, and dining-club subscribers at the Fishmarket. Respectable wealthy gents

---

[50] Horace *Satires* 1.4.33–8: *omnes hi metuunt uersus, odere poetas.* | *'faenum habet in cornu: longe fuge!* *dummodo risum* | *excutiat sibi, non hic cuiquam parcet amico;* | *et quodcumque semel chartis illeuerit,* *omnis* | *gestiet a furno redeuntis scire lacuque* | *et pueros et anus.*

[51] E.g. Herculaneum, junction of *decumanus maximus* and *cardo IV*: Wallace-Hadrill 2011.102, 166–8; Hartnett 2017.229–39. For some Pompeian examples, see Flower 2017.151–3, figs. II.21–2, plates 17 and 19.

[52] Martial 7.97.12; Horace *Satires* 2.3.25–6 (*frequentia compita*), 2.6.50 (*manat per compita rumor*), Propertius 2.20.22 (*de me et de te compita nulla tacent*), Ovid *Amores* 3.1.18 (*narrant in multas compita secta uias*), Juvenal 9.112–3 (*qui te per compita quaerat* | *nolentem*); cf. Cicero *Pro Murena* 13 (*maledictum ex triuio*), Horace *Ars poetica* 245 (*uelut innati triuiis ac paene forenses*), Juvenal 6.412 (*quocumque in triuio . . . narrat*).

[53] Hence the phrase 'a cross-roads poem', *carmen triuiale* (Juvenal 7.55)? Cf. also Virgil *Eclogues* 3.26–7 (*in triuiis . . . disperdere carmen*), Calpurnius Siculus 1.28 (*triuiali more . . . canit*).

[54] Plautus *Curculio* 467–80. The basilica (line 472) is unidentified: cf. Plautus *Captiui* 815, Livy 26.27.3 (no basilicas yet in 210 BC). The Fishmarket (line 474) was on the north-east side of the Forum: Livy 26.27.3 (burned in 210 BC), 27.11.16 (rebuilt the following year), 40.51.5 (redeveloped in 179). The Pool (line 477) was the *lacus Curtius* in the middle of the Forum: Pliny *Natural History* 15.78, cf. Livy 7.6.1. For the Old Shops, see n. 37 above.

walk about in the lower Forum; in the middle by the channel, they're nothing but show-offs. Above the Pool are confident malicious talkers who boldly slander other people for no reason, though there's plenty that could truly be said about themselves. By the Old Shops, that's where they give and take at interest.

We have no equivalent for the world of Catullus a century and a half later, except for a couple of comments from Caelius Rufus, reporting on the city's gossip for Cicero in 51 BC:[55]

On 24 May the ones by the Rostra – and may it be *their* death! – had spread it around that you were dead. All over the Forum and the city the rumour was very strong that you'd been murdered on the road by Quintus Pompeius.

I don't want you to think Favonius was passed over by the people in the colonnade. All the best people didn't vote for him.

No doubt the latter group (*columnarii*), who knew who had voted for whom at the recent elections, were like those sitting outside the 'randy pub' at the ninth column from Castor and Pollux.

It has been thought that Catullus was too sophisticated to be involved in such a *milieu*:[56]

It is impossible to imagine *him* reading his works to the Forum crowd. What the populace enjoyed was turgid stuff like Volusius' *Annales*, and he despised their taste just as his master Callimachus had....[57] Whenever Catullus talks of poetry, whether his own or his friends' or his enemies', he has written works in mind, either *pugillaria* and *tabelli*, on which presumably they were first distributed, or *libelli* and *uolumina*, in which form they were found on the booksellers' shelves.[58]

The scholar who made that over-confident judgement soon found himself having to explain away what the poet says about his friends in poem 47:[59]

---

[55] Caelius in Cicero *Ad familiares* 8.1.4, 8.9.5: *te a.d. VIIII Kal. Iun. subrostrani (quod illorum capiti sit!) dissiparant perisse. urbe ac foro toto maximus rumor fuit te a Q. Pompeio in itinere occisum . . . nolo te putare Fauonium a columnariis praeteritum; optimus quisque eum non fecit.*

[56] Wiseman 1982.38 = 1987.273 (regrettably endorsed by Lowrie 2010.285 and Feeney 2012.43).

[57] Catullus 95.10 (*at populus tumido gaudeat Antimacho*), Callimachus in *Anthologia Palatina* 12.43.4 (σικχαίνω πάντα τὰ δημόσια). Note the arbitrary assumption (1) that 'Antimachus' was a metaphorical reference to the Volusius of 95.7–8 and (2) that Callimachus was talking about poetry rather than boys who were too readily available.

[58] *Pugillaria/codicilli*: Catullus 42.4–5 and 11–12. *Tabelli*: 50.2. *Libelli*: 1.1–2 and 8, 14.12. *Volumina*: 22.5–8, 95.6. Books in general: 14.17–19 (booksellers), 14b.2–3, 36.1 and 20, 44.21, 95.7–8. *Scribere*: 22.5 and 16, 36.7, 44.18, 50.4.

[59] Wiseman 1982.40–1 = 1987.275–6; Catullus 47.6–7 (*mei sodales | quaerunt in triuio uocationes?*).

> It would be dangerous to take this poem as evidence that Veranius and Fabullus were literally cadging invitations on the street corner. But it is not inconceivable.

Of course it isn't, and it's not 'dangerous' either: it's what the poet says, and we are not entitled to ignore it. It fits with the places he went looking for Camerius in poem 55, and with Lesbia handling great-hearted Remus' grandsons 'at the cross-roads, in the alleys' in poem 58.[60] Both those items are in Schafer's **Ax** sequence and therefore probably not in the published collection (Section 2.5 above), but they are still good evidence for the world the short poems belong in. All over Rome there were places those poems might find an audience.

All this (to repeat) is social history,[61] not literary criticism. But I think the critics would be wise to take account of it, and not think *only* about books and readers.

---

[60] Catullus 55.3–8 (Wiseman 1980 = 1987.176–86), 58.4–5 (*nunc in quadriuiis et angiportis | glubit magnanimi Remi nepotes*).
[61] Detailed argument in Wiseman 2015 and 2017.

CHAPTER 4

What Were the Long Poems?

Such informal, ad hoc audiences were appropriate for short poems, easily memorized, but major works required something different. Here too the practice of the time has been obscured by the natural bias of literary criticism towards texts and readers. Texts needed papyrus, and papyrus had to be imported; texts needed scribes, and scribes were expensive; in Rome, as everywhere else in the ancient world, texts did not define literature. Poets, orators, satirists, philosophers, historians all performed to an audience before publishing to a readership.[1] And once again we may ask, 'What audience, where?'

4.1 Turning to the Social

It ought to be good news that 'recent criticism of Latin poetry has turned toward the social'.[2] In the chapter entitled 'Performance' in the *Oxford Handbook of Roman Studies*, Michèle Lowrie put it like this:[3]

> Scholarship in the late twentieth and early twenty-first centuries has taken a turn toward performance because of the intersection this concept affords between actual media of representation and performativity in the pragmatic sense.... What the concept of performance allows is the pragmatic link between art and society, whether performance is conceptualized literally as an event before an audience, distanced through reading, or regarded even more abstractly as the development, playing out, and reflection about a role over a lifetime. Suetonius reports that Augustus himself asked on his deathbed whether he had played well in the mime of life (*Aug.* 99). This

---

[1] Wiseman 2015 offers contemporary evidence, set out in chronological order from the origins of the Roman city-state in the seventh century BC.

[2] Lowrie 2010.289.

[3] Lowrie 2010.282–3, citing work by Fowler, Farrell, Williams, Starr, Horsfall, Johnson, Markus, Zorzetti, Habinek, Lendon, Gleason, Gunderson, Wray, Oliensis and Krostenko.

anecdote neatly demonstrates the intersection between public discourses of power, the media, and self-awareness.

I have to confess I find that a bit too abstract.[4] Yes, by all means let performance be 'conceptualized literally as an event before an audience'; but does it have to be 'distanced through reading'? And when Augustus made that comment about the mime of life, what sort of 'discourse' of 'the media' did he and those at his bedside have in their minds?

It says something about intellectual fashion when a handbook chapter on performance should be explicitly about 'elite literature outside drama'.[5] The conditions of such literature are clearly defined:[6]

> The main transition in the institutions supporting literature came in the late Republic, when libraries began to be made public, booksellers made book circulation more than an elite activity, and recitation began as a regular practice.... The mechanics of representation are a major preoccupation among the Augustans, and by their time the literary institutions had stabilized, though their patina remained new.

So when performance before a large public audience happens to be explicitly attested (Horace's *carmen saeculare* in June 17 BC), it is presented as 'the great exception', an 'anomaly'; 'its uniqueness makes it an interpretive challenge.'[7] The whole problem with this 'turn to the social' is that it concerns itself with only a very narrow stratum of Roman society, an 'elite' evidently restricted to those with a literary education and the resources to buy books or have them copied.

As always, it is a matter of social history. The sources have to be interrogated with particular care, because there was never any need to be explicit about what everyone knew and took for granted. For instance, no ancient author explains to us that the theatre and circus games (*ludi scaenici*

---

[4] What exactly does it mean to say that 'Roman literature is preoccupied by performativity' (Lowrie 2010.281)? Cf. McCarthy 2019.84: 'While there is good reason to believe that the poems of Catullus and Horace were recited and/or read aloud, that type of performance is not what my argument is aimed at illuminating. In place of this most literal meaning of the word "performance", my argument draws instead on the scholarship that has formulated performance as an act that takes place within the bounds of social and political life.'

[5] Lowrie 2010.287. The paragraph continues: 'Plautus and Terence were staged and new plays continued to be composed and performed into the Augustan period, when revivals became more prevalent, plays began to be composed for recitation, and theatre took a turn toward entertainment.' Literature for stage performance is not mentioned again.

[6] Lowrie 2010.281–2, cf. 285 ('The canon is a literary institution implying the codification arising through libraries').

[7] Lowrie 2010.288; see *CIL* 6.32323.139–49 (Thomas 2011.276). What is unique is the fortuitous documentation, not the event itself; there were hymns at every public festival, and somebody had composed them.

and *circenses*) were one of the defining privileges of Roman citizenship.[8] We have to infer it from a rhetorical manual of the fourth century AD that happens to quote a passage from a speech to the People by Gaius Fannius, consul in 122 BC:[9]

> If you give citizenship to the Latins, I suppose you think you'll have the same space you have now at public meetings, or when you're at the *ludi* or on public holidays. Don't you realise they'll monopolise everything?

It is too easy not to notice descriptions of the audience at the theatre festivals as 'the entire Roman People'.[10] All strata of society were there, and distinctions between them were resented:[11]

> 'The games have always been watched by all together. What has suddenly happened to make senators not want to have plebeians among them in the auditorium? Why should a rich man object to a poor man sitting next to him?'

It was 'where the whole of society met to do honour to the gods',[12] and the job of the magistrates in charge – plebeian aediles for the *ludi Ceriales*, *Florales* and *plebeii*, curule aediles for the *ludi Megalenses* and *Romani*, the urban praetor for the *ludi Apollinares* – was to find ways of instructing and entertaining everyone, educated and illiterate alike.[13]

How did the system work? For plays or other scripted shows, the magistrates would buy the text from the playwright (the curule aediles of 161 BC paid a record 8,000 sesterces for Terence's *Eunuchus*),[14] and hire the actors and performers to play it (in the 70s BC the star dancer Dionysia

---

[8] Though Cicero comes close, when his case happens to require it (*In Verrem* 2.5.36, *De haruspicum responso* 24).

[9] Iulius Victor in *Rhetores Latini* 402 Halm (*ORF* 32.3 Malcovati): *si Latinis ciuitatem dederitis, credo, existimatis uos ita, ut nunc constitistis, in contione habituros locum aut ludis et festis diebus interfuturos. nonne illos omnia occupaturos putatis?*

[10] Cicero *Pro Sestio* 118, 119, 122, 124, 125, *Philippics* 1.36, Pliny *Natural History* 36.119. See Rawson 1991.508 ('The games in Rome ... were central to its culture in innumerable ways'), 581 ('The theatre was one of the central institutions of Roman culture').

[11] Livy 34.54.6–7 (an imagined speech in 194 BC): *ad quingentesimum <quinquagesimum> octauum annum in promiscuo spectatum esse; quid repente factum cur immisceri sibi in cauea patres plebem nollent? cur diues pauperem consessorem fastidiret?* For the elaborate distinctions that eventually developed, see Rawson 1991.508–45.

[12] Rawson 1991.508; details of the various *ludi* in Bernstein 1998, with Wiseman 2008.167–74.

[13] Instruction: see, for instance, Varro *De lingua Latina* 6.18 (*docet populum*), Cicero *Pro Rabirio Postumo* 29 (*ut ... discamus*).

[14] Suetonius *Terence* 2; cf. Jerome *Chronica* Ol. 155.3 on Terence (*antequam aedilibus uenderet*), 156.3 on Pacuvius (*fabulas uenditauit*), Ovid *Tristia* 2.509–10 on mimes at Augustus' games (*inspice ludorum sumptus, Auguste, tuorum: | empta tibi magno talia multa leges*). L. Varius Rufus received one million sesterces for his tragedy *Thyestes*, produced 'at Augustus' games after the victory at Actium' (Hollis 2007.257–8, 277–8).

charged 200,000 sesterces for an appearance).[15] Note the inflation: the public games became ever more lavish and extravagant during the first century BC,[16] a phenomenon described by Livy, writing in the twenties, as 'madness that wealthy kingdoms would hardly tolerate'.[17] The process was surely accelerated by the creation in 55 BC of a huge new permanent theatre, with a vast auditorium and a stage 100 metres wide.[18] Before long the star performers and their riotous fans became a threat to public order; in 22 BC responsibility for all the games was transferred to the praetors, who had the authority to enforce security by military command.[19]

It is obvious that with big money available, acceptance for the programme became a highly competitive prize, and the magistrates' choice correspondingly contentious. It seems to have depended on a preliminary competition (*commissio*) to decide who would have the opportunity to present their work before the Roman People. The clearest evidence comes from the time of Augustus:[20]

> He objected to having anything written about him that was not serious and by the most outstanding authors, and he warned the praetors at the *commissiones* not to let his name become commonplace.

But the system was already in place in the late republic, as we know from two letters of Cicero at the time of the *ludi Apollinares* in July 44 BC:[21]

> I'd like you to give me detailed daily reports, right from the *commissio* itself, about how these games are received.

---

[15] Cicero *Pro Roscio comoedo* 23, cf. Aulus Gellius 1.5.3 (*notissima saltatricula*).

[16] See the extravagant innovations listed by Valerius Maximus 2.4.6 and Pliny *Natural History* 19.23, 21.6, 33.53, 35.27, 36.117, probably from Varro (frr. 309–14 Funaioli).

[17] Livy 7.2.13 (*res in hanc uix opulentis regnis tolerabilem insaniam uenerit*); cf. Seneca *De clementia* 1.26.2 (*apparentur licet magna impensa et regiis opibus*).

[18] Essential details in Sear 2006.133–5.

[19] Dio Cassius 54.17.4–5 (στάσις of Pylades and Bathyllus), Macrobius *Saturnalia* 2.7.19 (*propter populi seditionem pro contentione inter se*); Dio Cassius 54.2.3–4 (22 BC), cf. Dionysius of Halicarnassus *Roman Antiquities* 2.19.4.

[20] Suetonius *Diuus Augustus* 89.3: *componi tamen aliquid de se nisi et serio et a praestantissimis offendebatur, admonebatque praetores ne paterentur nomen suum commissionibus obsolefieri.* The passage is regularly misunderstood, as if it referred to *commissiones* in the sense of competitive declamations in the rhetorical schools (Suetonius *Gaius* 53.2, *De grammaticis* 17.1), with which of course the praetors had nothing to do; for the true meaning, see Suetonius *Diuus Augustus* 43.5, Seneca *Letters* 84.10, Pliny *Letters* 7.24.6, *Panegyricus* 54.1.

[21] Cicero *Ad Atticum* 15.26.1 (*tecum ago ut iam ab ipsa commissione ad me quem ad modum accipiantur hi ludi … in dies singulos persequare*), 16.5.1 (*rumoris nescioquid adflauerat commissione Graecorum frequentiam non fuisse, quod quidem me minime fefellit*); Brutus, as urban praetor, was responsible for the games, but the assassins were all keeping out of Rome, and he was anxious about what the popular reaction to them would be.

He'd had a breath of some kind of rumour that there hadn't been many people at the *commissio* of the Greek games, which didn't surprise me in the least.

Cicero often went to stay in the country while the games were on, and the day of the *commissio* was the day he would leave Rome.[22]

These unobtrusive items are easy to miss, and easy to misinterpret. Their significance – and I would say their fundamental importance for understanding the literary culture of the first century BC – becomes clear once we understand that the poets who performed at the *ludi*, and competed for that privilege at the *commissiones*, were not only playwrights.

We know, for instance, that Varro's Menippean satires addressed an audience in a theatre,[23] that Philodemus' book on poetry defined the poet's job as 'enthralling the crowd',[24] that Lucretius had in mind at least the possibility of addressing the *uulgus*.[25] At Pompey's lavish games in 55 BC the poetic programme was chosen by Sp. Maecius Tarpa, who for Horace twenty years later was still the competition judge par excellence:[26]

> These things I play about with aren't meant to resound in the temple, in a competition with Tarpa judging, or to come back again and again as theatre shows.

His contemporary Cornelius Gallus named Valerius Cato and Vibius Viscus as the hard-to-please *iudices*.[27] It would be they who judged the *commissiones*, and decided who should perform to the great public audience at the theatre games.

---

[22] Wiseman 2015.82–5; Cicero *Ad Q. fratrem* 3.4.6 (*quo die ludi committebantur in Tusculanum proficiscens*), *De finibus* 3.8 (*ludis commissis ex urbe profectus*). The meaning is not 'at the start of the games', as usually translated, but something like 'once the games were programmed'; Cicero would leave as soon as he knew what the main items were going to be, not on the first day of the games themselves, when there would be dense crowds and a grand procession (Hanson 1959.81–6).

[23] Varro *Menippean Satires* 218 Astbury = Nonius 510L (*uosque in theatro . . .*), 355 Astbury = Nonius 593L (*ualete et me palmulis producite*); for satire as a performance genre, see Wiseman 2009.132–43.

[24] Philodemus *De poematibus* 1.161–2 (Janko 2000.373, 375): οἱ ψυχαγωγοῦντες τὸν ὄχλον . . . δεῖν τὸν μὲν σοφιστὴν ζητεῖν τὴ[ν] ἀλήθ[εια]ν, τὸν δὲ πο[η]τὴν τὰ [πα]ρὰ τοῖς πολλοῖς εὐδοκι]μοῦντα. διὸ [ταύτην τὴν λέξι]ν καλλίστην ἔ[λεγε, τὴν] τοὺς ὄχλους [ψυχαγωγο]ῦσαν. Philodemus was quoting the otherwise unknown Andromenides (Wiseman 2015.97).

[25] Lucretius 1.943–5 = 4.18–20: *quoniam haec ratio plerumque uidetur* | *tristior esse quibus non est tractata, retroque* | *uulgus abhorret ab hac . . .* He wrote for *mortalibus aegris* (6.1), not just the educated few.

[26] Cicero *Ad familiares* 7.1.1. Horace *Satires* 1.10.37–9: *haec ego ludo* | *quae neque in aede sonent certantia iudice Tarpa* | *nec redeant iterum atque iterum spectanda theatris*.

[27] Gallus *FPR* 145.8–9 Hollis (*non ego, Visce,* | *[. . .] Kato, iudice te uereor*); cf. Suetonius *De grammaticis* 11 for Cato, Horace *Satires* 1.10.83 (and ps.Acro *ad loc.*) for Viscus and his brother.

Horace didn't need to compete. He had the privilege of a private audience at the house of Maecenas, and people disliked him for it:[28]

> If I say 'I'm ashamed to recite my unworthy writings in crowded theatres and add weight to trifles', then someone replies: 'You're laughing – you keep your stuff for the ears of Jove, so confident that you alone distil poetic honey. You really fancy yourself.' I'm afraid to treat that sort of criticism with contempt, and in case he fights and I get cut by his sharp nails, I shout 'I don't like that venue', and ask for a break. For the games have given rise to alarming competitiveness and anger, and anger has given rise to grim feuds and deadly war.

Poets were expected to provide pleasure for everybody, not just the 'elite'.

All this information is readily available, but the 'turn to the social' has not noticed it.[29] What it shows is that the *ludi scaenici*, with their audience of the whole Roman People from top to bottom of the social and educational scale, were central to the literary culture of Catullus' time.

4.2 Scripts for Occasions

Two of Catullus' 'long poems', 62 and 67, were written in dramatic form. Necessarily, their presence as poems in a written collection is secondary, and there is no indication of the circumstances of their original performance.

That is particularly apparent in poem 62, where the antiphonal songs of the boys' and girls' choirs are an *epithalamium* for a totally unspecified marriage: 'there is nothing to tie it to a particular wedding or even a definite place.'[30] The contrast with the wedding song for Manlius Torquatus and Aurunculeia (poem 61) could hardly be more conspicuous.[31] That too was composed for performance, by a solo singer and two

---

[28] Horace *Epistles* 1.19.41–9 (to Maecenas): *'spissis indigna theatris | scripta pudet recitare et nugis addere pondus' | si dixi, 'rides' ait 'et Iouis auribus ista | seruas; fidis enim manare poetica mella | te solum, tibi pulcher'. ad haec ego naribus uti | formido et luctantis acuto ne secer ungui, | 'displicet iste locus' clamo et diludia posco. | ludus enim genuit trepidum certamen et iram, | ira truces inimicitias et funebre bellum.*

[29] Cf. Lowrie 2010.287–8, who treats the Horace passage just quoted (note *spissis theatris*) as the equivalent of Juvenal 1.1–14, satirical comment on a private *recitatio*.

[30] Thomson 1997.365; the poem is cited as *epithalamium* by Quintilian 9.3.16.

[31] Catullus 61.16–20 (*namque Iunia Manlio . . . nubet*), 83–4 (*Aurunculeia*), 209 (*Torquatus*). For the bride's name (Vibia Aurunculeia?), see Thomson 1997.348, where however the reference '*ILS* 7819 (Praeneste)' should read '*ILS* 7825 (Corfinium)'; the unfamiliar female *praenomen* at line 16 might easily have been 'corrected' to *Iunia*. See Section 2.6 above for the bridegroom: *pace* Du Quesnay 2021.172, it is not known which of the late-republican Manlii Torquati he was.

choirs,[32] but the stages of it are clearly marked: first at the home of the bride, a kletic hymn followed by the girls' song, then at the bridegroom's house, the boys' song followed by the *epithalamium* proper.[33] In poem 62 the rival songs seem to be delivered after the banquet at the bridegroom's house, and the victorious male choristers address the bride, who has evidently just arrived;[34] but who she is, and why she should need this lecture about obedience, is never explained.

It can only have been explained outside the text. It seems likely that what has come down to us as a poem in the written collection had once been part of something more extensive, an occasion to which Catullus' script for the two choirs was only a contribution. Was it a private commission, this time with someone else hired to do the hymn? Was it part of a drama, in which the choirs' formal antiphony was just one element?[35] There are many possibilities:[36] with no clues to guide us, we can only guess.

Poem 67 is more straightforward, a satirical dialogue with a house door in Verona exposing the scandalous affairs that went on within. As Ian Du Quesnay well observes, 'the poem seems best considered as an (urban) mime in elegiacs', though it isn't clear why this 'performance piece' should be intended only 'for the entertainment of local dignitaries at a local *conuiuium*'.[37] Why not a public performance at Verona's games, for a popular audience that would most enjoy the embarrassing revelations? Imagine the same sort of treatment given to prominent people in Rome, and it's easy to see why Cicero, on Trebatius' behalf, was nervous about 'our friend Valerius'.[38]

Recent work on poem 67 has gone in a quite different direction. In the collection as we have it, this exposé of Transpadane misbehaviour immediately follows the elaborate court poetry of Callimachus' *Coma Berenices*,

---

[32] Wiseman 2015.106–7; the contrary opinion is often repeated as a dogma, but never justified as a hypothesis. Cf. Du Quesnay 2021.172: 'there seems no reason to suppose that Poem 61 was not performed for the entertainment of the guests, possibly sung and accompanied by music.' Why only 'possibly', and why only the guests? Wedding processions were a public affair (Juvenal 6.78, *longa per angustos ponamus pulpita uicos*).

[33] Catullus 61.1–35 (hymn), 36–113 (girls' song), 114–83 (boys' song), 184–228 (*epithalamium*).

[34] Catullus 62. 3 (*surgere iam tempus, iam pinguis linquere mensas*), 59 (*et tu ne pugna cum tali coniuge, uirgo*); discussion in Agnesini 2007.66–75.

[35] The rest perhaps being danced: see Sections 6.3 and 6.4 below for the importance of danced scenarios in late republican theatre.

[36] Not confined to those discussed in Agnesini 2007.95–100.

[37] Du Quesnay 2021.176, cf. 184 on poem 17 as 'a performance piece designed to entertain and amuse local notables of the *colonia*'. Why only them?

[38] Cicero *Ad familiares* 7.11.2 (Section 2.7 above).

the translation Catullus sent to Hortalus in place of what he'd asked for (Section 2.6 above). In 2004 Marco Fantuzzi and Richard Hunter made a tentative suggestion:[39]

> In Poem 66 Catullus does not seem to have translated the final two verses of Callimachus' poem, although their wretched state of preservation makes any interpretation hazardous. Only the opening of the last Greek hexameter can be read, and even here there is room for disagreement about the punctuation:
>
> χ[αῖρε], φίλη τεκέεσσι
> 'Hail, [lady] dear to your children . . .'
>
> Almost certainly the lock here hails the deified Arsinoe, treated as 'mother' to Euergetes and Berenice, who were 'brother and sister' according to the terminology of the court. It is indeed easy enough to see why Catullus might have chosen to omit this final couplet. Nevertheless, it is to be noted that Poem 67 begins with an address to a door, which bears a certain similarity to the farewell to Arsinoe:
>
> o dulci iucunda uiro, iucunda parenti,
> salue, teque bona Iuppiter auctet ope,
> ianua . . .
>
> O you who bring pleasure to a sweet husband, pleasure to a parent, greetings, and may Jupiter increase your prosperity, door . . . (Catullus 67.1–3)

So far, so cautious, but they then go on:[40]

> The opening of 67 may in fact allude to – or should we say 'translate'? – the ending of the Greek 'Coma Berenices', as one of the many ways in which 66 and 67 are thematically connected.

No, of course we shouldn't say 'translate': the only word in common is *salue* for χαῖρε, and even that's in a different line.

Schafer now takes this implausible idea as a datum,[41] to illustrate 'the resonance of the Door with the Lock (both inanimate speakers) and the pointed contrast between the "high" social world of the Alexandrian court and the "low" world of naughty Transpadane adulterers'.[42] 'These

---

[39] Fantuzzi and Hunter 2004.476, referring to the end of *POxy* 2258.

[40] With a reference to *Catullan Questions* (Wiseman 1969.22), which offers only a single thematic connection (marriage).

[41] Schafer 2020.158: 'Now, however, we see that poem 67 is partially translated from Callimachus, and that it makes a pair with and asks to be read with and against poem 66.'

[42] Schafer 2020.156, explained by all the ways the plot of poem 67 does *not* correspond with that of Demetrius, Apame and Berenice (157).

connections', he says, 'are easily sufficient to draw poem 67 close to 66', though he admits that 67 'may need to be "Callimachean" in a broader sense' (whatever that means).[43] The vague terminology speaks for itself; when he says, rather endearingly, 'All of this, I trust, does in fact work,'[44] you don't have to be a hardened sceptic to disagree.

Fantuzzi and Hunter noted that the address to the door at the start of poem 67 'bears a certain similarity' to the address to the queen at the end of Callimachus' *Coma Berenices*. A far superior explanation was offered by Alex Agnesini in 2011: what appears in our texts as the opening couplet of poem 67 was probably the concluding couplet of poem 66.[45] The dialogue with the door would then start immediately with the vocative *ianua*, as we should expect. The two texts differ utterly in theme and tone, and there is not the slightest reason to think that poem 67, the script for a satirical performance at Verona, had anything to do with the poet's Callimachean gift to Hortalus.

As for that gift itself, it has been suggested that poem 66 was written as a political allegory,[46] or with reference to Hortalus' interest in the Egypt of his own time.[47] But it is clear from the covering letter, poem 65 (Section 2.6 above), that this was not what Hortalus had asked for, only what the poet was able to send instead. How did it happen to be readily available? Perhaps it was an exercise, evidence for something undeniable but otherwise unattested, the poet's extensive education in Greek literature. The person who owned the Sirmio villa – and other properties, including a farm near Tibur – could certainly afford the best available tutors for his promising sons.[48]

4.3   At the Games

Poem 63 has always been a problem for Latinists. Calling it 'remarkable' and 'extraordinary' or 'bizarre and haunting' is all very well,[49] but doesn't

---

[43] Schafer 2020.157, 158.

[44] Schafer 2020.158. 'Resonance', 'pointed contrast' and 'drawing close' are neither demonstrable nor refutable; empirical argument requires clarity.

[45] Agnesini 2011, and independently Du Quesnay 2012.181–3; the two lines are now printed as 66.95–6 in Fo 2018.196.

[46] Konstan 2007.83, referring to Pompey in 60 BC: 'Fanciful? Absolutely.'

[47] Du Quesnay 2012.156–62: in 57–56 BC Q. Hortensius was one of the leading *optimates* trying to prevent Pompey from getting the command to restore Ptolemy Auletes (Cicero *Ad familiares* 1.1.1, 1.2.1, 1.5b.2, 1.7.2). However, there is no reason to suppose that Hortalus was Hortensius (see Chapter 2, n. 152).

[48] Perhaps not quite as Raphael (2019.1) imagines it: 'We were tutored, my brother Manlius [*sic*] and I, by an old Greek slave, fifty-five at least, Solon . . .'

[49] Respectively, Butterfield 2021.153 and 154, Gaisser 2009.28.

do much to explain what this text actually *is*. As Ian Du Quesnay rightly says, 'poem 63 (*Attis*) is, formally, a narrative hymn',[50] but then the complications start:[51]

> The *Attis* was clearly an ambitious literary work and there is every reason to suppose it circulated separately. It has been suggested that the poem may have been written for performance at the Megalesia. But perhaps one should think of performance at the 'feasts and *conuiuia*' that were a conspicuous feature of the Megalesia rather than its being performed as part of the Romanised ritual itself.

There is a lot to unpack here. First, the premise that the text was a literary work circulated for readers, confusing its secondary use with its primary function. Second, the assumption that 'feasts and *conuiuia*' known from antiquarian sources were an inherently more likely context than the *ludi Megalenses* themselves.[52] Third, the pejorative description ('Romanised ritual') of a grand public festival celebrated since 191 BC at a Palatine temple that was linked by both legend and topography with the foundation of Rome itself.[53] I think there is a mindset behind these casually unargued judgements, one that sees Roman literature as the concern of an educated minority quite separate not only from the entertainment and instruction of the populace but also from the public religion of the Roman state.

It is surely paradoxical to identify a text as a hymn and then assume it was performed at a banquet, and yet the same is said of the hymn to Diana (poem 34) and the hymn to the marriage god (poem 61).[54] It seems that

---

[50] Du Quesnay 2021.173.

[51] Du Quesnay 2021.173, citing Wiseman 1985.205–6, 2015.108–9. For the 'feasts and *conuiuia*', see Ovid *Fasti* 4.353–4, *Fasti Praenestini* = Degrassi 1963.126–7 (*nobilium mutitationes cenarum solitae sunt frequenter fieri*), Aulus Gellius 2.24.2 (*antiquo ritu*), 18.1.11 (*quam ob causam patricii Megalensibus mutitare solitae sint*).

[52] Note the past tenses in the *Fasti Praenestini* and the second Gellius passage (previous note). In the late republic, senators were often out of town during these games (Wiseman 2015.83–4): see, for instance, Cicero *In Clodium et Curionem* fr. 19 Crawford (*eis qui mense Aprili apud Baias essent et aquis calidis uterentur*).

[53] Livy 29.14.14, 29.37.2, 36.36.3–4 (*in Palatio*, 191 BC). The goddess honoured with the temple and games was called *mater Idaea* (Livy 29.10.5, 29.14.5), *mater deum* (29.11.7), *mater magna* (29.37.2) or *mater magna Idaea* (36.36.3), and Ida was the birthplace of Aeneas (Hesiod *Theogony* 1008–10); she was identified as Rhea (Ovid *Fasti* 4.201), the name given to the mother of Romulus and Remus (Livy 1.3.11); the temple was next to that of Victoria (cf. Livy 29.14.14), which was directly above the Lupercal (Dionysius of Halicarnassus *Roman Antiquities* 1.32.3–5), where the twins were suckled by the she-wolf.

[54] Du Quesnay 2021.172 (n. 32 above) and 189 ('Poem 34 may have been commissioned by Manlius Torquatus for a feast or entertainment which he organised as *XVuir sacris faciundis*'); for poem 34, see Zetzel 1992.48–51 and Wiseman 1992.62–3.

even a scholar well aware of the importance of oral delivery still feels constrained to imagine an 'elite' audience. Of course, there was nothing to stop dinner guests from singing a hymn, or having one sung for them, but the *triclinium* was not self-evidently the place for it. A hymn (which was also a prayer) would typically be sung with a sacrifice at the altar, addressing the divinity in the temple or the sacred grove;[55] but it would be no less appropriate at the theatre games, where there was also an altar,[56] and where the divinity was always present to watch.[57]

For the *ludi Megalenses* in particular we happen to have precisely contemporary eyewitness evidence. Here is Lucretius on the subject of sense perception, describing the effect of coloured awnings 'stretched across great theatres':[58]

> They stain the audience there below in the auditorium, and the whole sight of the stage, the senators and the Mother of the Gods, and make them ripple in their own colour.

The senators were in the *orchestra*, and the goddess was in the seat of honour at the front of the auditorium; her presence was symbolized by the turreted crown from her cult statue (Fig. 4.1), replaced afterwards with due ceremony by the aedile in charge.[59] Later in the same book Lucretius used the theatre for another illustration, how people who spent all day at the games saw dancers and heard music even in their dreams.[60] Combining these two precious scraps of evidence, we must suppose that at times during the seven days of the *ludi Megalenses* the goddess in her theatre would be watching danced performances.

Was Catullus 63 one of them? Even within the text itself there is good reason to think it was:[61]

> One apparently puzzling feature of the poem, the disappearance of Attis' companions after line 38, is more easily explicable if the poem was written

---

[55] Temple: Vitruvius 4.5.1 (*uti qui adierint ad aram immolantes aut sacrificia facientes spectent ad . . . simulacrum quod erit in aede*). Grove: e.g. Catullus fr. 1 (the hymn to Priapus), Virgil *Aeneid* 8.285–305 (*tum Salii ad cantus incensa altaria circum . . . consonat omne nemus*).

[56] Lucretius 2.416–7 (*cum scena croco Cilici perfusa recens est | araque Panchaeos exhalat propter odores*), Josephus *Jewish Antiquities* 19.87 (ἔθυσε τῷ Σεβαστῷ Καίσαρι, ᾧ δὴ καὶ τὰ τῆς θεωρίας ἤγετο); Hanson 1959.86–90.

[57] E.g. Cicero *De haruspicum responso* 24 (*in ipso matris magnae conspectu*), Arnobius *Aduersus nationes* 7.33 (*Flora si suis in ludis flagitiosas conspexerit res agi*); Hanson 1959.13–17, Goldberg 1998.

[58] Lucretius 4.78–80: *namque ibi consessum caueai subter et omnem | scenai speciem patrum matrisque deorum | inficiunt coguntque suo fluitare colore.* See Colin 1954 for line 79, where the manuscripts have the meaningless *patrum matrumque deorum*.

[59] Varro *Menippean Satires* 150 Astbury = Nonius 119L (*dum e scena coronam adlatam inponeret aedilis signo deae*); Wiseman 1974.159–60.

[60] Lucretius 4.978–83 (Section 6.3 below).   [61] Wiseman 1985.200.

Fig. 4.1 The presence of the goddess. Detail of a relief showing the temple of Magna Mater, Villa Medici, Rome (D-DAI-ROM-77.1753, Christoph Rossa); in the centre of the pediment is the goddess's throne with her turreted crown on it.

for performance: the chorus could retire to the periphery and leave the 'centre stage' to the chorus leader (protagonist or *archigallus*), which would be obvious to an audience as it is not to a reader.

I would no longer add 'or *archigallus*':[62] hymns sung and danced by the goddess's eunuch priests in her 'Phrygian rites' are not at issue here.[63] But

---

[62] I.e. *archigallus matris deum magnae Idaeae et Attis* (*CIL* 6.2183), probably described by Varro in his *Menippean Satires* (121 Astbury): 'He shines like the dawn in his long purple robe, he wears a crown of gold that gleams with jewels, filling the place with light.'

[63] They were always in Greek (Servius on *Georgics* 2.394), and the Phrygian rites (ὀργιασμοί) seem to have been forbidden to Roman citizens anyway (Dionysius of Halicarnassus *Roman Antiquities* 2.19.5).

that doesn't affect the argument. When the poet describes Attis' companions as a *chorus*, it isn't necessarily metaphorical; on the contrary, the text works best as the libretto for a virtuoso dancer and singer supported by a dancing chorus, with an orchestra of drums, pipes and cymbals beating out that frenetic rhythm.[64] Since we know that the goddess's *galli* were played and danced in both Greek and Roman theatres,[65] there is no reason to doubt that Catullus' text 'must surely have been for performance at the games of the Great Mother'.[66]

In a previous chapter (Sections 2.5 and 2.6 above) it was argued that the collection as we have it represents Catullus' body of work from early spring 56 to early spring 54 BC.[67] The *ludi Megalenses* within that period took place on 4–10 April 55 BC, and the curule aediles responsible for them were probably Gnaeus Plancius and Aulus Plautius.[68] Of course no one can *know*, but I think it's likely that those ambitious gentlemen hired a top-class song and dance troupe and commissioned Catullus to provide a galliambic script to accompany their performance.

Later that year, probably in early September,[69] Pompey as consul put on lavish games for the dedication of his huge stone theatre.[70] He entrusted the programme to Spurius Maecius,[71] who would have to commission acts elaborate and spectacular enough to do justice to that enormous stage and keep that enormous audience entertained. My guess is that one of them was what we call poem 64:[72]

> There is a narrator, maybe the poet, maybe an actor, maybe singing, maybe reciting; there is a large *corps de ballet*, male and female; there are solo and small-group singers, male and female; and there is a *prima donna assoluta* whose role explodes into the narrative as a spectacular *tour de force*.

---

[64] Catullus 63.30, with lines 8–11, 21–2 and 28–9 for the music; cf. Thomson 1997.372 on 'the poet acting as a sort of tragic *choragus*'.

[65] Dioscorides 1691–6 Gow-Page (*Anthologia Palatina* 11.195), Suetonius *Diuus Augustus* 68 (*in scaena*); Attis is portrayed on stage in a wall painting in the 'Casa di Pinario Cereale' at Pompeii (Vermaseren 1977.66, plate 47).

[66] Wiseman 2015.108; the chorus of dissent (Harrison 2005.20 n. 23, Bremmer 2005.59, Harder 2005.82 n. 33, Nauta 2005.100) failed to distinguish between the *ludi Megalenses* watched by the Roman People (Cicero *De haruspicum responso* 22–5) and the Phrygian ritual carried out by the Great Mother's *galli* (n. 63 above).

[67] Expressed in a different idiom by Schafer 2020.191–2: 'Catullus represents himself composing **B** during the composition of **A**. . . . The three Catullan books coherently and fully dramatize their own composition.'

[68] Cicero *Pro Plancio* 17, 53; Broughton 1986.158. At the time of the previous year's *ludi Megalenses* Catullus was still abroad (poem 46).

[69] Nisbet 1961.199: immediately before the *ludi Romani* (cf. Cicero *In Verrem* 1.31)?

[70] Cicero *Ad familiares* 7.1.2, *In Pisonem* 65, Asconius 1C and 16C, Dio Cassius 39.38.1–2

[71] Cicero *Ad familiares* 7.1.1 (n. 26 above).　　　[72] Wiseman 2015.109.

That notion can, I think, be justified by a systematic exploration of how Roman literature interacted with Roman show business (see Chapter 6 below). Latinists, however, dismiss it as mere speculation,[73] so let's see whether their account of poem 64 is any more helpful.

The traditional explanation is that poem 64 is an 'epyllion', indeed the defining example of that genre.[74] The trouble is, 'epyllion' is not a genre attested by any ancient source. It is a modern idea, and one that evidently meets a need:[75]

> A book that declares so positively that there *is* such a widespread genre, and promises to deliver a tidily organised history of it, has an enduring appeal: it is much more satisfying to feel that a word in scholarly discourse refers to something in a comprehensible way than to be told that it does not actually apply to anything very much.

Some scholars have done their best to avoid the word: for them the poem is 'a mannered miniature *epos*', indeed a *Kleinepos*.[76] But that does no more than redefine the problem, since such miniature-*epos* poems are not attested either.[77] So perhaps, as a (more or less) narrative poem in hexameters, it should simply count as an epic? That's how Schafer sees it: 'poem 64 is of course thoroughly epic'.[78] But it still won't do, because epic was defined by the fact of being *long*:[79] not necessarily as long as the *Iliad* or *Odyssey*, said Aristotle, but at least the length of a tragic trilogy.[80] In fact no literary definition yet put forward is even remotely satisfactory.

Schafer sees 61–64 (**B**) as 'a poetry book consisting of "a handful of longer poems in various meters"',[81] but it cannot be the same sort of book as 1–51 (**A**) or 65–116 (**C**), because the **B** poems 'do not (as far as we can see) have or presuppose occasions within the depicted Catullus' world'.[82]

---

[73] See, for instance, Gowers 2016.14 on 'Wiseman … speculating, sometimes wildly, about the original performance context of many canonical texts'; she doesn't say what counts as 'wild'.

[74] See Trimble 2012 for a very helpful deconstruction of 'the ever expanding set of scholarly uses of this obstinately ineradicable word'.

[75] Trimble 2012.75, referring to Crump 1931.

[76] Lyne 1978.169 = Gaisser 2007.112; Syndikus 1990.100–3.

[77] Callimachus *Aetia* 1.5 (ἔπος δ' ἐπὶ τυτθὸν ἐλ[ίσσω]) doesn't describe a genre.

[78] Schafer 2020.154, cf. 225 on the poem 'set[ting] itself a problem of theodicy – as is generically appropriate for an epic poem to do'.

[79] Aristotle *Poetics* 24 (1459b22–3): τὸ ἐπεκτείνεσθαι τὸ μέγεθος.

[80] Aristotle *Poetics* 24 (1459b20–2): εἰ τῶν μὲν ἀρχαίων ἐλάττους αἱ συστάσεις εἶεν, πρὸς δὲ τὸ πλῆθος τραγῳδιῶν τῶν εἰς μίαν ἀκρόασιν τιθεμένων παρήκοιεν. Aeschylus' *Oresteia* trilogy is just under 4,000 lines long, nearly ten times the length of Catullus 64.

[81] Schafer 2020.134; it is not clear who is being quoted.

[82] Schafer 2020.189, cf. 192: 'The four poems of **B** take the reader progressively away from his world, whether this is understood as the Roman Republic of his lived reality or the fictionalized version of

In particular, 'there is a gap between the values expressed by the narrator of poem 64 and those which we can reasonably attribute to the Catullus who speaks elsewhere'.[83] But it is only a problem for those whose presumptions are literary. If the narrator was presenting a *spectacle*, lavishly produced with music and dance at the *ludi scaenici*, what he did at the end as an 'epilogic speaker' was provide the audience with a properly conventional moral lesson, exactly what a public festival required.[84]

Schafer rightly notes that 'Bacchus['] retinue of Maenads (64.254–64) look and sound so much like the troop of *Gallae* led by Attis (63.6–38)',[85] but doesn't ask what all the raucous music was for or why the *Gallae* were called a *chorus*. Later, he draws attention to 'the presence of cognitive response':[86]

> The woven image of the topless Ariadne (63–67), spectated upon by the human guests at the wedding (*spectando*, 267–8), and clearly the central interest of the voyeuristic narrator of the ecphrasis (50–266), is primarily a metapoetic focalization of artistic arousal, perhaps only secondarily an instance of it.

Why not forget the polysyllabic terminology and imagine a naked actress, spectated upon by a real audience whose voyeuristic central interest she literally was? That hypothesis (Section 6.9 below) concerns the realities of Roman life, not literary genres. To refute it requires another hypothesis that explains the phenomena better, and I don't think metapoetic focalization does the job.

4.4   The Hardest Case

What were the long poems? The answers suggested so far are these:

> 61: private commission, script for solo singer and two choirs
> 62: (?) public or private commission, script for two choirs
> 63: public commission, script for dancer-singer and dancing chorus
> 64: public commission, script for dancer-singers and dancing choruses
> 65: letter of apology to Hortalus, introducing
> 66: translation of Callimachus, (?) study exercise
> 67: (?) public commission, script for satirical dialogue

---

it presented in poems 1–51.' I think that betrays a restricted view of what his world of lived reality actually was.

[83] Schafer 2020.228–9, referring to 64.384–408. 'If the authorial voices of **B** are to be integrated with themselves, let alone with those of **A** and **C**, it will not be in favor of the epilogic speaker of 64 taken at face value' (Schafer 2020.229).

[84] See Rawson 1991.570–81 for the theatre as moral instruction. I think what the 'epilogic speaker' did at both 63.91–3 and 64.384–408 was bring the audience down to earth after the overwhelming visual and auditory experience of the performance.

[85] Schafer 2020.152.   [86] Schafer 2020.188.

68a: letter of apology to Mallius (? Manlius).

The hardest case is 68b. Explanation, *pace* Schafer and much of the literature, has to start with the fact that the poem is about Allius, and *not* Mallius/Manlius.[87] There is no reason at all to link it with 68a.

The opening passage is an address to the Muses, but not a request for inspiration. The poet knows exactly what he is going to say:[88]

> Goddesses, I cannot fail to tell in what matter Allius helped me, and with how great services he helped, lest time, in flight through centuries of forgetting, should cover this devotion in blind night; but I'll tell you, and you in turn tell many thousands and make this paper speak when it is old.

The only other place where Catullus refers to writing on papyrus is in poem 35, the letter to his friend Caecilius in Novum Comum.[89] So was 68b a letter too? It was certainly meant to be read by Allius, to whom the last twelve lines are addressed in the second person.[90]

Not all letters were written for the attention of one person only. A few passing comments in Cicero's correspondence provide important evidence. First, in his long and detailed account to Atticus of the trial of Clodius in 61 BC, he wrote:[91]

> I don't feel that I am bragging offensively when I talk about myself in your hearing, especially in a letter which I don't wish to be read to other people.

With some letters, we infer, he did wish that. Next, in March 49 BC, soon after Pompey and the optimates had left Italy, Cicero wrote to Caesar, carefully setting out his own position in the conflict.[92] He arranged for

---

[87] Catullus 68b.41, 50, 66, 150. Schafer 2020.12 ('following a long tradition, I take *Allius* in [68b] as pseudonymous for *Mallius* in [68a]'), 155–6 (treated as a fact); *contra* (e.g.) Wiseman 1974.88–90 and most recently Du Quesnay 2021.176. 'Allius' was a real name, but cf. Schafer 2020.105, equally casually categorizing Flavius, Suffenus, Thallus, Juventius, Furius and Aurelius as 'suspected or known to be fictional'; no argument is offered, but in a society where reputation mattered so much, the real names of real people couldn't just be used at random (Wiseman 1985.130–4).

[88] Catullus 68b.41–6: *non possum reticere, deae, qua me Allius in re | iuuerit aut quantis iuuerit officiis, | ne fugiens saeclis obliuiscentibus aetas | illius hoc caeca nocte tegat stadium: | sed dicam uobis, uos porro dicite multis | milibus et facite haec carta loquatur anus.*

[89] Catullus 35.2 (*uelim Caecilio, papyre, dicas* . . .); Theodorakopoulos 2007.321. For papyrus (*charta*) as epistolary material, see, for instance, Cicero *Ad Q. fratrem* 2.15.1 (best quality), *Ad familiares* 7.18.2 (reused).

[90] Catullus 68b.149–60, esp. 149–50 (*hoc tibi, quod potui, confectum carmine munus | pro multis, Alli, redditur officiis*), 155 (*sitis felices et tu simul et tua uita*). The passage echoes the opening address to the Muses: 68.42/150 (*officia*), 50/151 (*nomen*).

[91] Cicero *Ad Atticum* 1.16.8 (trans. D. R. Shackleton Bailey): *non enim mihi uideor insolenter gloriari cum de me apud te loquor, in ea praesertim epistula quam nolo aliis legi.*

[92] Cicero *Ad Atticum* 9.11a; for the contrast with his private opinion, see Wiseman 2009.193–5.

copies to be made, and was pleased a few days later when Atticus reported that the letter had become public knowledge;[93] clearly he had wanted it to be 'read to other people' as widely as possible. Finally, in June 44 BC he wrote to Atticus about how well young Marcus was doing as a student in Athens: 'really his own letter is so affectionately and classically written that I should not mind reading it before an audience'.[94]

The *ad familiares* collection contains some fine examples of letters that must have been intended to reach more people than just the addressee. The account of Pompey's games to Marcus Marius at Pompeii was no doubt written in the hope that Marius would share it with his villa-dwelling neighbours; he even refers by name to Marius' man Protogenes, who would have the job of reading it to them.[95] On the political side, the letter to the historian Lucius Lucceius, setting out Cicero's claim to fame in the turbulent years from 63 to 57 BC, and that to Lentulus Spinther, justifying his change of direction in 56, both much too long to be mere correspondence, were surely also aimed at a much wider optimate audience.[96] These elaborate compositions were works of art in their own right;[97] and so too, *mutatis mutandis*, was Catullus' poem 68b.

When Cicero wrote that he'd be willing to read young Marcus' letter *in acroasi*, what sort of occasion did he have in mind? We may get an idea of it from Varro's satires, where someone claims that Diogenes' knowledge of literature was 'enough both for everyday use and for an *acroasis* of fine gentlemen'.[98] In Rome, the gentlemen might be meeting in a grand town house like that of Cicero himself on the Palatine. That house had a *palaestra*, an architectural form consisting of three porticos with *exedrae* 'where philosophers, rhetoricians and other lovers of literature might sit and debate'.[99] Or perhaps they might be in the *exedra* of a portico at a country house in the Alban hills.[100] Even if venues quite so luxurious were beyond the means of equestrians like Catullus and (presumably) Allius,

[93] Cicero *Ad Atticum* 8.9.1: *epistulam meam quod peruulgatam scribis esse non fero moleste, quin etiam ipse multis dedi describendam.*

[94] Cicero *Ad Atticum* 15.17.2 (trans. D. R. Shackleton Bailey): *et mehercule ipsius litterae sic et* φιλοστόργως *et* εὐπινῶς *scriptae ut eas in uel in acroasi audeam legere.*

[95] Cicero *Ad familiares* 7.1.3; cf. *Ad Atticum* 16.2.6 on Atticus' man Salvius.

[96] Cicero *Ad familiares* 5.12, 1.9.

[97] Cicero *Ad Atticum* 4.6.4 for the Lucceius letter as *ualde bella.*

[98] Varro *Menippean Satires* 517 Astbury = Nonius 373–4L: *Diogenem litteras scisse cum usioni quod satis esset, tum quod etiam acroasi bellorum hominum.*

[99] Cicero *Ad Atticum* 2.4.7 (*palaestrae Palatinae*), cf. *Brutus* 10 (*cum inambularem in xysto*), 24 (*in pratulo propter Platonis statuam*). See Vitruvius 5.11.2 on *palaestra* design: *constituantur autem in tribus porticibus exedrae spatiosae habentes sedes in quibus philosophi, rhetores reliquique qui studiis delectantur sedentes disputare possint.*

[100] Like that of L. Crassus at Tusculum: Cicero *De oratore* 1.28 (*cum in ambulationem uentum esset*), 2.12 (*in porticu*), 3.17 (*in eam exedram*).

occasions like that are still what we should have in mind when we try to imagine how Catullus hoped poem 68b would be received.

What makes it such a hard case is the mismatch between the furtively adulterous subject matter and the elaborate mythological apparatus employed to narrate it.[101] And that must have caused a problem for Allius when he received it: many people would admire the composition, but how many would also condone the deception of Lesbia's husband?

Again, Cicero's correspondence offers an analogy. After the Ides of March in 44 BC, Cicero rationalized his delight at the death of Caesar by imagining the murderers as Homeric heroes who killed for glory.[102] In June that year, keeping out of Rome like Brutus and Cassius, he wrote *De Gloria*.[103] He sent the text to Atticus, asking him to keep it safe, find reliable guests and just read them a couple of extracts at dinner.[104] No doubt in other circumstances he would have asked him to organize an *acroasis*. Not so much was at stake for Allius, of course, but even he must have had a decision to make about how widely his praise-poem could be publicized.

Well aware of his dilemma, the poet tactfully asked the Muses to do the job: 'I'll tell *you*, and *you* must tell everyone else, and make this paper I'm writing on now speak of Allius' deed long into the future.'[105]

4.5 Art and Life

The social world in which Catullus shows himself enmeshed is constructed by the poet, and the degree to which it is useful to align that construct with historical reality is a matter of critical debate.

—Cynthia Damon

The theme of the book, moreover, is not at all what Mr Wilson describes: the theme is myself.... If he means the narrator, then it is me, because I have painstakingly indicated throughout the book that the hero is myself.

—Henry Miller

---

[101] To borrow a phrase from Schafer (2020.2), here if anywhere we are 'at the seam between his poetry and his lived reality'.

[102] Cicero *Ad Atticum* 14.4.3 (*nostri* ἥρωες *quod per ipsos confici potuit gloriosissime et magnificentissime confecerunt*), 14.6.1 (*cum heroibus nostris*), 14.11.1 (*nostri illi non heroes sed di*), 15.12.2 (*erga nostros* ἥρωας); cf. *Philippics* 2.25 (*gloriosissimi facti*), 117 (*fama gloriosum*).

[103] Cicero *Ad Atticum* 15.14.4 (Tusculum, 27 June), 15.27.2 (Arpinum, 3 July), 16.2.6 (Puteoli, 11 July), 16.3.1 (Puteoli, 17 July), 16.6.4 (Vibo, 25 July). See Aulus Gellius 15.6.3 for his use of *Iliad* 7.91 (τὸ δ' ἐμὸν κλέος οὔ ποτ' ὀλεῖται becoming *mea semper gloria uiuet*), as if the murder of an unarmed man were equivalent to the single combat of Ajax and Hector to decide the war.

[104] Cicero *Ad Atticum* 16.2.6: *custodies igitur, ut soles, sed notentur eclogae duae quas Saluius bonos auditores nactus in conuiuio dumtaxat legat.*

[105] Catullus 68b.45–6 (n. 88 above).

The first of these quotations, from Cynthia Damon in the *Cambridge Companion to Catullus* (2021), represents what most Latinists would, I think, take for granted; the second, Henry Miller's response to Edmund Wilson's review of *Tropic of Cancer* (1938), is a reminder that the critics don't always get it right.[106] In Rome too, autofiction was a puzzle: Ovid scolded his audience for believing everything he told them about Corinna,[107] but still took Catullus' poetry as a real confession of adultery.[108]

If there is one point in the whole Catullan collection where the reader gets the sense of authentic experience vividly recalled, it is surely the passage in 68b at the end of the long and complex eulogy of Laodamia, who came to the house of her husband Protesilaus as the poet's mistress came to the house of Allius:[109]

> In no way, or only a little, falling short of her, my bright one brought herself into my arms, while Cupid running about this way and that shone bright in his saffron tunic. Although she is not content with Catullus alone, still I'll put up with my discreet mistress's rare deceits, so as not to be too tiresome, as idiots are.... Yet she didn't come escorted on her father's arm, to a house fragrant with Assyrian scents, but gave me stolen gifts that miraculous night, taken from her own husband's own embrace.

It is an extraordinary document. Turning a furtive affair into a mythological event, presenting the comparison in such formally symmetrical architecture, even appealing to the family values of inheritance and legitimate offspring,[110] the poem records the delusion of a great love. So too the deliberate disruption of that symmetry, for the poet to mourn the death of his brother at Troy,[111] documents an abrupt change of attitude.

---

[106] Damon 2021.8; Wilson 1952.708–9, quoting Miller's letter of 18 May 1938.

[107] Ovid *Amores* 3.12.19 and 43–4: *nec tamen ut testes mos est audire poetas ... et mea debuerat falso laudata uideri | femina; credulitas nunc mihi uestra nocet.* Cf. *Tristia* 4.10.57–60 for his audience, the *populus*.

[108] Ovid *Tristia* 2.429–30: *multos uulgauit amores, | in quibus ipse suum fassus adulterium est.*

[109] Catullus 68b.131–40, 143–8: *aut nihil aut paulo cui tum concedere digna | lux mea se nostrum contulit in gremium, | quam circumcursans hinc illinc saepe Cupido | fulgebat crocina candidus in tunica. | quae tamen etsi uno non est contenta Catullo, | rara uerecundae furta feremus erae, | ne nimium simus stultorum more molesti. | ... nec tamen illa mihi dextra deducta paterna | fragrantem Assyrio uenit odore domum, | sed furtiua dedit mira munuscula nocte, | ipsius ex ipso dempta uiri gremio.*

[110] Catullus 68b.119–24; we know that such values mattered to him (72.3–4).

[111] Catullus 68b.91–100, surely a subsequent addition (Section 2.6 above).

The evidence in the text is unambiguous: 'Alas, brother, ... our whole house is buried along with you.'[112] Evidently, the brother had no children; family values now applied in earnest. It was time to give up high-society love affairs, and he had to explain to his friends what had happened:[113]

> At the time when the white toga was first given to me, when flowering youth was spending its happy spring, I fooled around enough. She knows me, the goddess who mixes sweet bitterness with anxieties. But this whole pursuit my brother's death has snatched away in mourning.... His death has made me drive from my whole mind all these pursuits and pleasures of the spirit.

'The theme is myself.' Here at least the poet was offering autobiography.

Catullus received his adult toga probably at the age of sixteen,[114] and probably on 17 March, the Liberalia.[115] Infuriatingly, we don't know which year that was, but since his father was rich (that villa) and well connected (host to Caesar), we can be pretty sure what happened. Escorted by friends and well-wishers,[116] Catullus *père* took his younger son down to the Forum and registered his name at the censors' archive in the *atrium Libertatis*;[117] then they processed up to the Capitol for a sacrifice at the altar of Iuventas in the precinct of the temple of Jupiter Optimus Maximus.[118] Gaius Valerius Catullus had become a free adult citizen – but not an independent one.

There must have been a generous allowance from his father,[119] attested indirectly by those who tried to cadge money from him.[120] The family

---

[112] Catullus 68b.94 (*tecum una tota est nostra sepulta domus*); the line is repeated from 68a.22, to Mallius/Manlius.

[113] Catullus 68a.15–20, 24–5: *tempore quo primum uestis mihi tradita pura est, | iucundum cum aetas florida uer ageret, | multa satis lusi: non est dea nescia nostri | quae dulcem curis miscet amaritiem. | sed totum hoc studium luctu fraterna mihi mors | abstulit. . . . | cuius ego interitu tota de mente fugaui | haec studia atque omnes delicias animi.*

[114] E.g. Persius 5.30–8 with the *uita Persi* (*cum esset annorum XVI*), Suetonius *Galba* 4.1 with Dio Cassius 56.29.5; seventeen was the age of legal adulthood and liability for military service (Aulus Gellius 10.28.1 = Tubero *FRHist* 38 F4, Plutarch *C. Gracchus* 5.1).

[115] Ovid *Fasti* 3.771–88, Cicero *Ad Atticum* 6.1.12; other dates are also attested.

[116] Appian *Civil Wars* 4.30.129, cf. Ovid *Fasti* 3.787 (*frequentia*).

[117] *Deductus in forum*: Augustus *Res gestae* 14.1, Seneca *Epistles* 4.2, Suetonius *Diuus Augustus* 26.2, *Tiberius* 15.1, *Nero* 7.2. The registration, a necessary stage, is not explicitly attested; see Livy 43.16.13 for the archive (*tabularium*) and its staff of *serui publici*; for the *atrium Libertatis* (Coarelli 2019.109–22), see Livy 45.15.6 (censors' office), Cicero *Ad Atticum* 4.16.8 (approximate position).

[118] *In Capitolium*: Suetonius *Diuus Claudius* 2.2, Servius on *Eclogues* 4.50, cf. Valerius Maximus 5.4.4. Altar of Iuventas: Dionysius of Halicarnassus *Roman Antiquities* 3.69.55, 4.15.5.

[119] The young M. Caelius and the clients of the loan shark Fufidius were less fortunate: Cicero *Pro Caelio* 36 (*filium familias patre parco ac tenaci*), Horace *Satires* 1.2.116–17 (*modo sumpta ueste uirili | sub patribus duris*).

[120] Catullus 23.26–7, 41.2, 103.1; for his attitude to money and honest dealing, see Wiseman 1985.103–7.

steward to whom he applied when his purse was full of cobwebs (13.7–8) probably balanced the young master's expenses against the profits of business affairs in Spain and Asia Minor.[121] The money wasn't being wasted; he would be studying, and getting himself known where it mattered, while his elder brother, probably called Lucius,[122] looked after the family interests abroad.

Nothing is known about this stage of his life, not even how long it lasted. Purely as a guess, we might say seven years: from the *toga uirilis* in (say) 63 BC to the next attested event, leaving Bithynian Nicaea and the good friends he had made on provincial service, in the spring of 56.[123] Clodia Metelli, the widowed lady so slandered by Cicero, had nothing to do with it (Section 1.1 above); the poet loved 'Lesbia', a younger Clodia not long married, in 56—55 BC, and the poems of that period were collected together as an ordered series of *libelli* in the spring of 54 (Section 2.5 above). Three words, *multa satis lusi* ('I fooled around enough'), cover the whole of his adult life before the event that changed everything.

That event may best be seen through the eyes of the poet's father. What did he think of young Gaius having an affair with a married lady in high society, and using his talent and education to celebrate it in verse? What did he think of young Gaius prominently taking sides in a volatile political world, and openly insulting the family's most distinguished acquaintance? Of course we don't know, but we can guess.[124] Caesar was magnanimous about the offence, but there was worse to come. The elder son died, with no children to carry on the line.[125] If young Gaius really cared about family, now was the time he had to act on it.

And it seems he did. The family survived and prospered for many generations,[126] and the simplest explanation is that young Gaius married and fathered at least one son before dying himself at the age of thirty. In the last five years of his life he employed his literary skill in a different way, writing satirical plays to be sold to the aediles or praetors for the public

---

[121] Catullus 13.8 (*plenus sacculus est aranearum*); *CIL* 15.4756 (Spain); *IG* 2².4159 with Cicero *Ad familiares* 13.65 (Asia Minor); Wiseman 1987.338–40, 2007.60–3.

[122] The praenomen most often used by the family (Wiseman 2007.62).

[123] Catullus 46.9–11: *o dulces comitum ualete coetus,* | *longe quos simul a domo profectos* | *diuersae uarie uiae reportant.* See Du Quesnay and Woodman 2021.1–2 on the dates; I assume for the sake of argument that the thirty-year life attested by Suetonius (Jerome *Chronica* on Ol. 180.3) was 79–49 BC.

[124] 'One wonders how on earth Catullus thought he could get away with embarrassing the family so blatantly' (Skinner 2007.3).

[125] Catullus 68a.22 = 68b.94 (n. 112 above); 'Catullus appears in this poem as, by implication, the last of his line' (Gale 2021.236).

[126] Details in Wiseman 2007.59–65.

games (Section 2.7 above). He already had some experience in writing for the stage, to judge by poems 63 and 64 (Section 4.3 above); at this point, the change of direction was probably something his father would approve of.[127] It may seem a comedown in literary-critical terms, but who are we to despise the act of a dutiful son?

This is not to suggest that Catullus renounced what he had done before. On the contrary, at this very time he collected all the work he wanted to preserve from the previous two years into an ordered series of *libelli*, of which the first and most conspicuous paid due respect to Caesar but also celebrated his love for 'Lesbia'. Another included the praise of Allius that he hoped the Muses would publicize, though now an address to dead Lucius interrupted it. Back in Rome and still writing ('I'm terrified of our friend Valerius,' said Cicero),[128] of course he wanted his work to be read and admired.

He died in Rome, and if his fifteenth-century biographer can be trusted,[129] the Roman People mourned him at his funeral.

* * *

Written by a young man on the make, *Catullan Questions* has been revisited by an old man in a hurry. These four chapters, 'a headlong kind of work',[130] were composed in immediate reaction first to Schafer (2020) and then to Du Quesnay and Woodman (2021). Those dates tell their own story: lockdown in the plague years certainly concentrated the mind. What follows in Part II, three free-standing studies written in less urgent times, may be regarded as supplementary material to a dense and demanding argument.

---

[127] Writing for the *ludi* was probably how the young Horace was able to make money: *paupertas impulit audax | ut uersus facerem* (Horace *Epistles* 2.2.51–2). Poetry for its own sake wouldn't do it, as Ovid's father pointed out: '*studium quid inutile temptas? | Maeonides nullas ipse reliquit opes*' (Ovid *Tristia* 4.10.21–2).

[128] Cicero *Ad familiares* 7.11.2 (Section 2.7 above).

[129] Jerome *Chronica* on Ol. 180.3 (*Romae moritur*). Gerolamo Squarzafico, on whom see Chapter 1, n. 32 above (from Suetonius' *De poetis*?): *anno uero aetatis suae XXX Romae moritur elatus moerore publico.*

[130] Jerome *Chronica* pref. 2 (*quicquid hoc tumultuarii operis est*), evidently echoing Catullus 1.8 (*quicquid hoc libelli*).

PART II

CHAPTER 5

How Gallic Were the Transpadanes?

Catullus' most recent biographer takes it for granted that he was a 'Gaul'.[1] She is in good company: Wilamowitz himself attributed the poet's wonderful ease of expression to his 'Gallic blood'.[2] But what is the evidence for this notion? It is true that Catullus was born and grew up in the province that was called 'nearer Gaul' or 'Cisalpine Gaul' or 'toga-wearing Gaul',[3] but he called his native people by a geographical, not ethnic, name – *Transpadani*, from north of the river Padus (Po).[4]

Dedicating his little book to a fellow Transpadane, Catullus pointedly called Cornelius Nepos an Italian, *Italus*.[5] Just as *Italia* and *Gallia* were mutually exclusive geographical areas,[6] so *Itali* and *Galli* were wholly distinct ethnic categories.[7] In Catullus' time the Gauls were still 'a race most hostile to the name of Rome', and war against them was always a struggle for survival.[8] Yet Cicero in 44 BC could describe *prouincia Gallia* as 'the flower of Italy, the bulwark of the empire of the Roman People, the ornament of its dignity'.[9]

---

[1]   Dunn 2016.17–18, 40, 44, 55, 112 (cf. 41 on Cornelius Nepos, 'a poet and historian from Gaul'); no evidence or explanation provided.

[2]   Wilamowitz 1921.139: 'admirabilis facilitas, quam Gallico sanguini deberi credo'.

[3]   Caesar *De bello Gallico* 1.24.3, 1.54.3, 2.1.1, 2.2.1, 5.1.5, 5.2.1 (*Gallia citerior*); 1.10.5 (*citerior prouincia*), 6.1.2 (*cisalpina Gallia*); Hirtius *De bello Gallico* 8.23.3, 8.54.3 (*Gallia citerior*); 8.24.3, 8.52.1 (*Gallia togata*); Cicero *De inuentione* 2.111 (*citerior Gallia*), *Philippics* 3.13 (*prouincia Gallia*), 8.27 (*Gallia togata*); Catullus 43.6 (*prouincia*). Catullus born in Verona: Jerome *Chronica* on Ol. 173.2 ('87–6 BC', almost certainly misdated).

[4]   Catullus 39.13; so too Cicero *Ad familiares* 8.1.2, 12.5.2, Caesar *De bello ciuili* 3.87.4.

[5]   Catullus 1.5 (*unus Italorum*), cf. Pliny *Nat. Hist.* 3.127 for Nepos as a 'neighbour of the Padus'.

[6]   Bounded first by the river Aesis and then by the Rubicon: Strabo 5.1.11 (C217), 5.2.10 (C227); cf. nn. 19 and 20 below.

[7]   See, for instance, Tacitus *Annals* 11.23.2–3 on Italians as *consanguinei populi* and Gauls as *alienigenae*.

[8]   Sallust *Catiline* 52.24 (*Gallorum gentem infestissumam nomini Romano*), *Jugurthine War* 114.2 (*usque ad nostram memoriam . . . cum Gallis pro salute, non pro gloria certare*); Cicero *De prouinciis consularibus* 32–3. For traditional Roman fear of the Gauls, see Williams 2001.171–82.

[9]   Cicero *Philippics* 3.13 (trans. D. R. Shackleton Bailey): *est enim ille flos Italiae, illud firmamentum imperi populi Romani, illud ornamentum dignitatis*.

These apparent contradictions need to be resolved if we are to have any hope of understanding Catullus' background. I think it can be done, but it is not a simple story. Fortunately, we have the help of Strabo of Amaseia, a polymathic historian about twenty years younger than Catullus, who in his old age wrote seventeen books of *Geography*. The fourth and fifth dealt with the Gauls, or 'Kelts' (*Keltoi*).

5.1   Strabo on the Keltic Lands

Strabo begins his description of Europe in the far west. Book 3 of the *Geography* deals with Iberia, bounded by the Pyrenees. The subject of book 4 is 'the Keltic land beyond the Alps', a conspicuously repeated formula,[10] and then the Alps themselves. Since Strabo refers to rivers that flowed down into 'the Keltic land *within* the Alps',[11] the reader naturally assumes that this second tract of Keltic land will be the subject of the next book. But the next book begins: 'After the foothills of the Alps is the start of what is now Italy.'[12]

The author explains that the name of Italy 'advanced up to the foothills of the Alps, and took in addition the Ligurian land from the boundary of Etruria as far as the river Varus [between Nice and Antibes] and the sea there, and also Istria as far as Pola' (Fig. 5.1).[13] Those were the boundaries of Italy as established by Augustus.[14] Nevertheless, in book 5 Strabo sometimes used his previous terminology, referring to the great plain between the Alps and the Apennines as 'the Keltic land within the Alps'.[15] A recent commentator finds that anomalous,[16] but the reason for it is clear enough.

---

[10] Strabo 4.1.1 (C176), 4.4.6 (C199), 4.6.1 (C201): ἡ ὑπὲρ τῶν Ἄλπεων Κελτική. Cf. also 4.6.11 (C208), εἰς τὴν ἔξω Κελτικήν, and 6.4.2 (C287), τὴν δὲ Κελτικὴν ἅπασαν τήν τε ἐντὸς καὶ τὴν ἐκτός.

[11] 4.3.3 (C192), 4.6.5 (C203): ἡ ἐντὸς τῶν Ἄλπεων Κελτική.

[12] 5.1.1 (C209): μετὰ δὲ τὴν ὑπώρειαν τῶν Ἄλπεων ἀρχὴ τῆς νῦν Ἰταλίας. Also 5.1.2 (C210) and 5.1.3 (C211): σύμπασαν τὴν νῦν Ἰταλίαν ... περὶ τῆς νῦν Ἰταλίας ἁπάσης.

[13] 5.1.1 (C209): μέχρι τῆς ὑπωρείας τῶν Ἄλπεων προὔβη, προσέλαβε δὲ καὶ τῆς Λιγυστικῆς τὰ μέχρι Οὐάρου ποταμοῦ καὶ τῆς ταύτῃ θαλάττης ἀπὸ τῶν ὁρίων τῶν Τυρρηνικῶν καὶ τῆς Ἰστρίας μέχρι Πόλας. For the Varus see 4.1.9 (C184): ὁ δὲ Οὐᾶρος μέσος ἐστὶ τῆς Ἀντιπόλεως καὶ Νικαίας ... κατὰ τὸν νῦν ἀποδεδειγμένον ὅρον.

[14] Pliny *Natural History* 3.46 (*auctorem nos diuum Augustum secuturos*), 3.47 (*igitur ab amne Varo ...*), 3.129 (after Pola, *finis Italiae fluuius Arsia*). See Tozzi 1988.38–9 for this 'new reality'.

[15] 5.1.3 (C211): ἡ ἐντὸς τῶν Ἄλπεων Κελτική. 5.1.11 (C217): χώρα ... ἣν ἐντὸς Κελτικὴν καλοῦμεν. Cf. also 5.1.1 (C210): τοῖς ἐντὸς Ἄλπεων Γαλάταις.

[16] Roller 2018.215–16, suggesting a 'textual disruption' at 5.1.3 (C211). However, it is not true that 'the phrase "Keltike within the Alps" occurs nowhere else in the *Geography*', and there is no reason to think that it 'represents a remnant of a pre-Roman view'. Pre-*Augustan*, yes.

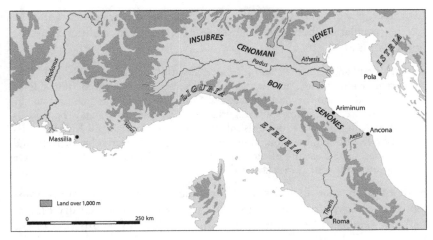

Fig. 5.1   The Keltic lands described by Strabo

Strabo's main sources for books 4 and 5 were Polybius, Artemidorus and Posidonius,[17] whose writings together spanned three generations, from about 150 to about 60 BC. Though he was constantly adding more recent evidence, it is easy to see how terminology appropriate to the second or early first century BC could survive in the structuring of his work. One such survival is his reference to 'Italy that is defined by the Apennines ... where they connect with the area around Ariminum and Ancona and define the breadth of Italy from sea to sea'.[18] That presupposes the middle-republican concept of *terra Italia*, the boundary of which on the Adriatic coast was the river Aesis a few miles north of Ancona;[19] beyond the Aesis was the *ager Gallicus*,[20] or in Greek 'the Keltic land within the Alps'.

---

[17] Polybius: cited at 4.1.8 (C183), 4.2.1 (C190), 4.6.11 (C208), 5.1.3 (C211), 5.1.8 (C214–15), 5.4.3 (C242). Artemidorus: cited at 4.1.8 (C183), 4.4.6 (C198), 5.2.6 (C224), 5.4.6 (C245). Posidonius: cited at 4.1.7 (C183), 4.1.13–14 (C188), 4.4.5 (C198), 5.1.8 (C214–5). See in general Biffi 1988.xxxvii–xlv; Tozzi 1988.39–40.

[18] 5.1.3 (C211): τῇ Ἰταλίᾳ τῇ ἀφοριζομένῃ τοῖς Ἀπεννίνοις ὄρεσι ... τὰ δὲ Ἀπέννινα ὄρη συνάψαντα τοῖς περὶ Ἀρίμινον καὶ Ἀγκῶνα καὶ ἀφορίσαντα τὸ ταύτης πλάτος τῆς Ἰταλίας ἀπὸ θαλάττης ἐπὶ θάλατταν... 5.4.1–2 (C240): ἀρκτέον δὲ πάλιν ἀπὸ τῶν Κελτικῶν ὅρων ... τὰς τῶν Ὀμβρικῶν πόλεις τὰς μεταξὺ Ἀριμίνου καὶ Ἀγκῶνος.

[19] 5.1.11 (C217), 5.2.10 (C227); cf. 6.3.10 (C285), Artemidorus' use of the Aesis as a distance marker. See Harris 2007 for the origin of this concept, probably in the late fourth or early third century BC, and Bispham 2007.60–8 for its description as *terra Italia*.

[20] Cato *FRHist* 5 F46, Cicero *Pro Sestio* 9, Livy 24.10.3, 39.44.10, Pliny *Natural History* 3.112. See Polybius 2.17.4–8 for the Gallic peoples who occupied the plain of the Po, and 2.14.11, 2.16.5 and 2.19.13 for Sena Gallica, the Roman colony founded in 283 BC just north of the Aesis, as the southernmost point of the plain.

Strabo goes on to describe the basic geography of the region, and here too his oscillation between Augustan and republican realities must be borne in mind:[21]

> It is a plain, very fertile and interspersed with fruitful deep-soiled hills. The river Padus divides it roughly in the centre, so it is called 'this side of the Padus' and 'beyond the Padus'. 'This side' is all the area next to the Apennine mountains, plus Liguria [on the west coast], and 'beyond' is everything else. The former is inhabited by the Ligurian and Keltic peoples who live both in the mountains and in the plains, the latter by the Kelts and Veneti. The Kelts are of the same race as those beyond the Alps, but there are two different stories about the Veneti.

A description that includes Keltic peoples south of the Padus must represent a viewpoint already obsolete by the mid-second century BC.

A few sentences later Strabo mentions the Romans' extirpation of the Senones and the Boii (respectively, 283 and 191 BC); but 'beyond the Padus, the Insubres still exist'.[22] He knows that their capital Mediolanum, which used to be a village, 'is now a notable city'. That suggests that he is reporting the conditions of his own time, and it is sometimes assumed that his text genuinely attests the survival of the Insubres as an ethnic community.[23] But in what sense could Milan in the age of Augustus still be called Insubrian?

Strabo makes a point of the fact that the Kelts 'within the Alps', including the Insubres, were of the same race as the warlike Transalpine peoples whose barbaric way of life he described in the previous book.[24] The association of the Insubres with the Transalpine Gauls could be

---

[21] 5.1.4 (C212): ἔστι δὲ πεδίον σφόδρα εὔδαιμων καὶ γεωλοφίαις εὐκάρποις πεποικιλμένον. διαιρεῖ δ' αὐτὸ μέσον πως ὁ Πάδος, καὶ καλεῖται τὸ μὲν ἐντὸς τοῦ Πάδου, τὸ δὲ πέραν· ἐντὸς μὲν ὅσον ἐστὶ πρὸς τοῖς Ἀπεννίνοις ὄρεσι καὶ τῇ Λιγυστικῇ, πέραν δὲ τὸ λοιπόν. οἰκεῖται δὲ τὸ μὲν ὑπὸ Λιγυστικῶν ἐθνῶν καὶ τῶν Κελτικῶν, τῶν μὲν ἐν τοῖς ὄρεσιν οἰκούντων τῶν δ' ἐν τοῖς πεδίοις, τὸ δ' ὑπὸ τῶν Κελτῶν καὶ Ἐνετῶν. οἱ μὲν οὖν Κελτοὶ τοῖς ὑπεραλπίοις ὁμοεθνεῖς εἰσι, περὶ δὲ τῶν Ἐνετῶν διττός ἐστι λόγος. Note that the Loeb translation at this point has 'the former' and 'the latter' the wrong way round. 'This side' (ἐντὸς τοῦ Πάδου): also 5.1.10 (C216), 5.1.11 (C216), 5.1.11 (C217). 'Beyond' (πέραν τοῦ Πάδου): also 5.1.6 (C213), 5.1.9 (C216).

[22] 5.1.6 (C212–13): τούτους μὲν οὖν ἐξέφθειραν ὕστερον τελέως Ῥωμαῖοι [so too Pliny *Natural History* 3.116] ... Ἴνσουβροι δὲ καὶ νῦν εἰσί ... πέραν τοῦ Πάδου.

[23] Williams 2001.126 ('the Cenomani and Insubres ... were still in some sense existing as ethnic communities') and 214 ('the persistence of the Insubres and Cenomani as communities into the late Republic'); however, Strabo offers no support for the survival of the Cenomani.

[24] 4.4.5 (C197–8) = Posidonius fr. 274 E–K (an eyewitness account). Transalpine (ὑπεράλπιος): 4.3.3 (C192), 4.6.3 (C203), 514 (C212), 5.1.12 (C218); Polybius (2.15.8–9, 2.19.1, 2.21.5) translates the Latin term *Transalpinus*. For 'the civilizing of the barbarians under Roman rule [as] a unifying historical theme of the *Geography*', see Woolf 1998.50–3 on Strabo book 4.

exploited by Cicero as late as the 50s BC,[25] just about the time the young Virgil was getting what must have been a good classical education at Mediolanum.[26]

Terrifying barbarians or civilized Italians? Those ambiguous late-republican attitudes presuppose the assimilation of the Cisalpine Gauls into Roman culture, but do not explain how it came about. Strabo has not been much exploited for this puzzling question, but I hope a close reading of one particular passage, and careful attention to its implications, may help to make sense of it.

5.2 Roman Colonists

At the beginning of book 5, explaining how the term 'Italy' was extended as a result of Roman conquest, Strabo makes this statement:[27]

> At some late stage, after the Romans granted equal citizenship to the Italians [90 BC], it was decided to assign the same status to the Gauls and Veneti this side of the Alps, to call them all Italians and Romans, and to send out many colonies, some sooner, some later, than which it would be hard to name any better ones.

He has evidently compressed his source a little here (to what times do 'sooner' and 'later' refer?), but whichever colonies these were, Strabo regarded them as unsurpassed.

The reader expects these admirable places to be named in what follows, and indeed they are; in no other region of Italy is Strabo so generous with laudatory epithets (Fig. 5.2). Mediolanum is 'a notable city'; Verona 'also a large city'; Patavium 'the best of all cities in the region'; Ravenna 'the largest city in the marshes'; south of the Padus, Placentia, Cremona, Parma, Mutina and Bononia are 'illustrious cities'; and Dertona, like Mediolanum, a 'notable city'.[28] Strabo makes no distinction between the

---

[25] See his description of L. Piso's maternal grandfather as an *Insuber* (Cicero *In Pisonem* fr. ix = Asconius 5C), *Transalpini sanguinis* (Cicero *Post reditum in senatu* 15).

[26] Jerome *Chronica* Ol. 181.4 (*Vergilius sumpta toga Mediolanum transgreditur*, 53/2 BC); Servius on Virgil *Aeneid* pref. (*et Cremonae et Mediolani et Neapoli studuit*).

[27] Strabo 5.1.1 (C210): ὀψὲ δέ ποτε ἀφ' οὗ μετέδοσαν Ῥωμαῖοι τοῖς Ἰταλιώταις τὴν ἰσοπολιτείαν, ἔδοξε καὶ τοῖς ἐντὸς Ἄλπεων Γαλάταις καὶ Ἐνετοῖς τὴν αὐτὴν ἀπονεῖμαι τιμήν, προσαγορεῦσαι δὲ καὶ Ἰταλιώτας πάντας καὶ Ῥωμαίους, ἀποικίας τε πολλὰς στεῖλαι, τὰς μὲν πρότερον τὰς δ' ὕστερον, ὧν οὐ ῥάδιον εἰπεῖν ἀμείνους ἑτέρας.

[28] 5.1.6 (C213), 5.1.7 (C213); 5.1.11 (C216), 5.1.11 (C217). Cremona was north of the river, but Strabo counts it in his second category (ἐντὸς τοῦ Πάδου καὶ περὶ τὸν Πάδον); compare the Latin term *circumpadanus* (Livy 21.35.8; Pliny *Natural History* 8.190, 14.124, 18.101, 18.120).

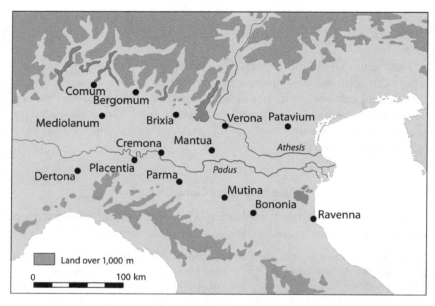

Fig. 5.2   The Roman colonies named by Strabo

Cispadane cities, colonies sent out long before,[29] and those in the
Transpadane region and the marshes of the delta. So Mediolanum,
Verona, Patavium and Ravenna seem to be among the 'later' colonies he
refers to.[30]

What Strabo wrote and what he evidently meant are clear enough.
Whether he was right is a different matter. To answer that, we must look
at the whole long history of Roman engagement with Transpadane Italy.

The Augustan consular *fasti* mark the first stage of the process with a
conspicuous chronological marker at what we call 225 BC: *Bellum
Gallicum cisalpinum*. It is the second of a series: the others are *Bellum
Punicum primum* (264), [*Bellum Pun*]*icum* [*secu*]*nd*[*u*]*m* (218), *Bellum
Philippicum* (200), [*Be*]*llum Antiochinum* (191), *Bellum Persicum* (171),

---

[29] Placentia and Cremona Latin colonies of 218 BC (Polybius 3.40.4–5, Livy *Epitome* 20), Parma and
Mutina citizen colonies of 183 (Livy 39.55.7), Bononia a Latin colony of 189 (Livy 37.57.7–8,
Velleius Paterculus 1.15.2), Dertona a citizen colony of c. 120 (Velleius Paterculus 1.15.5, with
Fraccaro 1957.127–30).

[30] Also Brixia, Mantua, 'Rhegium' and Comum, described at 5.1.6 (C213) as smaller than
Mediolanum and Verona – but still cities, not mere πολισμάτια like Opitergium, Concordia,
Atria and Vicetia (5.1.7, C214). 'Rhegium' must be an error for 'Bergomum' (Roller 2018.219).

Bellum Punicum tertium (149) and *Bellum Marsicum* (90).[31] The conquest of the Gauls this side of the Alps evidently counted as one of the great formative conflicts of the Roman republic.

The gains were all lost in the Hannibalic war, and the whole area had to be reconquered in the 190s BC. There were frequent further campaigns throughout the second century, with triumphs being won against Gallic peoples in the Alpine foothills as late as 117 (Q. Marcius Rex against the Stoeni) and 115 (M. Aemilius Scaurus against the Carni).[32] We happen to know that Rome's peace treaties with the Cenomani, Insubres and other Gallic peoples specified that no member of them could be accepted into the Roman citizenship.[33] At the time when Strabo's sources Polybius and Artemidorus were writing, the assimilation of the *Keltoi* was hardly conceivable. But it seems to have happened within two generations.

The stages of the process are attested by Asconius and Cassius Dio, reporting events in 89, 49 and 41 BC:

(1) ... Cn. Pompeius Strabo [consul in 89 BC], the father of Cn. Pompeius Magnus, founded Transpadane colonies. He did not establish them with new colonists, but gave the existing former inhabitants 'Latin' rights, so they could have the same rights as the other Latin colonies, namely to achieve Roman citizenship by [holding] magistracies.[34]

(2) Caesar accepted the authority [of *dictator*] as soon as he entered the city [in March 49 BC]. However, he did nothing dreadful in that capacity, but ... granted citizenship to the Gauls who live this side of the Alps beyond the Padus, whose governor he had also been.[35]

---

[31] *Inscriptiones Italiae* 13.1 (1947) 40, 44, 48, 50, 52, 54; the years 130–111 and 105–99 are missing, so it is not known whether the *bellum Iugurthinum* and *bellum Cimbricum* were marked in the same way.

[32] *Inscriptiones Italiae* 13.1 (1947) 85, respectively, *de Liguribus Stoeneis* and *de Galleis Karneis*; Livy *Epitome* 62 (*Q. Marcius consul Stynos gentem Alpinam expugnauit*), Orosius 5.14.5 (*Q. Marcius consul Gallorum gentem sub radice Alpium sitam bello adgressus est*); for the Carni, above Aquileia to the east, see Strabo 4.6.9 (C206), 5.1.10 (C216), Pliny *Natural History* 3.126–7.

[33] Cicero *Pro Balbo* 32: *etenim quaedam foedera exstant, ut Cenomanorum Insubrium Heluetiorum Iapydum, nonnullorum item ex Gallia barbarorum, quorum in foederibus exceptum est ne quis eorum a nobis ciuis recipiatur.* Detailed discussion in Haeussler 2013b.108–12.

[34] Asconius 3C: *quemadmodum ... Cn. Pompeius Strabo, pater Cn. Pompei Magni, Transpadanas colonias deduxerit. Pompeius enim non nouis colonis eas constituit sed ueteribus incolis manentibus ius dedit Latii, ut possent habere ius quod ceterae Latinae coloniae, id est ut per magistratus ciuitatem Romanam adipiscerentur.* Alerted by John Ramsey, in the final clause I have preferred Stangl's reading *per magistratus* to that of Clark's Oxford text (*petendo magistratus*); the citizenship was earned by serving as a local magistrate (Appian *Civil Wars* 2.26.98), not just by standing for election.

[35] Dio Cassius 41.36.2–3: καὶ ὃς ὑπέστη μὲν τὴν ἀρχήν, ἐπειδὴ πρῶτον ἐς τὴν πόλιν ἐσῆλθεν, οὐ μέντοι καὶ φοβερὸν οὐδὲν ἐν αὐτῇ ἔπραξεν, ἀλλὰ ... τοῖς Γαλάταις τοῖς ἐντὸς τῶν Ἄλπεων ὑπὲρ τὸν Ἠριδανὸν οἰκοῦσι τὴν πολιτείαν, ἅτε καὶ ἄρξας αὐτῶν, ἀπέδωκε.

(3) Both money and soldiers came to [the Triumvirs] also from *Gallia togata*, which had now been enrolled into the legal status of Italy, so that no one else on the excuse of being governor there should keep soldiers this side of the Alps.[36]

This paradox – that Rome should so quickly have welcomed her most dangerous enemies into her citizen body – has never been satisfactorily explained, and recent analyses, concentrating on 'ethnic identities' as inferred from the archaeological data, provide little assistance.[37]

The process of assimilation used to be called 'Romanization', but that term now requires careful glossing,[38] and even Greg Woolf's useful phrase 'becoming Roman' is used nowadays with a sceptical question mark.[39] Ralph Haeussler provides a useful summary of current thinking:[40]

> Was the integration of Cisalpine Gaul already achieved in the 40's BC? As we have seen, despite the integration into the Roman citizen body in 89/49 BC, archaeologically we can hardly define any aspirations for a Roman identity in north-west Italy in the Republican period. Instead, cultural expressions had a rather experimental and often contradictory character when people tried to negotiate their place in Roman Italy, as coinage, epigraphy, material culture, and funerary rituals reveal. Not until the Principate, however, do we recognize a society in which status acquired in Roman structures has become more important than locally acquired status, rendering local ethnicities almost meaningless.

But that leaves out the evidence of Catullus, always known as the poet of Verona,[41] who already in the 50s BC had 'negotiated his place' pretty

---

[36] Dio Cassius 48.12.5: καὶ αὐτοῖς καὶ ἐκ τῆς Γαλατίας τῆς τογάτης, ἢ καὶ ἐς τὸν τῆς Ἰταλίας ἤδη νόμον, ὥστε μηδένα ἄλλον προφάσει τῆς ἐνταῦθα ἀρχῆς στρατιώτας ἐντὸς τῶν Ἄλπεων τρέφειν, ἐσεγέγραπτο, καὶ χρήματα καὶ στρατιῶται ἦλθον. Also Appian *Civil Wars* 5.3.12 on the 'freeing of the Keltic land this side the Alps, according to the intention of the elder Caesar'. For *Gallia togata* cf. Hirtius *De bello Gallico* 8.24.3, 8.52.1–2.

[37] Haeussler 2007, 2013a, 2013b, 2015; Lomas 2007, 2015.

[38] 'Romanization (or any "ization") is not a package given by a more advanced imperial power to a primitive society that passively accepts the fruits of the greater culture. Rather, as Woolf (1998) has argued, it is about groups actively joining the debate as to what that cultural package is' (Isayev 2007.17).

[39] Compare the titles of Woolf 1998 and Haeussler 2013a and 2013b.

[40] Haeussler 2013a.63–4; full details in Haeussler 2013b, ch. 2. At 2013b.115 Haeussler offers a rather different perspective: 'In the late Republic, when societies across Italy were experiencing rapid upheavals, the grant of *ius Latii* to the *Transpadani* must have transformed people's identities and their social and cultural understandings.'

[41] Ovid *Amores* 3.15.7; Martial 1.61.1, 14.100, 14.152, 14.195; Pliny *Natural History* 37.48 (cf. pref. 1, *conterraneus meus*); Nonius 876L, Ausonius 1.4.2 OCT, Macrobius *Saturnalia* 2.1.8, Priscian *Gramm. Lat.* 2.16 Keil.

thoroughly in Roman society. Did he really think of himself as a Gaul of the Cenomani?

Asconius reports that when Cn. Pompeius Strabo founded *Transpadanae coloniae* in 89 BC, 'he did not establish them with new colonists, but gave the existing former inhabitants "Latin" rights'.[42] According to Strabo, the later colonies, like the former ones, were 'sent out', which seems to contradict Asconius' statement. On the strength of what Asconius says, it is almost universally assumed in modern scholarship that these were 'fictive colonies', and that the 'existing former inhabitants' were the indigenous peoples.[43] But I think that is unlikely.

One relevant text is Catullus' poem 17, addressed to a *colonia* that hoped to build a new causeway over its nearby marsh.[44] The context is certainly Transpadane, since the poet refers to 'a certain fellow-citizen' of his own, from Verona. Philip Cluverius in 1624 thought the description suited Mantua, but that suggestion is universally discounted because 'Mantua was not a Roman colony'.[45] Strabo evidently believed that it was,[46] but whatever the precise identification, Catullus' *colonia* does not sound like a community of indigenous Gauls or Veneti whose colonial status was merely 'fictive'.[47]

It seems likely that Strabo oversimplified what his source told him about the 'later' colonization of Cisalpine Gaul. In particular, his phrase 'at some late stage' (ὀψὲ δέ ποτε) suggests some chronological imprecision. But I don't think we should simply ignore, without argument or justification, the clear implication of what he says. If it is inconsistent with the passage in Asconius, then perhaps the passage in Asconius should itself be read more carefully. Who exactly were the 'existing former inhabitants' (*ueteres incolae manentes*) to whom Latin rights were granted in 89 BC?

5.3 After the Invasion

Just twelve years before Pompeius Strabo's consulship a cataclysmic event had taken place in Transpadane Italy. Poorly attested in the ancient

---

[42] Asconius 3C (n. 34 above): *non nouis colonis eas constituit sed ueteribus incolis manentibus ius dedit Latii.*

[43] See, for instance, Bandelli 1990.260–6, who gives the extensive previous bibliography, and Bispham 2007.173–5.

[44] Catullus 17.1–5: *O colonia, quae cupis ponte ludere longo ... sic tibi bonus ex tua pons libidine fiat.* The *palus* is emphasised at lines 4, 10–11 and 25–6.

[45] Ellis 1889.61, citing Cluverius, *Italia antiqua* p. 127.

[46] 5.1.6 (C213), with n. 30 above. Strabo of course does not distinguish between Latin colonies and *coloniae ciuium Romanorum*.

[47] For Catullus' view of Gauls cf. 42.8–9 (*mimice ac moleste | ridentem catuli ore Gallicani*).

sources, the Cimbric invasion is ignored or forgotten by modern historians,[48] but its impact must have been devastating.

The essentials of Livy's lost narrative can be recovered from the *Epitome* and from Florus and Orosius.[49] The Cimbri, Teutones and Tigurini, 'Gallic Germanic' peoples whose territory on the North Sea had been flooded, migrated south to find somewhere to settle. In 109 BC they asked the Roman Senate for land in Italy, and when rebuffed decided that they would take it anyway.[50] By 105, when they had routed three consular armies, the whole of Italy was terrified, expecting an invasion.[51] Marius was repeatedly elected consul to deal with the threat, which finally materialized in 102: the Teutones and Tigurini planned to move east from Narbonese Gaul and the Cimbri south from Noricum down the valley of the Athesis (Adige). Marius defeated the Teutones and Tigurini at Aquae Sextiae, but his consular colleague Quintus Catulus fled before the Cimbri, who advanced unhindered into Italy.[52] Having crossed the Athesis, presumably at or near Verona, they had the whole plain north of the Padus at their mercy.

The accuracy of this narrative is confirmed by Plutarch, who used the eyewitness accounts of Catulus and Sulla.[53] 'Three hundred thousand armed warriors were on the move with their women and children, looking for enough land to support such a huge multitude';[54] after the flight of Catulus, the Cimbri 'poured into a land empty of protection and ravaged it', and when Marius arrived with reinforcements in the early summer of 101, 'he crossed the Padus in an attempt to keep the barbarians out of Italy

---

[48] No mention, for instance, in Bandelli 1990, Lomas 2007 and 2015, or Haeussler 2013a; it is absent from the table of 'historic events affecting Northwest Italy in the 4th–1st centuries BC' at Haeussler 2013b.76.

[49] Livy *Epitome* 65, 67, 68; Florus 3.3.1–18 (1.38); Orosius 5.16.1–22, 6.14.2.

[50] Florus 3.3.3 (*quod nequiuerant precibus, armis petere coeperunt*), Orosius 5.16.1 (*gentes quae tunc ut imperium Romanum extinguerent conspirauerant*).

[51] Orosius 5.16.7 (*maximus tunc Romae ... metus fuit ne confestim Cimbri Alpes transgrederentur Italiamque delerent*), cf. Sallust *Jugurthine War* 114.2 (*quo metu Italia omnis contremuerat*). The defeated armies were those of M. Silanus in 109 BC and Q. Caepio and Cn. Mallius (separately) at Arausio in 105.

[52] Livy *Epitome* 68 (*Cimbri cum ... in Italiam traiecissent*), Florus 3.3.11 (*in Italiam prouoluti ueluti ruina descenderant*), Orosius 5.16.14 (*Italiae plana peruaserant*); *pace* Haeussler 2007.70, it is not true that 'Rome ... stopped the invasion of the Cimbri.'

[53] Plutarch *Marius* 11–27; Catulus *FRHist* 19 F1–3 (Plutarch *Marius* 25.6, 26.5, 27.4); Sulla *FRHist* 22 F7–9 (Plutarch *Sulla* 4.3, *Marius* 25.4, 26.3).

[54] Plutarch *Marius* 11.2: μυριάδες μὲν γὰρ αἱ μάχιμοι τριάκοντα σὺν ὅπλοις ἐχώρουν, ὄχλοι δὲ παίδων καὶ γυναικῶν ἐλέγοντο πολλῷ πλείους συμπεριάγεσθαι, γῆς χρῄζοντες ἢ θρέψει τοσοῦτον πλῆθος. Cf. Orosius 5.16.16 (*tanta ac tam terribilis multitudo*).

south of the river'.[55] The land north of the river was already theirs, a situation that had lasted seven or eight months by the time the combined armies of Marius and Catulus fought it out with the Cimbri on 30 July at the battle of Campi Raudii, and destroyed them.[56]

Marius had recruited his army 'not according to custom from the [property-owning] classes, but as the urge took each man, most of them assessed for their person alone'.[57] After their heroic efforts in saving the rest of Italy from invasion, those soldiers needed their reward. The following year (100 BC) the tribune L. Appuleius Saturninus provided it as part of his *popularis* legislative programme:[58]

> Appuleius brought in a law to divide up all the land which the Cimbri (a Keltic people) had seized in what the Romans now call Gaul; Marius, having driven them out, had taken the land into Roman ownership because it no longer belonged to the Gauls.

Despite Appian's evident confusion about 'what the Romans *now* call Gaul', it is obvious that this refers to the Transpadane territory that the Cimbri had occupied after the rout of Catulus' army.[59] After the victory Marius claimed it for Rome, to provide land for his deserving veterans.

When Saturninus' tribunate ended in violence and the tribune's own death, the Senate decreed that his legislation was invalid.[60] But it is inconceivable that the land was handed back to the indigenous Gauls and Veneti, or that the veterans did not get their reward. Michael Crawford makes an important inference from the revival of the *quinarius* coinage at this time:[61]

---

[55] Plutarch *Marius* 23.6, 24.2: τὴν δὲ χώραν ἔρημον βοηθείας ἐπιχυθέντες ἐπόρθουν . . . διαβὰς τὸν Ἠριδανὸν εἴργειν ἐπειρᾶτο τῆς ἐντὸς Ἰταλίας τοὺς βαρβάρους.

[56] Velleius Paterculus 2.12.5 (over 100,000 killed or captured), Florus 3.3.14 (65,000 killed); Plutarch *Marius* 26.4 for the date.

[57] Sallust *Jugurthine War* 86.2 (trans. A. J. Woodman): *non more maiorum neque ex classibus, sed uti quoiusque lubido erat, capite censos plerique.* On *capite censi* (citizens without property, *proletarii*), see Cicero *De republica* 2.40, Aulus Gellius 16.10.10.

[58] Appian *Civil Wars* 1.29.130: ὁ μὲν Ἀπουλήιος νόμον ἐσέφερε διαδάσασθαι γῆν ὅσην ἐν τῇ νῦν ὑπὸ Ῥωμαίων καλουμένῃ Γαλατίᾳ Κίμβροι γένος Κελτῶν κατειλήφεσαν, καὶ αὐτοὺς ὁ Μάριος ἔναγχος ἐξελάσας τὴν γῆν ὡς οὐκέτι Γαλατῶν ἐς Ῥωμαίους περιεσπάκει.

[59] So Fraccaro 1957.98–103, Gabba 1958.102; *contra* Brunt 1988.279, who believed that Appian's phrase meant Transalpine Gaul, and that it is 'not remotely plausible that the Cimbri had annexed any land' in the Transpadana. But the Cimbri came directly from Noricum into Italy; what land could they have occupied in Transalpine Gaul?

[60] Cicero *De legibus* 2.14 (*Appuleias leges . . . quae praesertim uno uersiculo senatus puncto temporis sublatae sint*), *Pro Balbo* 48 (*cum lege Appuleia coloniae non essent deductae*); for discussion, see Lintott 1968.136–8 and Dyck 2004.277–9.

[61] Crawford 1985.182–3; see Velleius Paterculus 1.15.5 for Eporedia, a citizen colony founded in the far north-west in 100 BC.

> If we look at the occasions on which Rome struck quinarii, a significant link
> with Gaul is apparent.... I should argue that the issues of 101 and 99–97
> are to be linked with Marius' colonising activity and with Saturninus' *leges
> agrariae*. The moderate issue of 101 suggests that Eporedia was by then
> envisaged for settlement, the enormous issues of 99–97 that the *lex agraria*
> of 100 was put into effect and that Rome struck money specially for the
> purpose, to finance the viritane settlement of Marius' veterans. Only if this
> took place is the tranquillity of the 90s comprehensible.

There was no trouble, because the veterans got their land. We even have
evidence, in this most ill-attested decade, for two of the commissioners (one
of them Marius' brother-in-law) who were appointed to divide it up.[62]

When the senators delivered their partisan judgement on Saturninus'
legislation, it was not his land law that particularly concerned them.
Previous agrarian legislation (that of Tiberius and Gaius Gracchus in
133 and 123 BC) had found the land to distribute to Rome's poor by
confiscating the illegally held estates of wealthy Romans in Italy. But the
lands Saturninus was offering had belonged to the Gauls and the Veneti
and were then taken by conquest, first by the Cimbri and then by Marius
for Rome. There was no reason why the Senate should object to those
lands being distributed, though its judgement on Saturninus' laws meant
that the legal status of the settlements was precarious.

The Gauls and Veneti dispossessed by the Cimbri could not just return
to their previous life. As Appian tells us, their land now belonged to Rome.
Only those who served as auxiliaries with Catulus' or Marius' armies could
expect to benefit from the land distributions, and even then only after
Roman claimants had been satisfied; everyone else would have to manage
as best they could on whatever land was left over.[63] The tribal centres they
had abandoned to the invaders would be developed as Roman towns and
cities. A decade later, in the new emergency of the 'Social War', Pompeius
Strabo regularized their disputed legal status by granting Latin rights to all
the 'existing inhabitants', whether newly settled Romans or subordinate
natives. The towns and cities were now officially Latin colonies – precisely
the 'later' Transpadane colonies described by Strabo as second to none.

For Marius' veterans Latin status was a demotion, which is why the full
enfranchisement of the *Transpadani* was such a contentious issue

---

[62] *CIL* 6.40955 (C. Caesar Strabo) and 41023 (C. Caesar *pater diui Iuli*): *Xuiri agris dandis adtribuendis iudicandis* (cf. Wiseman 1987.329–30 for the date).

[63] 'What the conquered had to offer, in the short or long run, was themselves as a demographic resource for Rome's further wars' (Purcell 1990.21).

throughout the next generation.[64] Early in 68 BC, coming back from a quaestorship in Spain, Marius' nephew Caesar paid them a visit:[65]

> He went to the Latin colonies, which were in a ferment about seeking citizenship, and might have urged them on to do something rash if the consuls had not, for that very reason, kept back for a while the legions that had been enrolled there for Cilicia.

The colonies were a good recruiting ground, and useful also for gaining electoral support, as Cicero noted in 65.[66] However, the *Transpadani* consisted not only of people like Vergilius Maro of Mantua and Titus Livius of Patavium,[67] but also of indigenous Gauls and Veneti who were less acceptable to conservative Roman opinion.

That, I think, is the explanation of their puzzling history: the inconsistent late-republican evidence reflects ambiguous attitudes to a mixed population. It seems to me that the current orthodoxy is mistaken in concentrating wholly on the indigenous inhabitants,[68] and the reason for the mistake is a failure to take account of the Cimbric invasion and its consequences. Once we recognize the substantial presence of veteran colonists from the 90s BC, we can begin to make sense of it all. Within two generations, they had constructed a regional society successful enough to enable even the indigenous part of the population to 'become Roman' too. In 41 BC, when the next great settlement of veterans came, the expropriations were resented north of the Padus in just the same way as anywhere else in Italy.[69]

Whether or not we call this process 'Romanization', the long-term reputation of the *Transpadani* shows how effective it was. The younger

---

[64] Dio Cassius 37.9.3 (dispute between the censors of 65 περὶ τῶν ὑπὲρ τὸν Ἠριδανὸν οἰκούντων); Cicero *Ad Atticum* 5.2.3 (Cicero expecting trouble *de Transpadanis* in 51), 5.11.2 and Plutarch *Caesar* 29.2 (a Transpadane flogged as a message to Caesar); Dio Cassius 41.36.2–3 (n. 35 above).

[65] Suetonius *Diuus Iulius* 8: *colonias Latinas de petenda ciuitate agitantes adiit, et ad audendum aliquid concitasset nisi consules conscriptas in Ciliciam legiones paulisper ob id ipsum retinuisset.*

[66] Caesar *De bello ciuili* 3.87.4; Suetonius *Diuus Iulius* 24.2 (Caesar's fifth legion); Cicero *Ad Atticum* 1.1.2 (*quoniam uidetur in suffragiis multum posse Gallia*).

[67] Jerome *Chronica* on Ol.177.3–4 (*Vergilius Maro in pago qui Andes dicitur haut procul a Mantua nascitur Pompeio at Crasso consulibus*), 180.2 (*nascitur . . . Titus Liuius Patauinus scriptor historicus*); add the historian Cornelius Nepos (n. 5 above).

[68] See above, nn. 37–40. Note Haeussler 2013b.108, 135 and 140–1 on cultural changes archaeologically detectable after about 100 BC. The obvious explanation, new veteran settlement, is ignored: 'People [were] adopting new forms of status display and new identities. This mirrors a period of social upheaval, eventually leading to a "rupture" in social expression in the second half of the first century BC' (Haeussler 2013b.141).

[69] Appian *Civil Wars* 5.12–13; details in Keppie 1983 (esp. 190–201 on the Transpadana), Osgood 2006.108–51. At Virgil *Eclogues* 1.70–1 the *impius miles* now owning Meliboeus' farm is described as a *barbarus*.

Pliny, a Transpadane from Comum, provides the classic text: in a letter of AD 97 he describes a neighbouring city (Brixia) as belonging to 'that Italy of ours which still retains and preserves much of the modesty, frugality and even rusticity of former times', and refers to Patavium as proverbial for maintaining high standards of moral probity.[70] Of course it is easy to be cynical about such claims, but modern scholars are in no position to disprove Pliny's well-informed belief.

For the present argument it is important to remember that these were also the perceived characteristics of Gaius Marius, and of the men who fought in his army. Sallust refers to Marius' industry and probity, Velleius to his rustic birth and integrity of life; for the elder Pliny, who approved of such people, he was 'a ploughman, a commander from the ranks'.[71] As even hostile sources make clear, he recruited men of his own type: 'some said he wanted to curry favour with men of low condition, since he owed to them his fame and advancement';[72] 'acting as one would expect a low-born man to act, he had forced the lowest class of citizens to enlist'.[73] In fact they were largely volunteers, and behind the disdainful phrases was a reality of hard work and disciplined endurance.[74]

The men of that army were settled in what Strabo called 'the later colonies' sent to the land of the Gauls and Veneti 'this side of the Alps'.[75] They helped to defend a frontier province still subject to raids from hostile neighbours.[76] What they created was the Transpadane Italy in which Catullus grew up.

5.4 What's in a Name?

Since the name 'Catullus' is much more commonly attested in the Transalpine provinces than elsewhere, it may well have been of Gallic origin; two men called M. Catullius who set up a dedication to the

---

[70] Pliny *Letters* 1.14.4 (*Brixia ex illa nostra Italia quae multum adhuc uerecundiae, frugalitatis atque etiam rusticitatis antiquae retinet ac seruat*); 1.14.6 and Martial 11.16.8 for Patavium; at 5.3.6 Pliny refers to the *sanctitas morum* of the Transpadanes Virgil and Cornelius Nepos. Full discussion in Syme 1968.135–6 = 1979.694–7.

[71] Marius: Sallust *Jugurthine War* 63.2 (*industria, probitas*); Velleius Paterculus 2.11.1 (*natus agresti loco . . . uitaque sanctus*); Pliny *Natural History* 33.150 (*ille arator Arpinas et manipularis imperator*).

[72] Sallust *Jugurthine War* 86.3 (trans. S. A. Handford): *alii per ambitionem consulis memorabant, quod ab eo genere celebratus auctusque erat.*

[73] Florus 3.1.13 (Loeb trans.): *cum pro obscuritate generis sui capite censos sacramento adegisset.*

[74] For the ethos Marius instilled, see Sallust *Jugurthine War* 85.33–4, 100.3–5, Plutarch *Marius* 13.1. Volunteers: Sallust *Jugurthine War* 86.2 (*uti quoiusque lubido erat*).

[75] Strabo 5.1.1 (C210), n. 27 above.

[76] Cf. Cicero *De inuentione* 2.111 (*in citeriore Gallia*) for *excursiones* and *latrocinia* in 95 BC.

Matronae at Comum in AD 103 were probably descended from a Gallic ancestor who Latinized his name on gaining Roman citizenship.[77] More often such enfranchisements resulted in the beneficiary bearing the *praenomen* and *gentilicium* of the Roman magistrate who made the grant, as in the case of the man Caesar chose in 58 BC as his emissary to Ariovistus:[78]

> The best plan seemed to be to send C. Valerius Procillus, a very well-educated young man of exceptional courage, whose father C. Valerius Caburus had been granted Roman citizenship by C. Valerius Flaccus [consul 93 BC].

A prominent figure in Transalpine Gaul, Procillus was 'Caesar's friend and host'.[79]

So too was the father of C. Valerius Catullus,[80] and the similar name suggests that he could have gained the citizenship from the same source. Flaccus' proconsular command in Spain was evidently extended to Transalpine Gaul and prolonged by the successive emergencies of the war of the allies and the Sullan civil wars.[81] There is no positive evidence for his presence in Cisalpine Gaul, but in the confusion of those times he could have been involved there too. It is conceivable, for instance, that he took part in the organization of the Transpadane centres as Latin colonies in 89 BC.

On the basis of nomenclature alone, a story could be created. In their surge down the Athesis valley and out into the fertile plain, the Cimbri in 102 BC may well have ignored the island/peninsula of Sirmio, off their immediate track and easy to defend. If the Cenomanian chieftain who held it then mustered his tenants and followers to fight as an auxiliary force with Marius' army, he would surely have kept his fiefdom when the lands were divided up for veteran settlement, and it certainly would have enhanced his standing as a local grandee in the years that followed, as the veterans' settlements were being turned into Roman towns. But when they were recognized as Latin colonies in 89 BC, keeping that status would require

---

[77] *CIL* 5.5252 = *ILS* 4819 (M. Catullius Mercator and M. Catullius Secundus); I am very grateful to John Morgan for pointing this out.

[78] Caesar *De bello Gallico* 1.47.4: *commodissimum uisum est C. Valerium Procillum C. Valeri Caburi filium, summa uirtute et humanitate adulescentem, cuius pater a C. Valerio Flacco ciuitate donatus est, ad eum mittere.*

[79] Caesar *De bello Gallico* 1.53.6 (*hominem honestissimum prouinciae Galliae, suum familiarem et hospitem*); cf. 1.19.3 (*principem Galliae prouinciae*), though there the *cognomen* is textually uncertain.

[80] Suetonius *Diuus Iulius* 73 (Section 2.5 above).

[81] Cicero *Pro Quinctio* 28 (*imperator* in Gaul, 85 BC), Granius Licinianus 39B (triumph *ex Celtiberia et Gallia*, 81 BC); Broughton 1986.211.

Roman citizenship. If C. Valerius Flaccus, ex-consul and *imperator*, happened to be the senior Roman in charge at the time, in getting the citizenship he would also get Flaccus' first two names.

That could be the story of the poet's father or grandfather – but if so, it is very surprising that his Gallic ancestry was not noticed either by ill-wishers at the time or in subsequent biography.[82] It is much more likely, I think, that the Gallic-sounding cognomen 'Catullus' is not significant after all,[83] and that 'C. Valerius' was simply the family name of a Roman veteran who occupied the Sirmio site and became a leading figure at the new Latin colony of Verona.[84] If you just want a story, however, you can take your pick: once again, as in Section 1.2 above on 'Lesbia', we are in the novelists' territory.

---

[82] Suetonius' biographies always begin with a careful account of the subject's background.

[83] One of the poet's contemporaries was the senator L. Tillius Cimber (Cicero *Philippics* 2.27, Appian *Civil Wars* 3.2.4), unlikely to be descended from one of the invading Cimbri.

[84] As suggested by Wiseman 1985.109.

CHAPTER 6

Why Is Ariadne Naked?

This chapter collects the evidence for a long and flourishing tradition of erotic entertainment on the Roman stage. First written to explain a puzzling passage in poem 64, it serves here to expand – and I hope justify – the hypothesis offered in Section 4.3 above about the nature of that problematic work.

At the beginning of the description of the coverlet on the bridal bed of Thetis in Peleus' palace, the poet presents us with Ariadne abandoned on the shore as Theseus sails away (64.60–70):

> quem procul ex alga maestis Minois ocellis,   60
> saxea ut effigies bacchantis, prospicit, eheu,
> prospicit et magnis curarum fluctuat undis,
> non flauo retinens subtilem uertice mitram,
> non contecta leui uelatum pectus amictu,
> non tereti strophio lactentis uincta papillas,   65
> omnia quae toto delapsa e corpore passim
> ipsius ante pedes fluctus salis alludebant.
> sed neque tum mitrae neque tum fluitantis amictus
> illa uicem curans toto ex te pectore, Theseu,
> toto animo, tota pendebat perdita mente.   70

At him afar Minos' daughter gazes out from the seaweed with grieving eyes, like a stone effigy of a bacchant – gazes out, alas, and heaves with mighty waves of sorrow, not keeping the delicate scarf on her golden hair, not covered by the light dress to veil her bosom, her milk-white breasts not bound by the smooth band, all of which had fallen from her whole body, and everywhere the waves of salt were playing with them before her feet. But she, not caring then what happened to the scarf or what happened to the floating dress, was hanging on you, Theseus, with all her heart, with all her will, with all her mind. She was lost.

But what has caused her clothes to fall off? There is nothing in the story to motivate this elaborate description. Why, in short, must Ariadne be naked?

6.1   The 'Common Kind' of Poetry

To find an answer, we must first ask what 'Catullus 64' actually is. A hexameter poem with mythological content, it is quite different in length and style from traditional epic. We call it an 'epyllion', but that is no help; the term is a modern invention with no ancient authority, and attempts to define it are essentially circular ('a poem like Catullus 64').[1]

Catullus' contemporaries would have found the poem easy to define, because ancient thought divided poetry into just three types: dramatic, narrative and a mixture of the two. The idea goes back at least as far as Plato,[2] and was still taken for granted in the schools of the later Roman empire. In the late fourth or early fifth century AD the grammarian Diomedes used it to begin his chapter on types of poems, *De poematibus*:[3]

> *poematos genera sunt tria. aut enim actiuum est uel imitatiuum, quod Graeci dramaticon uel mimeticon, aut enarratiuum uel enuntiatiuum, quod Graeci exegeticon uel apangelticon dicunt, aut commune uel mixtum, quod Graeci* κοινόν *uel* μικτόν *appellant. dramaticon est uel actiuum in quo personae agunt solae sine ullius poetae interlocutione, ut se habent tragicae et comicae fabulae; quo genere scripta est prima Bucolicon et ea cuius initium est 'quo te, Moeri, pedes'. exegeticon est uel enarratiuum in quo poeta ipse loquitur sine ullius personae interlocutione, ut se habent tres Georgici et prima pars quarti, item Lucreti carmina et cetera his similia.* κοινόν *est uel commune in quo poeta ipse loquitur et personae loquentes introducuntur, ut est scripta Ilias et Odyssia tota Homeri et Aeneis Vergilii et cetera his similia.*

There are three kinds of poetry: the 'active' or 'imitative' ('dramatic' or 'mimetic' in Greek), the 'narrative' or 'assertive' ('exegetic' or 'expository' in Greek), and the 'common' or 'mixed' (the same terms in Greek). The dramatic or active kind is that in which only characters act, without the intervention of any poet's voice, as in the case of tragic and comic plays; the first *Eclogue* is written in that mode, and the one beginning *Quo te, Moeri, pedes* [no. 9]. The exegetic or narrative kind is that in which the poet himself speaks, without the intervention of any character's voice, as in the case of three of the *Georgics* and the first part of the fourth, also Lucretius' poem and others like that. The 'common' kind is that in which the poet himself speaks and speaking characters are also introduced; that is how the *Iliad* and the entire *Odyssey* of Homer are written, and Virgil's *Aeneid* and others like that.

---

[1] See Baumbach and Bär 2012, esp. Trimble 2012 for Catullus 64 as the defining example, and Section 4.3 above.

[2] Plato *Republic* 3.392d–394d; cf. Aristotle *Poetics* 1148a.20–4.   [3] *Grammatici Latini* 1.482 Keil.

Diomedes went on to define three species of the *genus commune*,[4] the first of which was mythological poetry (*heroica*) like that of Homer and Virgil. It is obvious that Catullus 64 must belong in this category.

'The poet himself speaks, and speaking characters are also introduced.' Since the most conspicuous elements of the poem are the long speeches by Ariadne and Aegeus (64.132–201, 215–37) and the song of the three Parcae (64.323–81), it is reasonable to wonder how, and in what circumstances, those great set-pieces were delivered. Plato and Aristotle evidently assumed that the epic bard himself would impersonate all his speaking characters,[5] but that was not the only way it could be done. Some papyrus texts of Homer have marginal notes naming the speakers of each passage, including πο for 'the poet' (ποιητής), which suggests that the speeches were regarded as parts for different performers.[6] That is what Diomedes seems to imply (*personae loquentes introducuntur*),[7] and there seems to be no reason to rule it out in the case of 'poem 64'.

In *Catullus and His World* (1985) I noted that poem 64 'would provide a superb script for six performers: 256 lines for the narrator, 70 for Ariadne, 23 for Aegeus, and 59 for the three Fates'.[8] In a more recent book, I suggested that the poem may even be the libretto for a danced performance.[9] The purpose of this chapter is to justify that startling idea, by concentrating not on literary *ekphrasis* but on the history of public entertainment in Rome. What follows is essentially a synthesis of the primary evidence, and to make cross-reference easier I have numbered the passages discussed.

6.2 The *Ludi Florales*

I begin with a passage from Valerius Maximus, writing in the first century AD. Valerius was a kind of historian,[10] but not in the sense of providing a linear narrative. What he did was take historical episodes from all periods and

---

[4] *Grammatici Latini* 1.483 Keil, as emended by Usener 1892.615 = 1913.291: κοινοῦ *uel communis poematos species prima est heroica, ut est Iliados et Aeneidos; secunda est elegiaca, <ut est Callimachi et Properti, tertia iambica,> ut est Archilochi et Horatii.* The MSS read *secunda est eliaca, ut est Archilochi et Horatii*; Keil emended *eliaca* to *lyrica*, a much less satisfactory solution.

[5] Plato *Republic* 3.393a–c (ὡς τις ἄλλος ὤν), Aristotle *Poetics* 1448a.21–2 (ἕτερόν τι γιγνόμενον ὥσπερ Ὅμηρος ποιεῖ).

[6] Examples and discussion in Azzarello 2008. The common phrase ἐκ τοῦ ἰδίου προσώπου (e.g. Schol. *Iliad* 2.570a¹, 6.152b, 21.388a³) or *ex persona poetae* (e.g. Velleius Paterculus 1.3.2–3) implies that the poet was regarded as a dramatic character (πρόσωπον, *persona*).

[7] So too Proclus *Prolegomenon to Hesiod* 5.8–17 Gaisford: μικτὸν δέ, ἐν ᾧ ὅ τε ποιητὴς διαλέγεται καὶ πρόσωπα εἰσῆκται διαλεγόμενα, οἷον ἐν τῇ Ἰλιάδι ἐμφαίνεται.

[8] Wiseman 1985.127–8.

[9] Wiseman 2015.109–10, cf. 89–93 on poetry and dance performance in the late republic.

[10] For the allusions to Livy in Valerius' preface, see Wiseman 2008.258–60.

use them as object lessons for how to live one's life; arranged in categories according to particular moral concepts or ethical dilemmas, his historical extracts offered examples of behaviour for the reader to imitate or avoid.

The one that interests us comes under the heading *maiestas*, for which, in this context, something like 'moral authority' might be an adequate translation. Valerius' chosen exemplar is Marcus Cato, a statesman from three generations before his own time, who was famous both for conspicuous moral integrity and for his refusal, by suicide, to accept the clemency of Caesar in 46 BC. This particular episode in his life can be dated to April 55 BC.

1. Valerius Maximus 2.10.8

eodem ludos Florales quos Messius aedilis faciebat spectante, populus ut mimae nudarentur postulare erubuit. quod cum ex Fauonio amicissimo sibi una sedente cognosset, discessit e theatro ne praesentia sua spectaculi consuetudinem impediret. quem abeuntem ingenti plausu populus prosecutus priscum morem iocorum in scaenam reuocarunt.

While he was watching the games of Flora that Messius was presenting, the People were embarrassed to call for the actresses to undress. Informed of this by his good friend Favonius, who was sitting next to him, he left the theatre, so as not to impede by his presence the tradition of the spectacle. Accompanying his departure with great applause, the People then recalled to the stage its ancient custom of fun.

Twenty years or so later the same story was referred to in similar terms by Valerius' contemporary Seneca.

2. Seneca *Letters* 97.8

... Catonem inquam illum, quo sedente populus negatur permisisse sibi postulare Florales iocos nudandarum meretricum.

... the same Cato whose presence in the audience is said to have stopped the People allowing themselves the Floral fun of prostitutes undressing.

Given the emphasis on the Roman People in particular and the repeated use of the word 'fun' (*iocus*), I think it is reasonable to start our search for Roman public entertainment with the *ludi Florales*.

The first thing to note is that Valerius calls the naked-actresses spectacle an 'ancient custom' (*priscus mos*). In that context it is worth bearing in mind the iconography of the bronze *cistae* that were produced in Latium, including Rome, in the late fourth and early third centuries BC.[11] One of

---

[11] Details in Wiseman 2008.104–24, 2015.29–39.

Fig. 6.1 Erotic Euripides staged in Latium. 'Unrolled' frieze of a cylindrical bronze *cista* in the Villa Giulia Museum, Rome (inv. 13141, drawing by M. Tibuzzi © CNR), late fourth century BC: Battaglia and Emiliozzi 1990.273–7. The central scene shows, from left to right: Iphigeneia, the stag that will replace her on the altar, Calchas, the executioner, a female figure (Artemis?) looking out from a stage window, and Agamemnon. Note on the far right a young satyr dancing, a bearded satyr playing the pipes, and a naked girl with a mirror whose necklace and bracelet match those of the heroine.

them (Fig. 6.1) shows a scene from *Iphigeneia at Aulis*, with the heroine undressing. This type of erotic reinterpretation of traditional tragic themes is also attested in other areas of central Italy in the same period: for instance, a burlesque Andromeda from Campania, or the Euripidean version of Leda and the swan from Clusium in central Etruria.[12] At just about the time these artefacts were created, Rhinthon in Tarentum was producing plays on Euripidean subjects in a dramatic form called 'cheerful tragedy' (*hilarotragoedia*), for which 'Italian comedy' was an alternative name.[13] The Latin for 'cheerful tragedy' might be something like *tragoedia iocosa*; and certainly it was in that chronological context that the *ludi Florales* were introduced, and their 'ancient custom of *ioci*' established.[14]

Our best information about Flora's games comes from the goddess herself, as interviewed by Ovid in the fifth book of *Fasti*. In fact, since the games began on 27 April, Ovid first introduced her at the end of book 4.

---

[12] Andromeda: fourth-century BC jug in the Museo Archeologico Nazionale, Naples (inv. 164482), Trendall 1967 Campanian 2/138, Wiseman 2008.123. Leda and the swan (Euripides *Helen* 17–21, swan pursued by eagle): fourth-century BC cup (Clusium group) in the Musée d'art et d'histoire, Geneva (inv. 23471), Wiseman 2004 plate 8, 2008.113.

[13] *Suda* R171 4.295 Adler (ἱλαροτραγῳδία), Athenaeus 9.402b (τῆς Ἰταλικῆς καλουμένης κωμῳδίας). See Kassel and Austin 2001.260–74; cf. also Olson 2007.13–16, and Taplin 1993.49–52 on Rhinthon.

[14] Velleius Paterculus 1.14.8 (241 BC), Pliny *Nat. Hist.* 18.286 (238 BC).

3. Ovid *Fasti* 4.945–6

mille uenit uariis florum dea nexa coronis;
scaena ioci morem liberioris habet.

A goddess comes wreathed with many-coloured garlands of a thousand flowers; the stage has the custom of freer fun.

Notice again the word *iocus*, which recurs in adjectival form at the beginning of the interview: 'Be present, mother of flowers, to be honoured with fun-filled games!'[15] And the more specific phrase *liberior iocus* is used again when the poet wonders about the particular nature of the goddess's spectacle.

4. Ovid *Fasti* 5.331–2

quaerere conabar quare lasciuia maior
his foret in ludis liberiorque iocus.

I was trying to enquire why in these games there is greater sexiness and freer fun.

It seems clear that *iocus* suggests a particular kind of fun;[16] and the fact that Liber was the Roman name for Dionysus gives the adjective *liberior* an added connotation.[17]

A piping satyr presided over the erotic burlesque of Euripidean tragedy in Fig. 6.1; Flora's temple in the third century BC was built next to that of Liber, Libera and Ceres;[18] and in one mythological story the goddess was identified as Liber's mother.[19] The orgiastic elements of Liber's cult, ruthlessly controlled by the Senate and consuls in 186 BC,[20] appear in a Greek context in Ovid's poem, defined by the same concept of *iocus*.

5. Ovid *Fasti* 1.395–400

di quoque cultores in idem uenere Lyaei
et quicumque iocis non alienus erat,
Panes et in Venerem satyrorum prona iuuentus
quaeque colunt amnes solaque rura deae.
uenerat et senior pando Silenus asello,
quique ruber pauidas inguine terret aues.

---

[15] Ovid *Fasti* 5.183: *mater ades florum ludis celebranda iocosis.*
[16] Barchiesi 1997.133: 'Ovid uses the word *ioci* and its cognate terms to refer to a whole comic and sexual sphere in the *Fasti*.'
[17] See in general Wiseman 2008.84–139, 2015.29–45.
[18] Tacitus *Annals* 2.49.1: *eodem in loco* (the Circus Maximus).
[19] Ampelius 9.11: *Liberi quinque . . . secundus Liber ex Merone et Flora.*
[20] Livy 39.8–19; *CIL* I² 581 = *ILS* 18.

Gods too came together, those who honour Lyaeus and whoever wasn't averse to a bit of fun – Pans, and young satyrs prone to Venus, and the goddesses who haunt the rivers and the lonely countryside. Old man Silenus had come too on his hollow-backed donkey, and the one with the red member who scares the timid birds.

The last-mentioned participant was of course Priapus, whose frustrated attempt on the nymph Lotis is the first sexy story in Ovid's *Fasti*. When dealing with the Roman Liberalia in March, Ovid was more cautious, restricting himself to a harmless tale about Silenus discovering honey while accompanying Liber.

6. Ovid *Fasti* 3.737–8

ibat harenoso satyris comitatus ab Hebro
(non habet ingratos fabula nostra iocos) . . .

He was on his way from sandy Hebrus, attended by the satyrs (my story contains no unwelcome frolics) . . .

Clearly, *ioci* were the sort of thing satyrs normally got up to, but here Ovid keeps them respectable in his treatment of the Roman cult. Now that the Liberalia had been bowdlerized, if you wanted *liberior iocus* you had to go to the games of Flora.

The very particular nature of these games was often noticed. Martial used them as an analogy for the obscene language allowed in epigrams.

7. Martial 1, *praef.*

epigrammata illis scribuntur qui solent spectare Florales. non intret Cato
theatrum meum, aut si intrauerit spectet. uideor mihi meo iure facturus si
epistolam uersibus clusero:

nosses iocosae dulce cum sacrum Florae
festosque lusus et licentiam uolgi,
cur in theatrum, Cato seuere, uenisti?
an ideo tantum ueneras ut exires?

Epigrams are written for people who like to watch the games of Flora. Let Cato stay out of my theatre, or if he does come in let him watch. I think I shall be within my rights if I end this epistle in verse:

Since you knew about fun-loving Flora's sweet ritual,
The sportive games and the People's licence,
Why did you come to the theatre, stern Cato?
Or had you come just so that you could leave?

What else could he call her but *iocosa*? Three centuries later, Ausonius in his poem on the Roman festivals makes the same assumption about the audience.

8. Ausonius *De feriis Romanis* 25–6

nec non lasciui Floralia laeta theatri
quae spectare uolunt qui uoluisse negant.

Then there are the sexy theatre's Floral games, which people want to watch who say they didn't.

But there is nothing to suggest that attendance at the *ludi Florales* was in any sense restricted. On the contrary, as Valerius Maximus and Seneca both make clear (items 1 and 2), the audience was the Roman People itself.

That too is confirmed in Ovid's conversation with the goddess. She tells him that her games were instituted by plebeian aediles with the significant name of Publicius,[21] and he doesn't need her to tell him that their popular nature explains their permissiveness.

9. Ovid *Fasti* 5.347–52

scaena leuis decet hanc: non est, mihi credite, non est
illa cothurnatas inter habenda deas.
turba quidem cur hos celebret meretricia ludos
non ex difficili causa petita subest.
non est de tetricis, non est de magna professis,
uolt sua plebeio sacra patere choro.

A lightweight stage is proper for this goddess. She isn't, believe me she isn't, to be counted among the goddesses in tragic boots. As for why a troupe of prostitutes performs these games, the reason behind it isn't hard to find. She's not one of the frowners, she's not one of those who make big claims. She wants her rites to be open to a plebeian chorus.

And at this point our investigation must move in a different direction. What exactly does Ovid mean when he refers to Flora's girls as a *chorus*?

6.3   Theatre and Dance

As with many other aspects of the ancient world, the understanding of Roman performance culture is much hampered by the haphazard nature of our sources of information. The main bodies of evidence are: (1) twenty-

---

[21] Ovid *Fasti* 5.287–8, cf. 283 *populi*, 285 *publica*, 289 *populus*.

eight play-texts by the comic dramatists Plautus and Terence, dating from c. 205 to 160 BC; (2) the remains of the three great permanent theatres constructed in Rome in 55, 13 and 11 BC; and (3) ten tragic or quasi-tragic play-texts by (or attributed to) Seneca, datable to the 50s and 60s AD. But can we construct from them alone any kind of coherent 'history of Roman drama'? I think the answer is no.

The plays of Plautus and Terence are a wonderful survival, but they represent only one of the many different types of Roman comedy that are known to have existed. The Senecan corpus is a notorious interpretative problem, even giving rise to the paradoxical notion of 'recitation drama', not written for performance at all.[22] As for the theatres of Pompey, Balbus and Marcellus, their remains imply enormous stages, evidently designed for large-scale spectacle and certainly far bigger than any surviving play-text would require. Rather than focus on just these conspicuous but problematic items, it is better to look more widely for contemporary references to the experience of theatre-going, and see what they imply.

Our first witness is Marcus Varro, whose satires were written probably in the 70s BC.

10. Varro *Menippean Satires* 513 Astbury

crede mihi, plures dominos serui comederunt quam canes. quod si Actaeon occupasset et ipse prius suos canes comedisset, non nugas saltatoribus in theatro fieret.

Believe me, more masters have been eaten up by their slaves than by their dogs. If Actaeon had got in first and eaten his dogs before they ate him, he wouldn't be rubbish for dancers in the theatre.

It is worth remembering that the Actaeon story was one of the many mythological themes listed by Lucian in the second century AD as the repertoire of the *pantomimus* dancer.[23]

The following is a piece of repartee from a court case in 62 BC.

11. Aulus Gellius 1.3.3

sed cum L. Torquatus ... gesticulariam Dionysiamque eum notissimae salt-atriculae nomine appellaret, tum uoce molli atque demissa Hortensius 'Dionysia' inquit, 'Dionysia malo equidem esse quam tu, Torquate, ἄμουσος, ἀναφρόδιτος, ἀπροσδιόνυσος.'

---

[22] Zwierlein 1966; cf. Wiseman 2008.201–2, 2015.166–9, Kragelund 2016.69–99.

[23] Lucian, *Saltatio* 41 (Loeb ed. vol. 5 p. 252).

> When Lucius Torquatus . . . called him a mime-actress and a Dionysia (the name of a very well-known dancing-girl), Hortensius gently and quietly replied 'Dionysia? I'd rather be Dionysia than what you are, Torquatus – a stranger to the Muses, to Aphrodite and to Dionysus.'

All we know about Dionysia (her professional name is surely significant) is that Cicero claimed her fee was 200,000 sesterces for a single appearance at the *ludi scaenici*.[24]

A few years later, Titus Lucretius' argument about the nature of sense perception led him into a discussion of dreams and waking visions. He used as an example 'those who for many successive days have given constant attention to the *ludi*',[25] and his description of their experience is very striking.

12. Lucretius 4.978–83

> *per multos itaque illa dies eadem obuersantur*
> *ante oculos, etiam uigilantes ut uideantur*
> *cernere saltantis et mollia membra mouentis*
> *et citharae liquidum carmen chordasque loquentis*
> *auribus accipere et consessum cernere eundem*
> *scaenaique simul uarios splendere decores.*

> And so they have the same things before their eyes for many days, with the result that even when awake they seem to see dancers moving their soft limbs, and receive in their ears the liquid song of the cithara and its speaking chords, and see the same audience and with it the varied decoration of the stage in all its splendour.

This seems to be a view from the back of the auditorium, since it includes the audience as well,[26] but wherever the poet was sitting, what he saw was dancers and what he heard was music.

Thirty years later again, Sextus Propertius was reflecting ruefully on his susceptibility to beautiful women.

13. Propertius 2.22.4–6

> *o nimis exitio nata theatra meo,*
> *siue aliqua in molli diducit candida gestu*
> *bracchia, seu uarios incinit ore modos!*

---

[24] Cicero *Pro Roscio comoedo* 23 (Section 4.1 above).
[25] Lucretius 4.973–4: *et quicumque dies multos ex ordine ludis | assiduas dederunt operas* . . .
[26] As also at 4.78: *consessum caueai*.

Oh, theatres were made too much for my destruction, whether [a woman] spreads her white arms with a soft gesture or plays the varied measures with her mouth.

What exactly that last phrase means is not clear; but we do know that dancers in the theatre also sang, as the *mima* Cytheris sang the sixth *Eclogue*.²⁷

Ovid too recognized theatres as a source of temptation, and recommended keeping away from them as one of his cures for love.

14. Ovid *Remedia amoris* 751–5

at tanti tibi sit non indulgere theatris,
dum bene de uacuo pectore cedat amor.
eneruant animos citharae lotosque lyraeque
et uox et numeris bracchia mota suis.
illic adsidue ficti saltantur amantes . . .

What *should* be so important to you is not frequenting theatres until love has left your heart properly free. They weaken your resolve, the citharas, pipes and lyres, the voice and the arms that move to their own measures. That's where stories of lovers are constantly danced.

The reference to the dancers' repertoire takes us back to Varro on Actaeon (item 10). From the 70s BC to the turn of the millennium, these passages offer a consistent picture of what theatre meant in Rome: it meant song, dance and music.

In that context, Ovid's reference to the plebeian *chorus* at Flora's games (item 9) makes perfectly good sense. The actresses who took their clothes off – described equally as actresses and prostitutes (*mimae* and *meretrices*) – were dancers and singers, and it is possible to make an educated guess about some of the stories they danced and sang.²⁸ But how typical were they of Roman stage performances in general?

6.4 Show Business

It is evident that the *ludi Florales* were unusual in the level of obscenity they permitted, although the direct evidence comes from a much later period, and there is no way of telling how far things may have changed over time. Lactantius in the early fourth century AD claims that the games

²⁷ Servius on *Eclogues* 6.11: *adeo ut cum eam postea Cytheris cantasset in theatre* . . . For Cytheris as a *mima*, see Cicero *Philippics* 2.20, 58, 62, 69, 77.
²⁸ See Wiseman 2008.175–86 on Cloelia and Porsena, Hercules and Bona Dea, Lara and Jupiter.

of Flora were first founded by the bequest of a wealthy prostitute,[29] which
he says accounts for the type of entertainment provided.

15. Lactantius *Diuinae institutiones* 1.20.10

*celebrantur ergo illi ludi conuenienter memoriae meretricis cum omni lasciuia.
nam praeter uerborum licentiam quibus obscaenitas omnis effunditur, exuuntur
etiam uestibus populo flagitante meretrices, quae tunc mimarum funguntur
officio et in conspectu populi usque ad satietatem impudicorum luminum cum
pudendis motibus detinentur.*

True to the prostitute's memory, therefore, those games are celebrated with
every type of licentiousness. Quite apart from the freedom of language in
which every obscenity is poured out, the prostitutes are also stripped of
their clothes at the demand of the People. They then carry out the role of
actresses, and with their disgraceful movements are kept under the People's
gaze until shameless eyes are satisfied.

We may get some idea of what Lactantius did not want to describe from an
item in the *Historia Augusta*, written in the second half of the fourth
century AD.[30] The biography of Elagabalus contains this item.

16. HA *Elagabalus* 6.5

*Hieroclem uero sic amauit ut eidem inguina oscularetur, quod dictum etiam
inuerecundum est, Floralia sacra se adserens celebrare.*

As for Hierocles, he loved him even to the extent of kissing his genitals,
something shameful even to say, and stated that he was celebrating the
Floralia ritual.

It is possible, therefore, that what made the *ludi Florales* unique was the
obscenity of word and action that was permitted, and not merely the
nudity of the performers. That is an important distinction to make, if it
means that naked actresses as such could be acceptable in the mainstream
of Roman popular entertainment. Later evidence for dramatizations of the
judgement of Paris certainly suggests that they were.[31]

In the 20s BC, the historian Livy described the extravagance of the
theatre in his day as a madness that even opulent monarchies would hardly

---

[29] Lactantius *Diu. inst.* 1.20.6; cf. Minucius Felix *Octauius* 25.8, Cyprian *De uanitate idolum* 4. For
Flora as the name of a famous late-republican call-girl, see Philodemus 12 Sider (*Anth. Pal.* 5.132),
Varro *Men.* 136B, Plutarch *Pompey* 2.2–4.

[30] Cameron 2011.743–82, esp. 772: between AD 361 and 386.

[31] Apuleius *Metamorphoses* 10.31, Lucian *Dearum iudicium* 9–13 (Loeb ed. vol. 3 pp. 397–403),
Tertullian *Apologeticus* 15.2 (item 30 below).

tolerate.[32] That is consistent with the enormous stage in Pompey's theatre, and later in those of Balbus and Marcellus too. It is also consistent with the extraordinary success of the dancers Bathyllus and Pylades, and the new style of performance they introduced just about the time Livy was writing.[33] It was probably because of the huge popular following enjoyed by these new stars, and the resulting danger to public order, that the responsibility for the annual *ludi* was transferred in 22 BC from the aediles to the praetors, magistrates with *imperium* (the power of military command).[34]

The new style required a grand stage capable of accommodating a grand spectacle – not only the virtuoso dancer in the closed-mouth mask, but also an orchestra, a chorus to sing the words, and supporting actors to deliver solo speeches where necessary.[35] The great new permanent theatres may have been a necessary condition for its development. Already in the 50s BC there are hints of new approaches in the traditional (and very versatile) theatrical mode known as *mimus*,[36] perhaps as a consequence of exploiting Pompey's theatre. One useful piece of information may be inferred from the innovation that made the new style possible.

17. Jerome *Chronica*, Olympiad 189.3 (22/21 BC)

Pylades Cilex pantomimus, cum ueteres ipsi canerent atque saltarent, primus Romae chorum et fistulam sibi praecinere fecit.

Pylades, Cilician *pantomimus*: although the ancients used to dance and sing themselves, he was the first at Rome to have a chorus and pipe music accompany him.

Jerome's information came from Suetonius, and Suetonius in turn may have had it from Pylades' own treatise on his art.[37] Lucian's later essay on dance confirms the point.

18. Lucian *Saltatio* 29–30

ἔχει γὰρ πολλοὺς τοὺς ὑπὲρ αὐτοῦ βοῶντας. πάλαι μὲν γὰρ αὐτοὶ καὶ ᾖδον καὶ ὠρχοῦντο· εἶτ᾽ ἐπειδὴ κινουμένων τὸ ἆσθμα τὴν ᾠδὴν ἐπετάραττεν, ἄμεινον ἔδοξεν ἄλλους αὐτοῖς ὑπᾴδειν.

---

[32] Livy 7.2.13: *ut appararet quam ab sano initio res in hanc uix opulentis regnis tolerabilem insaniam uenerit.*

[33] Athenaeus 1.20d, Dio Cassius 54.17.4–5 (18 BC), Macrobius *Saturnalia* 2.7.18–19; cf. Lucian *Saltatio* 34 ('under Augustus').

[34] Dio Cassius 54.2.3–4, cf. Dionysius of Halicarnassus *Roman Antiquities* 2.19.4.

[35] Lucian *Dance* 29–30 (mask), 68 (support team).

[36] Cicero *Pro Rabirio Postumo* 35 (new mime plots from Alexandria), Bern scholiast on Lucan 1.543–4 (Catullus' περὶ μιμολογίων), Pliny *Nat. Hist.* 35.199 (Publilius Syrus *mimicae scaenae conditor*).

[37] Athenaeus 1.20d: Πυλάδην, οὗ ἐστι καὶ σύγγραμμα περὶ ὀρχήσεως.

> For [the dancer] has many people raising their voices on his behalf. In the past, they themselves both danced and sang, but later, because their heavy breathing as they moved disturbed the singing, it seemed better that others should sing as accompaniment for them.

So *mimi* and *mimae* danced and sang at the same time, but the demands of a more spectacular stage-setting now made it necessary to separate the silent 'all-mime' dancer (*pantomimus*) from the chorus and actors who sang the words.

As the *pantomimus* style became ever more ubiquitous, it came to specialize in tragic plots, and even, in a sense, to replace tragedy itself;[38] at the start of it, however, Pylades was the tragedy expert and Bathyllus specialized in 'more cheerful' themes.[39] In particular, Bathyllus' dance style exploited the traditional *kordax* (from Old Comedy) and *sikinnis* (from satyr-play); Bathyllus' *Satyr* is referred to by Persius, evidently as a well-known dance.[40] If the new 'all-mime' style admitted elements from comedy and satyr-play, then so too, presumably, did the dance tradition from which it evolved, the world of celebrity actresses with stage names like Dionysia and Cytheris.

6.5   Ovidian Scenarios

To try to imagine the sort of performance such *mimae* may have given, we may look back to Varro's passing comment (item 10) about the Actaeon story being danced in the theatre. Actaeon had been a character in the Athenian tragic repertoire from the very beginning, though his sight of the naked Artemis was probably a later development in the story.[41] It is important to remember Rhinthon and his 'cheerful tragedy' style, which had evidently not gone out of fashion; his was a familiar name in Rome in Varro's time, and *fabulae Rhinthonicae* featured among the various sub-genres of Roman comedy.[42] Perhaps the Actaeon performance was a *Rhinthonica*? That would at least be an economical hypothesis.

---

[38] Libanius *Orations* 64.112; Lada-Richards 2008.292–3.

[39] Seneca *Controuersiae* 3.pref.10, Athenaeus 1.20e (ἱλαρωτέρα).

[40] Athenaeus 1.20d, Persius 5.123, Plutarch *Moralia* 711f.

[41] Early tragedies: e.g. Phrynichus *Aktaion*, Aeschylus *Toxotides*, Iophon *Aktaion*; cf. Pollux 4.141 for Actaeon's special tragic mask, with antlers. Voyeurism first attested at Callimachus *Hymns* 5.107–16.

[42] See n. 13 above. Cicero *Ad Atticum* 1.20.3 (Rhinthon *PCG* F 12); Euanthius *De comoedia* 4.1, Donatus *De comoedia* 6.1 (*PCG* T 5). For Varro's own taxonomy of comic modes, see Diomedes *Gramm. Lat.* 1.489 Keil (Varro fr. 306 Funaioli).

How 'cheerful' it was — or perhaps we should say what type of *ioci* it involved — depends on whether it presented Actaeon as an involuntary voyeur, and his death truly tragic,[43] or as one who lusted after the goddess and climbed a tree deliberately to spy on her, like Pentheus spying on the Bacchae in Euripides.[44] In either case the goddess' nymph companions were an essential part of the plot.[45] Nymphs of all kinds always danced and frequently sang, and the normal collective noun for them was *chorus*.[46] So a danced version of this story must surely have featured two separate *corps de ballet*, a female one playing the nymphs and a male one playing Actaeon's hounds, and the order of events makes it practically inevitable that the opening dance scene would show Diana and the nymphs, first hunting and then undressing to bathe in the pool of Gargaphie.[47]

The classic telling of the Actaeon story is of course in Ovid's *Metamorphoses* (3.138–252), and it is from Ovid's narrative poems, *Metamorphoses* and *Fasti*, that I think the next stage in our enquiry may be inferred. The argument is necessarily a tenuous one, but I am encouraged by Ismene Lada-Richards' argument for the influence on the *Metamorphoses* of the new dance style of Pylades and Bathyllus.[48] I'm sure she is right, but I would not want to restrict the influence to just one form of stage performance.

Fortunately, we know that Ovid did sometimes take his material from the theatre. He says so explicitly in his narrative of Quinta Claudia and the coming of the Great Mother.

19. Ovid *Fasti* 4.326

mira sed et scaena testificata loquar.

What I shall tell you is amazing, but attested also by the stage.

---

[43] Callimachus *Hymns* 5.113 (οὐκ ἐθέλων); Ovid *Metamorphoses* 3.142 (*error*), 175 (*errans*), *Tristia* 2.105 (*inscius*).

[44] Hyginus *Fabulae* 180 (*Dianam lauantem speculatus est et eam uiolare uoluit*), cf. Diodorus Siculus 4.81.4–5. Tree: Nonnus 5.303–7, 475–8. Pentheus: Euripides *Bacchae* 1058–75.

[45] Ovid *Metamorphoses* 3.165–72, 178-81; Nonnus 5.307–11, 439–40, 460, 489–91.

[46] E.g. Horace *Odes* 1.1.31, 1.4.5, 3.4.25, 4.7.6; Virgil *Georgics* 4.460, 4.533, *Aeneid* 5.240, 9.112, 10.219; [Virgil] *Culex* 116; Propertius 1.17.26, 1.20.46; Ovid *Fasti* 1.512, 2.156, 2.590, *Metamorphoses* 2.441; Statius *Siluae* 1.3.77, *Thebaid* 2.521.

[47] Ovid *Metamorphoses* 3.156, cf. Herodotus 9.25.2–3.

[48] Lada-Richards 2013, esp. 143: 'Haunted by the exuberant physicality of pantomime's live bodies, Ovid's *Metamorphoses* testifies … to a profound *symbiosis* between dance and literary expression, gestural poetry and the poetry of words: deep in the poetic veins of the Ovidian epic pulses the blood of pantomime's greatest stars, the Nijinskis and Nureyevs of Augustan Rome.'

That was probably from a play, perhaps a *fabula praetexta* or *togata*,[49] but there is no obvious reason why Ovid should not have exploited danced narratives too.[50]

Many of Ovid's stories concern nymphs – Naiads, Dryads, Hamadryads, Nereids – with the protagonist quite often introduced as one of the group or *chorus*, as in the following three examples linked by a common phrase.

20. Ovid *Fasti* 2.153–4

inter Hamadryadas iaculatricemque Dianam
Callisto sacri pars fuit una chori.

Among the Hamadryads and lance-throwing Diana, Callisto was one part of the sacred chorus.

21. Ovid *Metamorphoses* 1.690–1

inter Hamadryadas celeberrima Nonacrinas
Naias una fuit, nymphae Syringa uocabant.

Among the Hamadryads of Nonacria there was one most famous Naiad; the nymphs called her Syrinx.

22. Ovid *Metamorphoses* 14.623–4

rege sub hoc Pomona fuit, qua nulla Latinas
inter Hamadryadas coluit sollertius hortos.

Under this king [Proca] there lived Pomona, than whom none among the Hamadryads of Latium cultivated gardens more skilfully.

Group scenes of nymphs are frequent in Ovid – gathering to listen to Peneus or Jupiter,[51] accompanying Eurydice or Scylla or Ino and her son,[52] serving in the palace of Achelous or Circe,[53] grieving for

---

[49] Wiseman 2008.194–7, 210–11; cf. Manuwald 2001.93–4, excluding it from the *praetexta* category on what seem to me quite inadequate grounds. See Wiseman 2008.210–30 for 'Ovid and the stage' in general.

[50] His own work was often 'danced for the People in the theatre' (*Tristia* 2.519, 5.7.25).

[51] Peneus, *Metamorphoses* 1.576: *undis iura dabat nymphisque colentibus undis.* Jupiter, *Fasti* 2.589–90: *conuocat hic nymphas Latium quaecumque tenebant | et iacit in medio talia uerba choro.*

[52] Eurydice, *Met.* 10.8–9: *nupta per herbas | dum noua Naiadum turba comitata uagabat.* Scylla, *Met.* 13.736–7: *ad pelagi nymphas pelagi gratissima nymphis | ibat.* Ino, *Fasti* 6.499: *excipit illaesos Panope centumque sorores.*

[53] Achelous, *Met.* 8.571–2: *protinus adpositas nudae uestigia nymphae | instruxere epulis mensas.* Circe, *Met.* 14.264: *Nereides nymphaeque simul.*

Narcissus,[54] admiring Marsyas' pipe-playing,[55] yearning after handsome Picus,[56] trying in vain to console Egeria.[57]

Sometimes they are in the company of satyrs, Pans and Silenus, the Dionysiac *thiasos* that in Latin is often described as a *chorus*.[58] We have already met (in item 5) the company 'not averse to *ioci*' who gathered at Dionysus' party on the occasion when Priapus tried his luck with the nymph Lotis; they also came to Cybele's party on Mount Ida ('a little story full of fun') when he even had his eye on Vesta.[59] The usual choreography between nymphs and satyrs was one of arousal, pursuit and avoidance,[60] but sometimes they joined together in mourning, as for Marsyas.[61]

Of course there can be no certainty that these Ovidian scenes reflect what he and his readers were familiar with from the contemporary stage. But it is worth remembering Bathyllus and his satyric use of the new style of 'all-mime', for which Plutarch offers as an example '[the nymph] Echo or some Pan or satyr revelling with Eros'.[62] Such themes were clearly part of a well-known repertoire.

We should also remember what Vitruvius, writing in the 20s BC, says about stage scenery.

23. Vitruvius *De architectura* 5.6.9

tragicae deformantur columnis et fastigiis et signis reliquisqe regalibus rebus; comicae autem aedificiorum priuatorum et maenianorum habent speciem . . . ; satyricae uero ornantur arboribus speluncis montibus reliquisque agrestibus rebus in topeodi speciem deformati.

Tragic [scenery] is designed with columns, pediments, statues and other things appropriate to palaces; comic [scenery] has the appearance of private houses with balconies . . . ; satyric [scenery] is decorated with trees, caves,

---

[54] *Met.* 3.505–7: *planxere sorores* | *Naides et sectos fratri posuere capillos,* | *planxerunt Dryades.*

[55] *Fasti* 6.706: *iamque inter nymphas arte superbus erat.*

[56] *Met.* 14.326–8: *ille suos Dryadas Latiis in montibus ortas* | *uerterat in uultus, illum fontana petebant* | *numina Naiades.*

[57] *Met.* 15.490–1: *a quotiens nymphae nemorisque lacusque* | *ne faceret monuere.*

[58] [Virgil] *Culex* 115–16; Horace *Odes* 1.1.31; Propertius 2.3.18, 2.32.38, 3.17.22; Ovid *Fasti* 3.764, 6.510, *Metamorphoses* 11.86; Statius *Thebaid* 4.379, 9.479.

[59] Dionysus, Ovid *Fasti* 1.395–400. Cybele, *Fasti* 6.320–4: *est multi fabula parua ioci* . . . | *conuocat et satyros et rustica numina nymphas;* | *Silenus, quamuis nemo uocarat, adest.*

[60] E.g. *Fasti* 1.405–14 (arousal), *Met.* 1.692–4 (pursuit of Syrinx), 14.637–41 (pursuit of Pomona), *Heroides* 5.135–9 (pursuit of Oenone).

[61] Ovid *Metamorphoses* 6.392–4: *illum ruricolae siluarum numina fauni* | *et satyri fratres et tunc quoque carus Olympus* | *et nymphae flerunt.*

[62] Plutarch *Moralia* 711f: Ἠχοῦς ἤ τινος Πανὸς ἤ σατύρου σὺν Ἔρωτι κωμάζοντος ὑπόρχημά τι.

mountains and other features of the countryside, to give the appearance of a designed landscape.

Later, describing mural painting, Vitruvius notes that the walls of large open areas like *exedrae* were decorated like stage scenery 'in the tragic, comic, or satyric manner',[63] and showed features like springs, woods, hills, caves, flocks, shepherds. That is important for us because of Ovid's constant association of nymphs and satyrs with the countryside. Jupiter explains the situation at the heavenly Senate meeting that starts the action of the *Metamorphoses*.

24. Ovid *Metamorphoses* 1.192–5

sunt mihi semidei, sunt rustica numina nymphae
Faunique satyrique et monticolae Siluani,
quos quoniam caeli nondum dignamur honore,
quas dedimus certe terras habitare sinamus.

'I have to think of the half-gods, the countryside powers, nymphs and Fauns and satyrs and mountain-dwelling Silvani. Since we don't yet think them worthy of heaven, we must certainly let them dwell in the lands we gave them.'

The nymphs too belonged on the stage in front of that 'satyric' scenery; not only the trees and mountains but the caves as well were part of their story.[64]

Another striking feature of Ovid's narratives is how often the female protagonists get out of their clothes.[65] Diana and her nymphs undress to bathe in the Actaeon and Callisto stories,[66] Arethusa undresses to bathe and gets pursued by the river-god,[67] Salmacis throws off her clothes to grapple with Hermaphroditus,[68] Atalanta strips off for her foot-race,[69] Scylla strolls naked along the beach,[70] Thetis rides to her grotto naked

---

[63] Vitruvius *De architectura* 7.5.2: *ut … patentibus autem locis uti exhedris propter amplitudines parietum scaenarum frontes tragico more aut comico seu satyrico designarent.*

[64] E.g. *Fasti* 6.115 (Cranae); *Met.* 3.155, 177 (Diana's nymphs), 11.234–7 (Thetis). For 'Bacchic *antra*', see, for instance, Livy 39.13.13, Plutarch *Moralia* 565f–566a, Athenaeus 4.148b (Socrates of Rhodes *FGrH* 192 F 2), Philostratus *Imagines* 1.14.3, Macrobius *Saturnalia* 1.18.3.

[65] Or have them blown open: cf. *Met.* 1.527 on Daphne (*nudabant corpora uenti*), *Fasti* 3.15–16 on Rhea Silvia (*uentosque accepit aperto | pectore*).

[66] Actaeon: *Met.* 3.178 (*sicut erant nudae*), 3.185 (*sine ueste*), 3.192 (*posito uelamine*). Callisto: *Met.* 2.459 (*nuda corpora*), *Fasti* 2.169 (*uelamina ponunt*).

[67] *Met.* 5.601–3: *sicut eram fugio sine uestibus; altera uestes | ripa meas habuit. tanto magis instat et ardet | et quia nuda fui sum uisa paratior illi.*

[68] *Met.* 4.356–7: *omni | ueste procul iacta.*   [69] *Met.* 10.578: *ut faciem et posito corpus uelamine uidit.*

[70] *Met.* 13.901: *sine uestibus errat harena.*

on dolphin-back,[71] the satyrs watch Venus comb her hair naked on the shore,[72] the goddesses present themselves naked to Paris on Mount Ida.[73] If these stories do indeed presuppose stage performances, that may confirm our tentative conclusion in Section 6.3 above that naked actresses were part of the mainstream of Roman show business.

6.6 Lupercalia

Despite the Cato story (items 1 and 2), what made the *ludi Florales* unusual was evidently not just the fact that the *mimae* undressed. In fact, it seems that the Romans of the first century BC were comparatively relaxed about nudity. There were ritual occasions when even respectable citizens might be seen naked: women on the Kalends of April, for the cult of Fortuna and Venus Verticordia,[74] and men at the Lupercalia on 15 February, when the young equestrians of the *sodalitas Lupercorum* showed themselves off to the Roman People as they ran around lashing everyone who came within range.[75]

By great good fortune we happen to have a contemporary illustration of the naked Luperci (Fig. 6.2).[76] It is part of a terracotta wall plaque, found near the so-called House of Livia at the western corner of the Palatine – just above the Lupercal, as it happens. Since these 'Campana plaques' seem to predate the redevelopment of the area for the building of the Apollo temple after 36 BC,[77] we may take this scene as evidence for the Luperci of the late republic rather than those of the Augustan age and later, who wore loincloths for modesty.[78]

It is clear that the Lupercalia ritual was a sexy show, a *iocus* in the Ovidian sense.[79] The Luperci could evidently demand that young women

---

[71] *Met.* 11.236–7: *quo saepe uenire | frenato delphine sedens, Theti, nuda solebas.*

[72] *Fasti* 4.141–2: *litore siccabat rorantes nuda capillos; | uiderunt satyri turba proterua deam.*

[73] *Heroides* 5.36, 17.117: *uenit in arbitrium nuda Minerua tuum; . . . tres tibi se nudas exhibuere deae.* Cf. Propertius 2.2.14, 3.13.38, and n. 31 above.

[74] Wiseman 2008.140–54, on Ovid *Fasti* 4.133–62.

[75] Valerius Maximus 2.2.9 (*spectaculo sui*), Cicero *Pro Caelio* 26 (*sodalitas*), *Philippics* 3.12 (*populo Romano inspectante*). Naked Luperci: Varro *De lingua Latina* 6.34, Livy 1.5.2, Ovid *Fasti* 2.267, 2.283–8, Justin 43.1.7 (Wiseman 1995.82–3).

[76] See Caterina Nasti in Paris, Bruni and Roghi 2014.100–1; cf. also Tortorella 2000.251.

[77] Velleius Paterculus 2.81.3, Dio Cassius 49.15.5; Wiseman 2019.128–31.

[78] Ovid *Fasti* 5.101 (*cinctuti*), Dionysius of Halicarnassus *Ant. Rom.* 1.80.1 (ὑπεζωσμένους τὴν αἰδῶ); cf. Valerius Maximus 2.2.9 (*cincti*), Plutarch *Romulus* 21.5 (ἐν περιζώσμασι).

[79] Livy 1.5.2 (*per lusum atque lasciuiam*), Valerius Maximus 2.2.9 (*iocantes*), Plutarch *Caesar* 61.2 (ἐπὶ παιδιᾷ καὶ γέλωτι), Dio Cassius 46.19.4 (ἐν τῷ παιγνιώδει τῶν γιγνομένων).

Fig. 6.2   The running Luperci. Terracotta 'Campana' plaque from the Palatine, in the
Museo Nazionale Romano, Palazzo Massimo, Rome (inv. 4359, su concessione del
Ministero della cultura – Museo Nazionale Romano), first century BC: von Rohden and
Winnefeld 1911, tav. xlviii,1. The standing older man on the left wears a mask with shaggy
hair attached, and presumably the runners did too.

bare their bodies for the lash,[80] and descriptions of the famous Lupercalia of 44 BC take it for granted that the Roman People were present en masse to watch what was going on.[81] Varro calls the Luperci *ludii*, performers, and it must be significant that the first (abortive) permanent theatre in Rome was to have been at the Lupercal.[82]

It was at the Lupercal itself that the day's events started, with a sacrifice of goats;[83] the run could take place only after the victims had been butchered and skinned, and the hides cut up into thongs to equip the Luperci with their lashes. While all that was going on, the Luperci themselves were getting ready with a good lunch and plenty of wine.[84] What we do not know is whether there was also entertainment for the crowd as they waited for the main event.

Ovid's first aetiology of the nakedness of the Luperci is presented as a story full of *iocus*. It concerns the god Faunus, whom the poet identifies with Pan,[85] and Hercules in bondage to the Lydian queen Omphale.

25. Ovid *Fasti* 2.303–8

> sed cur praecipue fugiat uelamina Faunus
> traditur antiqui fabula plena ioci.
> forte comes dominae iuuenis Tirynthius ibat;
> uidit ab excelso Faunus utrumque iugo.
> uidit et incaluit. 'montana' que 'numina' dixit,
> 'nil mihi uobiscum est: hic meus ardor erit.'

But as to why Faunus has a particular aversion to clothes, a story is handed down full of old-fashioned fun. It happened that the Tirynthian youth was travelling in attendance on his mistress. Faunus saw them both from a lofty ridge. He saw them and got hot. 'Mountain deities', he said, 'you've got nothing for me. This is going to be my flame.'

---

[80] Ovid *Fasti* 2.445–6: *iussae sua terga puellae | pellibus exsectis percutienda dabant.* (To be taken seriously, *pace* North 2008.151–3.)

[81] Cicero *Philippics* 2.85, 3.12; Nicolaus of Damascus *FGrH* 90 F 130.21.72–3; cf. Ovid *Fasti* 5.102 (*celebres uias*).

[82] Varro *Antiquitates diuinae* fr. 80 Cardauns (Tertullian *De spectaculis* 5.3): *sicut et Lupercos ludios appellant, quod ludendo discurrant.* Velleius Paterculus 1.15.3: *Cassius censor a Lupercali in Palatium uersus theatrum facere instituit.*

[83] Varro *De lingua Latina* 5.85, 6.13; Ovid *Fasti* 2.361, 445; Plutarch *Romulus* 21.4, Quintilian *Inst.* 1.5.66.

[84] Valerius Maximus 2.2.9: *epularum hilaritate ac uino largiore prouecti.* Cf. Cicero *Philippics* 3.12, 13.31 (Antony as drunken Lupercus).

[85] Ovid *Fasti* 2.423–4, 3.84, 4.650–3; cf. Horace *Odes* 1.17.1–4. See Wiseman 2008.52–83 for a diachronic analysis of 'the god of the Lupercal'.

That wonderfully economical opening seems to presuppose a scene with Faunus and his usual playmates the nymphs ('mountain deities'),[86] into which Omphale and Hercules suddenly appeared, she gorgeous with perfumed hair and gilded bosom, he submissively holding her parasol. The rejected nymphs must have left the stage to Omphale's regal retinue,[87] among whom the lecherous Faunus lurked unobserved.

At this point the scene becomes one of Vitruvius' 'satyric' caves.

26. Ovid *Fasti* 2.313–16

> *iam Bacchi nemus et Tmoli uineta tenebat,*
> *Hesperus et fusco roscidus ibat equo.*
> *antra subit tofis laqueata et pumice uiuo;*
> *garrulus in primo limine riuus erat.*

And now [Omphale] was reaching the grove of Bacchus and the vineyards of Tmolus, and dewy Hesperus was riding his dusky steed. She enters a cave, its ceiling panelled with tufa and living pumice; right at the entrance there was a babbling stream.

While the staff busily prepare the banquet, Omphale and Hercules undress and then dress again in each other's clothes, as the following day's Bacchic festival requires. The cross-dressing scene is funny and sexy, but Faunus does not witness it. He is keeping out of sight, and reappears only when all the stage business is finished and the queen, her slave and her retinue have retired to sleep.

On stage it is night, and pitch dark; but of course the audience can see Faunus blundering this way and that with his hands outstretched, shrinking from the bed with the lion-skin and finding the one with the soft fabrics.

27. Ovid *Fasti* 2.345–50

> *ascendit spondaque sibi propiore recumbit*
> *et tumidum cornu durius inguen erat.*
> *interea tunicas ora subducit ab ima;*
> *horrebat densis aspera crura pilis.*
> *cetera temptantem subito Tyrinthius heros*
> *reppulit ...*

Up he gets and lies down on the bed closer to him, and his swollen member was harder than his horn. All the time he's drawing up the tunic from its

---

[86] Horace *Odes* 3.18.1: *Faune nympharum fugientum amator ...*
[87] *Fasti* 2.317 (*ministri*), 333 (*comites*), 351 (*comites*), 355 (*qui uidere*).

hem. Rough legs were bristling with thick hair. As he tried the next stage the Tirynthian hero suddenly shoved him off.

The denouement comes with sudden lights and shouts and laughter. And that is why Faunus doesn't like clothes, and summons people naked to his rites.

It is true that there is no direct evidence for such a play, and the Ovid passage is perfectly intelligible without the need of inferring one. Nevertheless, I follow the example ironically recommended by a great historian, Sir Ronald Syme:[88]

> The dearth of reliable evidence encourages constructive fiction – or, as sober historians style the process, 'rational conjecture'. When other practitioners take that path, it becomes 'idle or barren speculation'.

My own 'rational conjecture' depends on the recognition of two neglected facts: that mythological dance-drama was familiar on the Roman stage (item 10 above), and that Ovid sometimes used stage performance as a source for his own stories (item 19 above). Once those data are given their due weight, other puzzling evidence can begin to make sense.

6.7 Atalanta on Stage

As an example, I turn to another of Ovid's naked heroines, Atalanta, who is explicitly attested as a character on the Roman stage.[89]

Three main stories about Atalanta were known in Rome.[90] First, she took part in the hunt for the Calydonian Boar, and Meleager, who killed the boar, gave her its skin (the victor's prize) because he was in love with her; second, Milanion, who was also her admirer, earned her love by long and devoted service; and third, Hippomenes married her, having overcome her foot-race challenge by distracting her with golden apples.[91] All three stories were told with an explicitly sexual dénouement. The emperor Tiberius had a special room dedicated to an old-master painting showing Atalanta 'obliging Meleager with her mouth', presumably in return for the gift of the boar skin. According to Ovid, Milanion admired Atalanta's legs, and the reward for his devotion was to make love to her with one of her

---

[88] Syme 1991.165 (from a lecture on Marguerite Yourcenar's *Mémoires d'Hadrien*).
[89] Ovid *Metamorphoses* 10.578; *CIL* 6.37965.21 (item 28 below).
[90] The complex mythographical tradition is analyzed in Gantz 1993.335–9.
[91] (1) Hyginus *Fabulae* 174.5; (2) Propertius 1.1.9–16, Ovid *Ars amatoria* 2.185–90; (3) Ovid *Metamorphoses* 10.560–680, Hyginus *Fabulae* 185.1–4.

legs on each shoulder. As for Atalanta and Hippomenes, they were so eager for sex that they used the temple of Magna Mater, and were metamorphosed into lions for their impiety.[92]

Atalanta was a stage character already in the fifth century BC, though whether in tragedy or satyr-play is unclear.[93] Two Roman plays about her are attested in the first century BC: a satyr-play of some sort by L. Pomponius, otherwise better known for his *fabulae Atellanae*,[94] and a play by Ovid's contemporary Gracchus, the sole surviving fragment of which implies a tragic scene setting.[95] Midway between those two items, in the 40s BC, the poet Cornelius Gallus evidently cast himself as Milanion the patient lover,[96] and as everyone knew, his hard-hearted Atalanta was herself a mime-actress who may well have played the part on stage – none other than the famous Cytheris.[97]

We now go forward 200 years or more, to consider a quite different body of evidence, the high-relief sculpture of Roman sarcophagi in the second and third centuries AD.[98] The choice of mythological subjects was evidently influenced by the stage, as suggested by the actors' masks that sometimes appear in the iconography.[99] Masks also appear frequently as the front corners of sarcophagus lids; one fine example in the Louvre (Fig. 6.3), with closed-mouth masks signifying *pantomimus*, also features the Ovidian themes of Diana and Actaeon on the sarcophagus itself and Nereids and sea-gods on the lid.[100]

The story of Meleager and the boar of Calydon was a favourite theme for the sarcophagi sculptors, with more than 200 examples surviving.[101] Atalanta's role is often tragic, grieving at Meleager's deathbed, but there are also hints of the less decorous parts of her story. An example from the necropolis below St Peter's basilica (Fig. 6.4) shows Meleager and Atalanta indoors, after the hunt, when he has given her the boar's hide; he is

[92] (1) Suetonius *Tiberius* 44.2 (by Parrhasios, c. 400 BC); (2) Ovid *Amores* 3.2.29–30, *Ars amatoria* 3.775; (3) Ovid *Metamorphoses* 10.686–704, cf. Hyginus *Fabulae* 185.6 (temple of Jupiter Victor).

[93] Pollux 7.31 (*TGrF* 9 F2) for Aristias' *Atalante*.

[94] Porphyrio on Horace *Ars poetica* 221: *satyrica coeperunt scribere, ut Pomponius Atalanten uel Sisyphon uel Ariadnen*. There is no reason to doubt this testimony (cf. Wiseman 1988.2–3).

[95] Priscian *Grammatici Latini* 2.206 Keil (Hollis 2007.334–6): *o grata cardo, regium egressum indicans*.

[96] Inferred from Virgil *Eclogues* 10.52–61 and Propertius 1.1.9–16 (Rosen and Farrell 1986).

[97] Servius on *Eclogues* 10.1, cf. *De uiris illustribus* 82.2; Gallus called her 'Lycoris' (Ovid *Amores* 1.15.29–30, *Ars amatoria* 3.537, Martial 8.73.6).

[98] Wiseman 2015.177–9; full details and discussion in Zanker and Ewald 2012.

[99] See, for instance, Zanker and Ewald 2012.79 fig. 67 (Creusa and Medea, Basel Museum of Ancient Art), 236 fig. 213 (Apollo and Marsyas, Doria-Pamphilj Gallery).

[100] Zanker and Ewald 2012.52 fig. 39; cf. n. 35 above for the closed mouth.

[101] Zanker and Ewald 2012.359–69.

Fig. 6.3   The death of Actaeon. Roman sarcophagus in the Louvre, Paris (inv. MA 459),
second century AD: photo © RMN-Grand Palais (museé du Louvre)/René-Gabriel Ojeda.
Lid: *Seethiasos* between closed-mouth masks. Main scene: right-hand lunette, Diana
bathing; left-hand lunette, Actaeon attacked by his own hounds. Note the ithyphallic
Priapus on the right of the Actaeon scene.

evidently suggesting, to judge by his body language, that one good turn
deserves another.[102]

Atalanta was a familiar figure on the Roman stage at this time, as we know
from a very remarkable document of the first or second century AD, a large
marble plaque, worthy of a senator's *cursus honorum*, on which a certain Aulus
Allius composed the epitaph of his freedwoman and concubine Allia Potestas.[103]
In fifty heartfelt but not always metrical hexameters, he gave a frank and loving
description of her excellent qualities, not only moral but physical as well.

28. *CIL* 6.37965.21

quid crura? Atalantes status illi comicus ipse.

As for her legs, she had the real comic stance of Atalanta.

What sort of comedy did Allius have in mind? It is not likely to have been
that of Menander and Terence, played by male actors in masks.

However, Rome knew many other types of comedy, and it is worth
recalling at this point a neglected observation from Suetonius' lost history
of the Roman *ludi*.[104]

---

[102] Zanker and Ewald 2012.248 fig. 223 (Koch 1975.131 no. 146) – presupposing the story painted
by Parrhasios (n. 92 above)?
[103] Discussion and illustration in Gordon 1983.145–8 and fig. 65; improved translation and
commentary in Horsfall 1985.
[104] Discussed more fully in Wiseman 2014.

Fig. 6.4   Meleager and Atalanta after the Calydonian boar hunt. Detail of a sarcophagus in the necropolis beneath St Peter's basilica, Rome, second century AD: Koch 1975.131 no. 146, reproduced by permission.

29. Diomedes *De poematibus* 14.5 (Kaibel 1899.61), *GL* 1.491–2 Keil

primis autem temporibus, sic uti adserit Tranquillus, omnia quae in scaena
uersantur in comoedia agebantur. nam et pantomimus et pythaules et choraules
in comoedia canebant. sed quia non poterant omnia simul apud omnes artifices
pariter excellere, siqui erant inter actores comoediarum pro facultate et arte
potiores, principatum <sui> sibi artificii uindicabant. sic factum est <ut>,
nolentibus cedere mimis in artificio suo ceteris, separatio fieret reliquorum. nam
dum potiores inferioribus qui in communi ergasterio erant seruire dedignantur,
se ipsos a comoedia separauerunt, ac sic factum est ut exemplo semel sumpto usus
quisque artis suae rem exequi coeperit neque in comoediam uenire.

Originally, as Tranquillus asserts, everything that [now] happens on stage
was performed in comedy. For the *pantomimus*, the *pythaules* and the
choraules used to sing in comedy. But because not everything could be
equally excellent in the performance of everyone, those among the comedy
performers who had greater ability and skill each claimed the artistic
primacy for himself. So it came about that the *mimi* were unwilling to
yield to the others in their own speciality, and so there was a split from the
rest. For since, being more skilled, they were not prepared to serve the less
skilled in the work they shared, they separated themselves from comedy;
and so it happened that once the precedent had been established, the
practice of each speciality began to follow suit, and not appear in comedy.

Although it is not clear what exactly is being described here, or when it was
supposed to have happened, Suetonius' formulation suggests that by the second
century AD the broad concept of 'comedy' might be thought of as including
the performances of *mimi* and *mimae*, now proudly independent of the original
archaic genre. If so, the 'comic stance' to which Allia Potestas' legs were likened
might mean the style of a dance-actress playing Atalanta's erotic role.

6.8 Venus on Stage

Much of our best information about the Roman stage comes from
Christian sources. Here, for instance, is Tertullian in AD 197, on the
subject of pagan literature.[105]

30. Tertullian *Apologeticus* 15.1–2

cetera lasciuiae ingenia etiam uoluptatibus uestris per deorum dedecus operan-
tur. dispicite Lentulorum et Hostiliorum uenustates, utrum mimos an deos
uestros in iocis et strophis rideatis, moechum Anubin et masculam Lunam et
Dianam flagellatam et Iouis mortui testamentum recitatum et tres Hercules

---

[105] Cf. Tertullian *De pallio* 4.1 for Lentulus the *mimographus*; Hostilius is otherwise unattested.

famelicos inrisos. sed et histrionum litterae omnem foeditatem eorum designant.
luget Sol filium de caelo iactatum laetantibus uobis, et Cybele pastorem suspirat
fastidiosum non erubescentibus uobis, et sustinetis Iouis elogia cantari et
Iunonem Venerem Mineruam a pastore iudicari.

The other great authors of indecency are at work for your enjoyment even
through the gods' disgrace. Have a good look at the entertainments of
writers like Lentulus and Hostilius: in the fun and the cleverness, is it the
mime-actors you're laughing at, or your own gods? Anubis as an adulterer,
the Moon-goddess changing sex, Diana getting spanked, Jupiter deceased
and his will being read, three starving Herculeses – all objects of laughter.
And even the pantomime-dancers' texts point out the gods' degradation:
you enjoy it when the Sun-god is grieving over his son's fall from the sky;
you don't blush when Cybele is sighing for her disdainful shepherd-boy;
you put up with it when the charge-sheet against Jupiter is the subject of
song, and when the shepherd is making his judgement on Juno, Venus
and Minerva.

The same double attack, on the mime farces and the *pantomimus* bal-
lets,[106] is continued a few years later by another Christian polemicist.

31. Minucius Felix *Octauius* 37.12

in scaenicis etiam non minor furor et turpitudo prolixior: nunc enim mimus uel
exponit adulteria uel monstrat, nunc eneruis histrio amorem dum fingit infligit;
idem deos uestros induendo stupra suspiria odia dedecorat.

In stage shows the madness is no less and the baseness more prolonged: now
it's a mime-actor either narrating adulteries or acting them, now it's a
languid pantomime-dancer causing desire as he imitates it – and by taking
on their sex acts, their sighings and their enmities, he brings disgrace on
your gods.

For Tertullian, the stage had its own particular vicious nature: just as the
Circus was characterized by hysteria (*furor*) and the arena by cruelty
(*saeuitia*), so the theatre represented indecency (*lasciuia* or *impudicitia*).[107]
   A famous passage in Tertullian's *De spectaculis* reports Pompey's answer
to the traditionalists who objected to the idea of a permanent theatre.

---

[106] For *histrio* = *pantomimus*/ὀρχηστής, see Tacitus *Annals* 1.77.2–4, Suetonius *Diuus Augustus* 45.4;
   Tacitus *Annals* 1.54.2, 4.14.3 (~ Dio Cassius 56.47.2, 57.21.3), Macrobius *Saturnalia* 2.7.12–19
   (~ Dio Cassius 54.17.4–5), 5.17.5.
[107] Tertullian *De spectaculis* 10.4 (*lasciuia*); 17.1, 17.5–6, 20.5, 29.5 (*impudicitia*).

32. Tertullian *De spectaculis* 10.5

... Veneris aedem superposuit et ad dedicationem edicto populum uocans non theatrum sed Veneris templum nuncupauit, cui subiecimus, inquit, gradus spectaculorum.

He built a temple of Venus on top of it, and when he summoned the People by edict to the dedication he referred not to a theatre but to the temple of Venus, 'to which,' he said, 'we have added steps for spectators to sit'.

Of course that suited Tertullian's case very well: the theatre was quite rightly the shrine of Venus, the citadel of all vices, presided over by the goddess of *libido*.[108] And it may be that his point was more than just rhetorical opportunism.

We happen to know from contemporary evidence that the presiding goddess of Pompey's theatre was Victoria;[109] very soon, however, the deity was reidentified as Venus Victrix.[110] That was probably the result of Pompey's defeat at Pharsalus, where Caesar had vowed a temple to Venus Victrix and used her name as his watchword before the battle.[111] The very distinctive iconography of the victorious goddess, seen from behind and carrying a helmet or sword, identifies her on the denarii minted by the conqueror of Egypt, *Caesar Diui filius*, in 29 BC (Fig. 6.5).[112]

But Venus was not only the bringer of victory; she was also a victor herself, in the famous beauty contest on Mount Ida that was so popular a theme for the stage.[113] And since she presided over Rome's first and greatest purpose-built theatre, we may guess that she was honoured in all the theatrical styles, including that of *liberior iocus*.

With that in mind, we may turn to a neglected body of evidence from Tertullian's own time, the bronze mirrors with high-relief decoration that

---

[108] Tertullian *De spectaculis* 10.3 (*theatrum proprie sacrarium Veneris est*), 10.5 (*arcem omnium turpitudinum*), 10.6 (*libido*).

[109] Aulus Gellius 10.1.7, quoting a letter from Tiro to Cicero: *cum Pompeius, inquit, aedem Victoriae dedicaturus foret, cuius gradus uicem theatri essent ...*

[110] Pliny *Nat. Hist.* 8.20: *Pompei quoque altero consulatu dedicatione templi Veneris Victricis ...*

[111] Appian *Civil Wars* 2.68, 2.76; cf. Plutarch *Pompey* 68.2.

[112] Schmidt 1997.211–12 (iconography); Sutherland 1984.59 no. 250a (*denarii*).

[113] Rightly noted by Sauron 1987.462–3. See item 30 and nn. 31 and 73 above.

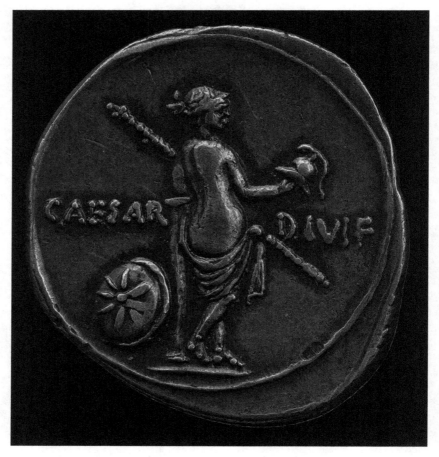

Fig. 6.5   Venus Victrix. Denarius of Imp. Caesar Divi f., 29 or 28 BC, British
Museum (inv. 28478.45). Reverse: Venus Victrix. © The Trustees of the
British Museum.

were in vogue in the second century AD.[114] Among the subjects illustrated
were the three Graces, Bacchus and Ariadne, Nereids on sea monsters –
and Venus Victrix surrounded by Cupids.[115] Two recent additions to the
corpus may be relevant to our theme.

[114] See Zahlhaas 1975, esp. 38–43 for the date.   [115] Zahlhaas 1975.32–3, 37–8 (Taf. 20–1).

Fig. 6.6 Venus and Priapus. Princeton University Art Museum: Roman gilded bronze mirror: Venus Victrix surrounded by three Erotes and a herm of Priapus; late first century A.D., gilt bronze; diam. 3.7 cm (1 7/16 in.); museum purchase, gift of Mitchell Wolfson, Jr., Class of 1963; y1985-1.

The first (Fig. 6.6), now in Princeton,[116] shows not only Venus Victrix and the Cupids but also an ithyphallic Priapus carrying a sceptre. Venus and Priapus are joined, perhaps literally, in a puzzling passage of Martial, where he warns his female readers in advance that the rest of the book will contain obscene words.

33. Martial 3.68.7–10

... sed aperte nominat illam
quam recipit sexto mense superba Venus,

---

[116] Princeton University Art Museum, inv. y1985-1; I am very grateful to Dr J. Michael Padgett, the Museum's Curator of Ancient Art, for his assistance.

custodem medio statuit quam uilicus horto,
opposito spectat quam proba uirgo manu.

[Terpsichore] openly names what proud Venus receives in the sixth month, what the bailiff sets up as a guard in the middle of the garden, what a well-brought-up girl looks at with her hand in front of her face.

The relative pronouns are all feminine, showing that the unspoken noun they refer to is *mentula*, but the particular allusion is to Priapus and his permanently threatening erection. It is just possible that by *sexto mense* Martial meant not June but August, the sixth month (*Sextilis*) in the old republican calendar; in that case the otherwise unattested ritual mentioned in line 8 could be part of the annual celebration of Venus Victrix at Pompey's theatre on the twelfth of that month.[117]

The other new mirror (Fig. 6.7), now in Boston,[118] shows a quite different scene. Here, Venus is being 'horsed' – or as the *Oxford English Dictionary* glosses it, 'elevated on a man's back in order to be flogged', a punishment normally used for schoolboys, as in a well-known wall painting from Pompeii.[119] Recent scholarship attributes this scene to the Lupercalia, where ladies might indeed be treated in this way;[120] but the iconography makes that very unlikely. The shield on the stand on the left, the sword on the stand in the centre, and the two Cupids (one holding her legs, the other keeping the score) show that this must be Venus Victrix; and since the flagellant has one shoulder bare and may be wearing a cap, he is evidently Vulcan, the blacksmith god, Venus' long-suffering husband.[121]

---

[117] Degrassi 1963.190–1 (*Fasti Amiternini*): *Veneri Victrici Hon(ori) Virt(uti) Felicitati in theatro marmoreo.* For the original numbering of the months, see Varro *De lingua Latina* 6.33–4.
[118] Vermeule and Comstock 1988.79–81, no. 95.
[119] *OED* 'Horse, v.', 4(b); the Pompeii school scene is illustrated in Wrede 1995.347.
[120] Wrede 1995.345–6, Tortorella 2000.245–6. See scholiast on Juvenal 2.142: *aut catomus* [i.e. κατ' ὤμους] *leuabantur aut a manibus uapulabant.* For a later parallel, cf. Matteo Bondello, *Novelle* (1554) 4.16, on the courtesan Isabella da Luna: 'hoisted on to the shoulders of a brawny sergeant'.
[121] Compare (e.g.) Hölscher 1988.382, no. 213 (Città Castellana c. 40 BC); Brommer 1978.42 fig. 16, 229 no. 5 (contorniate medallion, AD 152). The significance of the codex and styluses in the exergue, and the figure in the open cabinet at the top (hard to make out, but identified as Minerva by Vermeule and Comstock 1988.79), is not at all clear.

Fig. 6.7 Flagellation of Venus Victrix. Museum of Fine Arts, Boston: 'Mirror with Erotes and Silenos [*sic*] punishing a nude female; Roman imperial period, first or second century A.D., gilt bronze; sculpture in stone and bronze (MFA), no. 095; William E. Nickerson Fund, 1986.750.'

We know from Tertullian (item 30) that there was a stage scenario in which Diana for some reason received treatment similar to this, and the erotic flagellation of females may well have been a traditional theme of mime. One of the surviving fragments of Decimus Laberius certainly suggests that.[122]

34. Aulus Gellius 16.7.4 (Laberius fr. 59 Panayotakis).

tollet bona fide uos Orcus nudas in catomum.

Orcus in good faith will lift you up naked on the shoulders.

---

[122] See Panayotakis 2010.374–5 for *catomum* = κατ' ὦμον (cf. n. 120 above).

The addressees are female, perhaps the 'weaving-women' of the title of the play, and the predicted flagellation will evidently happen in the underworld. We don't know whether Laberius presented the spectacle to be seen on stage, but it seems clear that his successors two centuries later would have had no scruples about doing so.

6.9 'Epyllia'

Laberius brings us back at last to Catullus' time (Section 2.7 above). After this long and circuitous argument, I hope the idea that poem 64 could have been performed on stage may no longer seem absurd. There are features in the poem that may suggest a danced performance of the type we inferred from the Ovidian evidence in Section 6.5 above: not only the bare-breasted sea-nymphs confronting the Argonauts in the opening scene (lines 16–18) but also the sudden appearance of Iacchus and his satyrs and maenads, with their deafening music of horns and pipes and drums (251–64).

Ovid may even offer direct evidence for a dance drama on Ariadne. In *Fasti*, where he has to account for the constellation called 'Ariadne's crown', he composes a little sequel to Catullus' scenario in poem 64.[123] Ariadne is on the shore again, complaining again about betrayal – this time by Bacchus himself, who she believes is in love with an Indian princess.

35. Ovid *Fasti* 3.471–4

en iterum, fluctus, similes audite querellas!
en iterum lacrimas accipe, harena, meas!
dicebam, memini, 'periure et perfide Theseu!'
ille abiit; eadem crimina Bacchus habet.

'Again! Waves, listen to the same complaints. Again! Sand, receive my tears. I used to say, I remember, "Forsworn and faithless Theseus!" He's gone, now Bacchus incurs the same charge.'

Ariadne quotes her own speech in Catullus 64 – but why does she say *dicebam*? Elsewhere, in two separate passages, Ovid has Mars quoting what Jupiter said in Ennius, and of course he uses the perfect *dixisti*.[124] Ariadne's surprising use of the imperfect is emphasized by its repetition a

---

[123] Ovid *Fasti* 3.459–516, esp. 3.473 (~ Cat. 64.132–5), 3. 475 (~ Cat. 64.143); Wiseman 2015.160–1.
[124] *Fasti* 2.488, *Met.* 14.815 (~ Ennius *Annals* 54–5 Skutsch, quoted in Varro *De lingua Latina* 7.6).

few lines later: asking Bacchus why he saved her on the previous occasion, she says *quid me ... seruabas?* (3.479–80).

I think the explanation may be that Ovid and his readers knew Catullus' Ariadne narrative not just as a text in a book but as a performance seen on stage. She said what she said, and Bacchus did what he did, each time the piece was played, and so she reports it here in the imperfect tense.

We must remember that before the new 'all-mime' style was introduced by Pylades and Bathyllus, leading roles were played by performers who both danced *and* sang (items 17 and 18 above), and that the dancer Dionysia commanded big fees for what she offered (item 11). If Ariadne was played by a *prima donna* like her, the loss of her clothes in the scene on the shore becomes another example of a familiar phenomenon: an actress naked on stage for no obvious reason except the spectators' enjoyment.

In that context, it is worth thinking about two other 'epyllia', each written by a friend of Catullus, Calvus' *Io* and Cornificius' *Glaucus*.[125] Both poems are lost, but Ovid's treatment of the respective themes may reflect their influence. Io was a nymph, daughter of the river-god Inachus, loved by Jupiter and transformed into a heifer by jealous Juno. In Ovid's *Heroides* she is rhetorically addressed by Hypermnestra.

36. Ovid *Heroides* 14.99–100

quaeque modo ut posses etiam Ioue digna uideri
diues eras, nuda nuda recumbis humo.

You who once had everything, so you could even seem worthy of Jupiter, now lie naked on the naked ground.

(Why emphasize the nakedness? An animal would hardly be wearing clothes.) And the following is Ovid's account of her return to human form.

37. Ovid *Metamorphoses* 1.743–5

de boue nil superest, formae nisi candor, in illa;
officioque pedum nymphe contenta duorum
erigitur.

Nothing bovine is left in her except the whiteness of her form; the nymph stands up, content to use two feet.

---

[125] For fragments (text and translation) and discussion, see Hollis 2007.51–2 and 60–8 (*Io*), 150–3 (*Glaucus*).

What was in the poet's mind, I suggest, was not so much a heifer as an actress wearing a horned headdress and nothing else.[126]

As for Glaucus, a fisherman metamorphosed into a sea-god, in Ovid he falls in love with Scylla as she walks naked on the shore after swimming with the sea-nymphs.[127] We know he was a character in a dance-drama because we know one of the men who played him – no less a personage than L. Munatius Plancus, consul in 42 BC.

38. Velleius Paterculus 2.83.2

... *cum caeruleatus et nudus caputque redimitus arundine et caudam trahens genibus innixus Glaucum saltasset in conuiuio.*

... although at a private party [Plancus] had danced Glaucus on his knees, painted blue, naked, his head crowned with reeds, dragging a fish-tail.

In Ovid, the fish-tail was what put Scylla off: she thought he was a monster.[128] But no – he was the leader of a *chorus*, a company as sportive and picturesque in their watery world as the Dionysiac *thiasos* was on land. Virgil brings them on as Neptune's retinue.

39. Virgil *Aeneid* 5.822–6

tum uariae comitum facies, immania cete
et senior Glauci chorus Inousque Palaemon
Tritonesque citi Phorcique exercitus omnis;
laeua tenet Thetis et Melite Panopaeaque uirgo,
Nisaee Spioque Thaliaque Cymodoceque.

Then came his escort in its varied forms, huge sea-monsters and Glaucus' ageing dancers and Ino's son Palaemon and the swift Tritons and all of Phorcys' army; on the left side were Thetis and Melite and the maiden Panopaea, Nisaee and Spio and Thalia and Cymodoce.

The euphoniously named females on the left side were of course Nereids.[129] We have a fine first-century BC visual impression of the scene (Fig. 6.8) on the so-called altar of Domitius Ahenobarbus, a large

---

[126] Io's horns are constantly referred to: Propertius 2.33.9, Virgil *Aeneid* 7.789, Ovid *Amores* 1.3.21, *Heroides* 14.90, *Metamorphoses* 1.641, 740, Valerius Flaccus 4.406. Compare Actaeon (n. 41 above for his antlered mask in tragedy): Ovid *Metamorphoses* 3.139, 194, 200.

[127] Ovid *Metamorphoses* 13.733–7 (*pelagi gratissima nymphis*), 899 (Nereids), 901 (*sine uestibus*).

[128] *Metamorphoses* 13.912–19.

[129] Homer *Iliad* 18.38–40. Cf. also Virgil *Georgics* 1.437, *Aeneid* 5.239–40.

Fig. 6.8   Nereids and sea-monsters. Marble relief of *Seethiasos* from S. Salvatore in Campo, Rome, late second or early first century BC: Staatliche Antikensammlung und Glyptothek Munich (inv. GI 239), photograph by Renate Kühling. The marine scene occupied three sides of the base for a statue group; the fourth side (in the Louvre) probably shows the enrolment of citizens for the proposed new colony of Neptunia in 123 BC (Maschek 2018).

monument from a site in the southern Campus Martius, probably the temple of Neptune *in circo Flaminio*.[130]

Plancus' party performance was an early example of something that becomes more familiar under the Julio-Claudians: high-status Romans imitating the virtuoso professional performers they so much admired.[131] It may well be that he chose Glaucus because Cornificius had made the theme popular at just that time. The two men were exact contemporaries, at the same level of senatorial *dignitas*;[132] but since modern historians don't think much about poets, and literary scholars are more interested in intertexts than dancing senators, the compartmentalization of classical studies has meant that Plancus' performance is never mentioned in connection with Cornificius' poem.

If Catullus 64 was indeed a mime libretto, it was a remarkably varied and ambitious one, and even though it contained erotic elements it was not comic in the usual sense. But that need not surprise us. Catullus' contemporary Publilius Syrus, described by Pliny as 'the founder of the mimic stage' (which I suspect means pioneer of a style of mime that could fill the stage in Pompey's theatre),[133] was famous for his improving moral

---

[130]   Torelli 1982.5–9 (from S. Salvatore in Campo), Viscogliosi 1996; cf. Livy 28.11.4, *CIL* 6.8423 (*in circo Flaminio*); Pliny *Nat. Hist.* 36.26 (statue group by Scopas *delubro Cn. Domitii in circo Flaminio*).

[131]   Gaius Caesar was expert at 'stage dancing and singing' (Suetonius *Gaius* 11, Dio Cassius 59.5.5), 'imitated the *pantomimi* rather than watching them' (Seneca *De ira* 1.20.8) and impersonated gods 'as if in the theatre' (Philo *De legatione* 78–9); cf. also Tacitus *Annals* 11.31.2 on the Dionysiac masquerade of Silius and Messallina. Lady Diana Cooper (Section 1.2 above) had a successful career as a stage and film actress in the 1920s.

[132]   Probably both praetors in 45 BC, as inferred from their proconsulships the following year: Cicero *Ad familiares* 12.23.1 (Cornificius), *Philippics* 3.38 (Plancus).

[133]   Pliny *Nat. Hist.* 35.199 (*mimicae scaenae conditor*); cf. Section 6.4 above.

sententiae, of which a large anthology survives.[134] Seneca gives an idea of his versatility.

40. Seneca De *tranquillitate animi* 11.8

> *Publilius tragicis comicisque uehementior ingeniis, quotiens mimicas ineptias et uerba ad summam caueam spectantia reliquit, inter multa alia coturno non tantum sipario fortiora et hoc ait: 'cuiuis potest accidere quod cuiquam potest.'*

> Publilius was more vigorous than the authors of tragedies and comedies whenever he left the absurdities of mime and the lines that were aimed at the back of the auditorium. Among many things more powerful than tragedy, never mind comedy, he says this: 'What can happen to someone can happen to anyone.'

That sort of thing was applauded by theatre audiences, who took it for granted that the stage was for moral instruction as well as entertainment.[135] The closing lines of poem 64 would be a good example of that.

6.10   Conclusion

The erotic performance of mythological stories was a very old tradition. Its first attestation is the song of Demodocus at the Phaeacian games, probably composed just about the time when the Iron Age community at the crossing-point on the Tiber was first turning itself into a city-state with an *agora*, under the Greek name of Rhōmē.[136] The Romans were demonstrably familiar with Greek culture from at least the sixth century BC,[137] and 300 years later they had evidently appropriated the mythological-burlesque style of Rhinthon's 'Italian comedy'.[138]

Erotic entertainment was part of Roman culture as far back as the evidence allows us to see, associated at first with the cult of Liber, the Roman Dionysus;[139] and even after the Senate clamped down on the Bacchic cult in 186 BC, it continued to feature in the *ludi scaenici*, particularly those of Flora. The extent to which it was embedded in the

---

[134] Duff and Duff 1934.3–111; detailed discussion in Giancotti 1967.275–462.
[135] Seneca *Epistulae* 108.8–9 (*non uides quem ad modum theatra consonant* . . .), cf. 8.8–10 (Publilius again); see in general Rawson 1991.570–81.
[136] Homer *Odyssey* 8.266–369. City-state: Cornell 1995.92–7 (first Forum paving c. 625 BC), Wiseman 2015.10–19. Rome as Ῥώμη: Plutarch *Romulus* 1.1 ('founded by Pelasgians'); also Hyperochus of Cumae *FGrH* 576 F3 (Festus 328L), Ateius Praetextatus fr. 14 Funaioli (Servius on *Aeneid* 1.273), Solinus 1.1 ('originally Valentia, translated into Greek by Evander').
[137] Evidence and discussion in Wiseman 2004.13–36, 2015.14–19.
[138] See above, nn. 13 and 42.
[139] Evidence and discussion in Wiseman 2004.63–118, 2015.29–45.

Roman experience is indirectly attested by Tertullian's *De spectaculis*: that work was not a polemic directed against pagans, but a sermon addressed to fellow-Christians who saw no harm in enjoying the Roman games.[140] Evidently, the naked girls on the theatre stage were still an integral part of their world, an ancient custom of fun, *priscus mos iocorum* (item 1 above), just as Valerius Maximus had put it two centuries earlier.

Some classicists will reject a priori the notion that poems like Catullus 64 had anything to do with such performances. But as in *The Roman Audience* (Wiseman 2015), I have tried to suggest that the common ground of social and literary history requires a more holistic treatment than it normally receives. The evidence is scattered and enigmatic, but that does not excuse us from the duty of trying to make sense of it.

---

[140] Tertullian *De spectaculis* 1.1–3, 2.1–2.

CHAPTER 7

Clodia
Some Imaginary Lives

Not a question this time: left to the end as a mere period piece, this chapter chronicles some literary consequences of the historical error the original *Catullan Questions* tried to correct.[1] It was written a long time ago – before *I, Claudius* was televised,[2] and long before classical 'reception' studies became an industry – but a kind remark by my contemporary Susan Treggiari, in a book on one of Clodia's contemporaries,[3] makes me think it might be worth revisiting. Remember, though, that the fictions discussed below were all based on a fallacy; a historically credible story of Catullus and 'Lesbia' has yet to be told.

* * *

> It is strange that none of our novelists or imaginative writers have taken as their subject this brilliant circle, and given body and substance to the intrigues and plots, the banquets and revels, the singing-parties and the yachting-parties, the life in Clodia's mansion and gardens on the Palatine and by the shore and on the waters at Baiae. Not even does Cleopatra make a more striking portrait than would Clodia herself with her large burning eyes, her patrician grace and beauty, her savage loves and hates, her Claudian pride, her Claudian recklessness, and her Roman heartlessness. Surely here is a subject for romance, romance too which would not stray very far from the domain of actual history.
>
> —Robert Yelverton Tyrrell, 1890[4]

Though Tyrrell held the Chairs of Greek and Latin at Dublin (and that of Ancient History too, before he retired), his chief recreation, according to

---

[1] See Section 1.1 above.   [2] BBC, 27 September–6 December 1976.
[3] Treggiari 2019.298–311, a wonderful appendix on 'Servilia in some modern English novels'.
[4] Tyrrell and Purser 1890.xliii–xliv; for Tyrrell, see now Beard 2002.106–15. (He was wrong about Clodia's gardens, which weren't on the Palatine: Cicero *Pro Caelio* 36.)

Who's Who, had always been 'light literature and the drama'. But at that time it was perhaps too much to hope for a novel on Clodia and her lovers, even on Catullus, with whose 'Lesbia' she was confidently identified.

Only twelve years earlier, commenting on Catullus' poem about his meeting with Lesbia at Allius' house, H. A. J. Munro had shown a fine Victorian sense of propriety:[5]

> The 'amour-passion', what phlegmatic Verulam flouts at as 'the mad degree of love', is once more master of his soul. This mighty force is able to purify and sublimate his furious passion for a tainted adulteress, false even to her paramour. We almost excuse the outrage of his likening her to so noble and pure a heroine as Laodamia; we almost forgive his unmeasured praises of a man guilty of as base an action as a gentleman could well commit, who lent his house to conceal an adulterous intrigue between a woman of high rank and a vicious youth, and covered with dishonour one of the noblest and most virtuous patricians of the time.

On the political side, however (and Clodia was often thought to have shared her brother's *popularis* sympathies), the Victorians might have produced something startling if the Professor of History at University College London, a Benthamite radical in that college's best traditions, had been an 'imaginative writer'.

Indeed, unkind critics might say that E. S. Beesly's articles on Catiline and Clodius in the *Fortnightly Review* in 1865 and 1866 showed more imagination than historical responsibility in their splendidly iconoclastic defence of the 'leaders of the Popular Party'.[6] Beesly himself would have indignantly denied any adherence to the despised fraternity of literary men (who stick together 'like game-preservers or Whitechapel thieves'),[7] but his Social Positivist polemics were to be a source of inspiration to men of letters concerned with just the 'petty and personal' minutiae of history that he held in such contempt.

* * *

[5] Munro 1878.181 (citing Francis Bacon, Baron Verulam, whose essay 'Of Love' was published in 1612). Metellus Celer was not a patrician – an uncharacteristic error.

[6] For more detail, see Wiseman 1998.121–34 (a lecture given to the Beesly Society at UCL on 27 October 1994).

[7] Beesly 1865.184 = 1878.36; cf. Beesly 1866.434 = 1878.67, on Clodius' adoption in 59 BC: 'If there is a childish way of explaining a political movement, a literary man will generally adopt it. He is irresistibly attracted by what is petty and personal, as he is repelled and alarmed by the idea of an orderly evolution of human affairs.'

Tyrrell never got his 'romance'. A guide to historical fiction published in 1914, the year of his death, has nothing on Clodia, Catullus or Caelius Rufus. The same is true of a similar survey published in 1929.[8] In that year, however, a young Australian poet and classical scholar, recently arrived in London, published his complete translation of Catullus through the Fanfrolico Press, of which he was joint proprietor.

This was Jack Lindsay (1900–90), who was just beginning to undergo a 'painful and prolonged process of inner change' – from romantic existentialism via Freud to Marxism – at the same time as an emotionally destructive sadomasochistic relationship with 'Elza'. He abandoned the press and began an isolated and poverty-stricken life with her, moving from house to house in the west country and trying to find a way to make his living with his pen. In 1932 he began to read about Roman history in the Truro public library, led by his interest in Catullus to the first century BC. An Oxford undergraduate (unnamed in Lindsay's autobiography) sought out the recluse, became one of the only two guests to cross his threshold in ten years and began to supply him with books from his college library.

One of them was Beesly's *Catiline, Clodius, and Tiberius* (1878), 'a book which had a decisive effect on my thinking'. The result was that Lindsay abandoned his original plan to write a biography of Caelius Rufus and began instead a novel on Catiline (*Rome for Sale*, 1934), turning it into a trilogy with *Caesar Is Dead* (1934) and *Last Days with Cleopatra* (1935). As 'a pendant to the trilogy, making the direct link with Catullus and Clodia', he then produced a novel on Caelius Rufus (*Despoiling Venus*, 1935), and finally a companion piece on Catullus (*Brief Light*, 1939), written to absolve a commitment to his publishers.[9]

The main drawbacks of Lindsay's Roman novels may be seen from his own words:[10]

> In choosing the Caesarian revolution as my theme I had in a sense been exploring the poems of Catullus, which had always meant a great deal to me: finding myself through the discovery of their social and political implications, or rather of the dialectical relation between their intense personal definition and the larger aspects. While from one angle I had begun by trying to grasp the historical events as projections or facets of the poet's passionate personality, in the process of realization I was forced to

[8] Baker 1914.324–5; Nield 1929.6–7.
[9] Lindsay 1962, esp. pp. 229–31, 249, 278. See also the foreword to the final volume of the trilogy, and Lindsay's paragraph in Vinson 1972.772.
[10] Lindsay 1962.244–5.

invert this effort and explore the roots of personality in the social process. A set of tensions was thus set up between outer an inner reality, through which I sought to define the full structure of movement. While in one way the story was an allegory of my own struggles, in another and more important way it was a vehicle through which those struggles were enlarged.. . .

He criticizes Robert Graves for writing *I, Claudius* 'without any central idea or any effort to build the social picture', but it is precisely the abstract central idea – a teleological preoccupation with emerging world orders – that weakens his own novels and prevents him from doing what the historical novelist surely must do: recreate the past in its own terms. Unlike Mary Renault with her *kaloikagathoi*, or Zoé Oldenbourg with her Crusaders, Lindsay never allows himself to get fully into the value system of his chosen period, because he has contemporary values too much on his mind.[11]

Similarly, Graves is criticized for not putting his own experiences into his historical novels; for Lindsay, on the other hand, the autobiographical element was all-important. As he says, his novels were partly an attempt 'to analyse my own motivation and to understand what moved Elza'.[12] To read the Caelius and Catullus novels in conjunction with his own autobiography is a moving experience, but without that extra dimension they fall flat, the personally significant incidents and dialogue appearing merely arbitrary.[13] The trilogy is much better (especially the second book), but despite its imaginative merits the impression remains that Lindsay's short stories of the ancient world (*Come Home at Last*, 1936) are more successful than his novels precisely because they have less room for abstract theorizing and less need for filling out with autobiographical material.

Clodia appears in *Rome for Sale* and more briefly in *Caesar Is Dead*, and is naturally a major character in *Despoiling Venus* and *Brief Light*. Dark, shortish, coarse, big-hipped and with a tendency to fat, she has much in common with Elza and is hardly at all the proud aristocrat embodying old Rome, as she is supposed to appear in the trilogy. Her uncontrollable temper and moods of gloom are clearly from the same source, as is the

---

[11] 'I felt all kinds of correspondences with the present day' (Lindsay 1935, foreword); Lindsay 1962.234–5, 240–1, 244 (on the trilogy), 243 (on *I, Claudius*), 213, 271 (on his own method).
[12] Lindsay 1962.261, cf. 187 on Graves.
[13] Forty years later he was unrepentant (Jack Lindsay to author, August 1975): 'I should be ready to take any significant novelist and show how there is a vital relation between his work and his or her personal conflicts, whether the theme is historical or contemporary. But thank you all the same for the work and thought you put into the analyses.' See now Treggiari 2019.299–301 on Lindsay.

baby daughter who takes up her time.[14] Only in *Caesar Is Dead*, where Lindsay uses his imagination to recreate her – ageing unwillingly in her Tiber gardens, denying Ticida, her daughter's lover, the pleasure of being able to boast that he had had 'Lesbia', and at last dramatically expiating her long-regretted cruelty to Catullus – does the reader feel they have had any insight into what made the real Clodia tick.

As for her jealous quarrels with Caelius in *Despoiling Venus* and her unjust emotional browbeating of Catullus in *Brief Light*, they certainly have the painful immediacy of the real thing – but it is not the reality of Clodia's Rome. The Catullus we know from the poems would have resented such treatment all right, but his indignation would surely not have weakened, as Lindsay makes it, into a sense of guilt followed by groveling capitulation. Similarly, Caelius, the most acute political observer of his day in Cicero's opinion,[15] is saddled with a view of Roman politics as a complicated muddle that patently stems from his creator's attempt to interpret the sources in the light of Beesly's schematic 'parties' and his own disenchantment with capitalism. In the end, Lindsay himself is more interesting than his characters, and they too often exist only as pale reflections of his own life.

* * *

Three years after Lindsay's trilogy, W. G. Hardy (1895–1979) became head of the department of Classics at the University of Alberta in Edmonton.[16] He had already written two historical novels on Old Testament themes, and in that year, 1938, he published a fictional biography of Clodia called *Turn Back the River*. Indeed he dedicated it to Clodia as well, as if to a contemporary, for his purpose was explicitly to 'body forth the living past' and emphasize its modernity. So his Clodius calls Clodia 'Sis', his proletarians speak uneducated American English, and his characters refer to boom and depression, the struggle of the masses and plundering capitalism. 'The New Deal' is even suggested as a slogan for Cicero's consular candidature.

Here too the influence of Beesly's essays is clear: for Hardy, Catiline was a romantic idealist revolutionary, and the guilds (*collegia*) were a secret revolutionary organization lacking only a leader. The politics are as anachronistic as Lindsay's, but at a much more superficial level. The love

---

[14] The historical Clodia did indeed have a daughter in real life (Shackleton Bailey 1960.96–7).
[15] Cicero *Ad familiares* 2.8.1: πολιτικώτερον *enim te adhuc neminem cognoui.*
[16] On Hardy, see now Treggiari 2019.305–7.

interest, too, suffers in contrast with Lindsay, being novelettish and melodramatic, and though Hardy scores over his predecessor in the tightness of his plot, it is achieved by a heavy-handed use of the omniscient-author convention as dramatic ironies and simultaneities are pointed out. Fate controls his characters – or rather 'the Design', for Hardy is an associate member of that school of historians castigated by Isaiah Berlin, who 'feel that abstract nouns deserve capital letters, and tell us that Tradition or History (or "the Past" or "The Masses") are wiser than we'.[17]

Most of his story covers the years before Clodia is known to history. She is given a fierce love-hate relationship with Catiline, and a part in every major political event: having avoided a fate worse than death from Spartacus' slaves and had a brief affair with her rescuer (Caesar), she is made responsible for the political alignment of 70 BC, for Cicero's election as consul (to spite Catiline) and for the betrayal of the conspiracy; she is present at the conspirators' secret meeting at Laeca's house, and eventually (but too late) won over to their 'ideals'. Only the short final part, after Catiline's death in 62, deals with Caelius Rufus, Catullus, and the period of her life for which there is historical evidence.

Twenty years later, however, Hardy returned to Clodia and devoted another novel (*The City of Libertines*, 1957) to just those years, 62–54 BC. It is a much better book than the first. The plot is even more tightly constructed, with the Clodia-Catullus-Caelius narrative ingeniously interwoven with the political history,[18] and 'the Design' is replaced by the Good Goddess and the Furies, avenging, respectively, Clodius' sacrilege and the death of Metellus Celer. In *Turn Back the River*, Clodia was made to poison Metellus because he had struck her daughter (borrowed from Lindsay?); now she murders him because he beat her after her night with Catullus at the house of Manlius,[19] a characteristically economical expedient.

But the main plot of the earlier book is still taken for granted. Clodia is still essentially political, 'seeking power' and using her brother (at first) as a tool; the traumatic effect of her supposed relationship with Catiline is still an essential part of her motivation, in particular for her domination by Caelius, in whom she sees Catiline returned to life. Her depravity (as depicted by Cicero) is made out to be entirely the fault of Caelius'

---

[17] Hardy 1938.174, 202, 375, 383–4; Berlin 1954.9.

[18] At some cost to accuracy: the Clodian violence in 61 (Cicero *Ad Atticum* 1.14.5, 1.16.5) is greatly exaggerated, and Catullus is made one of the chief gang leaders.

[19] Like Lindsay, Hardy assumes (indefensibly) that the whole of 'Catullus 68' is a single poem addressed to Manlius Torquatus.

influence,[20] her real nature that of a great patrician lady, emancipated but not promiscuous, a political power but conscious of her inherited responsibilities.

In the meantime a very different Clodia had appeared, this one every bit as immoral as Cicero painted her and with an added taste for gladiators. She was the creation of Sir Pierson Dixon, GCMG, CB (1904–65), whose novel *Farewell, Catullus* was published in 1953. Classical Fellow of Pembroke for a short time in his twenties, the author had entered the Foreign Office in 1929; by the time the book appeared he was Deputy Under-Secretary of State and about to go to the United Nations as the British Permanent Representative. His Clodia is almost as political as Hardy's, but, not surprisingly, her politics are portrayed without any of Beesly's romanticizing of the *populares*.

For Dixon, Clodia's brother is an evil anarchist, and the guilds are sinister underground groups of organized workers who could paralyze Rome with strikes; it is they who demand, and bring about, the death of the conservative Metellus Celer. But the political background, like other necessary information, is expounded too didactically and not digested into the story. Some things are well done, such as the local colour for Catullus in Bithynia (Sir Pierson served at the British Embassy in Ankara in 1936), but the novel as a whole is not a success.

After the Australian poet, the Canadian classicist and the English diplomat, at last in 1965 Clodia found an author to whom the novel was a professional concern. Robert De Maria (1928–), whose doctoral dissertation at Columbia had been on the Utopian novel in England, became professor of English at Dowling College, New York, in 1965 and published his *Clodia* the same year. His lack of classical expertise, resulting in a higher than usual rate of historical inaccuracy,[21] is compensated by the subtle character-drawing, particularly in the elusive, contradictory nature of his Clodia. Demanding both love and hate, she hides behind 'the fog of her own fear and pride and restless arrogance', yet needs Catullus to restore her innocence – and in the process destroys his. De Maria's Cicero sums her up:[22]

---

[20] Hardy ingeniously interprets Caelius' *in triclinio Coa* (Quintilian 8.6.52) and Cicero's *frequentissima celebritate et clarissima luce laetatur* (*Pro Caelio* 47) as evidence of Clodia's final public degradation at Caelius' hands.

[21] Not that the classicists are free from it: for instance, Lindsay confuses the Bona Dea with the Magna Mater, Hardy makes Hortensius prosecute Clodius in 61, Dixon gives Catullus an anachronistic 'blood-baptism' (*taurobolium*) in Bithynia.

[22] De Maria 1965.230.

She is afraid of being trapped, of being kept in a cage as women have been for centuries. She fancies herself a liberated, sophisticated animal. Much of her behaviour is outrageous because this is her way of announcing her independence to the world. But there is a price these modern women must pay – a price they calculate for themselves. They lose the satisfaction of being put down, which is an age-old female pleasure.... She wants to be possessed, yet wants to be the possessor.

Caelius (and Cicero too, we are told) could handle her by not allowing her to dominate; Catullus could not. His possessiveness, his emotional self-deception and his attempt to force her into his own idealized conception are portrayed with a finesse beyond any of De Maria's predecessors.[23]

But still, the book is flawed. The inaccuracies are there, not only in detail but on major points – the character of Cicero, the career of Caesar – which add up to a falsification of the historical period. It seems that real novelists with real scholarly standards are as rare as philosopher kings. Only a distinguished few can do justice to what the evidence allows us to know, and at the same time create a character (like Marguerite Yourcenar's Hadrian) that ranks as a great artistic achievement in its own right.

The latest version of the Clodia story fails signally on both counts. *Death on the Appian Way* (1974), the fifth novel written by Kenneth Benton, CMG (1909–99) after his retirement from the diplomatic service in 1968, covers the years 63–52 BC as narrated by Caelius Rufus. But he is a trivial Caelius, innocuous as a high-spirited undergraduate, and his Clodia is worthy of him, petite and kittenish, imperious only to the extent of stamping her little foot; amateur theatricals are the limit of their depravity.[24] The plot soon becomes dominated by the character of Milo, pictured as a gigantic ex-gladiator with an unexpected taste for Ciceronian oratory ('Balls of Bacchus! The whole bleeding speech is beautiful') – an enjoyable travesty that serves only to emphasize the unhistorical superficiality of the whole.

* * *

To what extent were these five authors aware of one another's work? Hardy's debt to Lindsay is unmistakable, quite apart from the independent influence of Beesly's essays on each of them. Clodia's daughter, mentioned

---

[23] We are also well rid of Clodia's supposed political power: as De Maria rightly makes her say (1965.226), 'I am only a woman, a spectator.'
[24] That is how Benton interprets the *ludi* for which Caelius used the gold he borrowed from Clodia (Cicero *Pro Caelio* 53).

above, was not the only Lindsay invention taken over by Hardy: the proletarian boss of *Rome for Sale*, rejoicing in the name of Nacca, reappears as Bocca in *Turn Back the River*; Caelius' contemptuous presentation of a *quadrans* in *Despoiling Venus* is transferred to Catiline in Hardy's version;[25] and such arbitrary details as Curio's rouged face and the supposed Etruscans in the hills above Lake Garda turn up in both authors.

Significantly, Lindsay's and Hardy's are the only versions that deny the reality of Clodia's incest with her brother. For the former, it was presumably not valid as a reflection of his own life, and the latter must have been glad to avoid saddling his heroine with it. Dixon, however, implicitly, and De Maria and Benton openly, admit the incest. De Maria and Benton are also at one in attributing the death of Metellus Celer to Clodius, presumably out of jealousy. Clodia's predilection for gladiators is common to Dixon and De Maria, but the appearance of a Dixon–De Maria–Benton 'tradition' independent of the Lindsay-Hardy one is illusory. Eranna, for instance, Catullus' devoted slave girl in Lindsay's *Brief Light*, reappears in Dixon as Poppaea and in De Maria as the dumb Thalia, in each case as a foil for Clodia's jealousy. And the flogging of Clodia by Metellus in Hardy's second novel is reflected by De Maria in an aside ('Perhaps he should beat me,' his Clodia remarks), and this in turn is taken over by Benton: 'Perhaps he ought to have beaten you.' 'He did, once. And then apologized, so it didn't work.'[26]

The most revealing example of the borrowing technique comes in the treatment of Clodius' discovery at the rites of the Good Goddess. In *Rome for Sale*, Clodia lightheartedly warns him:[27]

> If you're found out, I'll disown you and let the women emasculate you on the spot. I'm sure that's the penalty. I'll propose it myself. So beware.

If anything, the appropriate penalty would be blinding,[28] but Hardy, with his taste for threatened sexual violence, predictably picked up Lindsay's hint. In his first book there is just a passing reference – Clodius 'only escapes castration by the grace of Abra, Pompeia's maid' – but in the second it becomes a major melodramatic scene ('The knives! Gelded! No, not that! Not that!'), as the bound Clodius awaits his fate in terror. Finally, with Benton we descend to the merely vulgar: 'They tore my dress off and

---

[25] It is curious that all the authors reject the picturesque, and credible, origin of the name 'Quadrantaria' given by Plutarch (*Cicero* 29.4). In Hardy's second book it is an empty insult coined by Catullus; this version is taken over by Dixon, while Benton ascribes the invention to Caelius, who is characteristically made to repent of it.

[26] Hardy 1957.225–6; De Maria 1965.184; Benton 1974.90.   [27] Lindsay 1934.132.

[28] Cicero *De haruspicum responso* 38, with Devereux 1973.40–4.

found what they were looking for, and then – I tell you, I thought they were going to castrate me, and ran like mad.'[29]

One of the details of the common stock – the fair-haired, blue-eyed, Celtic Catullus of Lindsay, Hardy and De Maria – may perhaps be traced to H. W. Garrod in the introduction to his *Oxford Book of Latin Verse*;[30] from this kind of source, too, the novelists' borrowings are sometimes blatant. For example, Hardy's Catiline in *Turn Back the River* scathingly refers to the Metelli, the Cottae and the Torquati as 'men whose ancestors were warming chapped hands and stinking of garlic when mine were patricians'. Warming chapped hands? Why does that sound wrong, but familiar? Beesly, of course:

> L. Sergius Catilina was sprung from one of the most ancient patrician families of Rome. His ancestors had been consuls and decemvirs when the Metelli and the Domitii were clapping their chopped hands and throwing up their sweaty nightcaps on the Aventine or Mons Sacer.

Not even Hardy could make Catiline himself quote Shakespeare.[31] It may also have been from a too literal interpretation of Beesly that Hardy produced his portrait of Cicero as a fatuous puppet in the hands of the *boni* against Catiline,[32] an absurdity, corrected in his second book, that contrasts strangely with the heroic Cicero of De Maria, brave and wise, a symbol of civilization against animal violence. In each case the historical data have been subordinated to the novelist's requirements.

Finally, two details in Benton, neither exploited for the purposes of the plot, may betray a more recent non-fictional origin. First, his Clodia waxes sarcastic about 'a men's world' and tells Caelius that 'women are beginning to get what they want'; second, Clodius is supposed to have drafted a law in 52 decreeing the mass liberation of slaves. It is true that Clodia as an emancipated woman is standard material, and that Clodius as a freer of slaves (an idea evidently garbled from two passages in the *Pro Milone*) had made an inconspicuous appearance in one of Lindsay's novels,[33] but my guess is that Benton was specifically influenced by a recent, and distinguished, source.

---

[29] Hardy 1938.353, 1957.18; Benton 1974.55.

[30] Garrod 1912.xvi ('Celtic influence' in Transpadane Italy), xix ('Celticism' in Virgil), xix and xxiv (Catullus' 'Celtic temperament'). The tacit premise, certainly false (see Section 5.3 above), is that the *Transpadani* of the mid-first century BC were ethnic Gauls.

[31] Hardy 1938.184; Beesly 1865.176 = 1878.19; cf. *Julius Caesar* 1.2.243–4. Beesly was certainly aware that the Torquati were patricians too.

[32] Cf. Beesly 1866.422 = 1878.42: 'I cannot forget ... that he hired himself to do the work of a vile party.'

[33] Lindsay 1939.321 ('Clodius ... threatening mysteriously to raise the slaves and create a new kind of equalitarian [*sic*] state'); cf. Cicero *Pro Milone* 87 and 89, with Asconius 52C, who gives the real, undramatic, meaning (Treggiari 1969.265–6).

In the *Sunday Times Magazine* for 9 March 1969 there appeared an article on Clodius and Clodia by Brigid Brophy (1929–95). Her final section is worth quoting at length:[34]

> What I have called the left wing at Rome is often called the democratic party. In a modern sense, however, there was not a democracy at all, because two sections of the population were utterly disenfranchised: women and slaves. Clodia and Clodius were, respectively, their partisans.
>
> The frustration the siblings experienced was one that's common today when people with rational arguments to put or just rights to assert feel that 'the system' denies them a route to an unprejudiced public hearing or to expression in political power. Their protest has to be made in terms of gesture. As the frustration builds up, the gestures become more conspicuous.
>
> Psychologically, I don't doubt, Clodia's compulsive sexual promiscuity expressed the fact she was in love with her brother. But she turned the quirks of her personal psychology to rational and social account. She was in the habit of charging her lovers a *quadrans* – the small coin that was the admission charge to the public baths: comment, by telling gesture, on women's status at Rome.
>
> Clodius was driven to gestures less defensible because violent. All the same, his was a small-scale violence if you compare it with the violence perpetrated by the system he was protesting against, which treated human beings as things. Clodius intended, in the praetorship he didn't live to win, to legislate to make freedmen citizens. But he also, Cicero says, explicitly promised liberty to slaves.

Brophy goes on to suggest that Clodius deserves to be considered as the inventor of democratic socialism. She concludes:

> Had Clodius achieved power, Cicero told a jury, the goodies [i.e., the *boni*] wouldn't have been able to call their goods their own and would have been handed over to their own human goods, their slaves. When Milo was prosecuted for the affray, Cicero's defence was that to kill Clodius was a public service. Nowadays I think it looks more as if Milo killed Rome's last and best hope, and delivered the civilized world over to the inevitability of Caesar and the Caesars.

Not even Beesly went as far as that.

* * *

[34] Brophy 1969.37.

However much historians may cavil at her interpretation, a novel on Clodia by the author of *Flesh* and *King of a Rainy Country* would be worth all the others put together.[35] But major writers (to exclude Lindsay unkindly from their company), if they deal with Clodia's story at all, have conspicuously avoided making it the subject of a full-scale novel, no doubt instinctively avoiding the pitfalls of melodrama and triviality. Four examples show how they preferred to work.

Marcel Schwob (1867–1905), polyglot scholar and littérateur, was already a major literary figure in Paris by his middle twenties as a result of his work on Villon and his collections of short stories: Edmond de Goncourt was enthusiastic about his 'magical' evocations of antiquity;[36] Colette found his work so perfect it made her skin tingle.[37] In July 1894 he began contributing to *Le Journal* a series of pieces on historical characters, from Burke and Hare to Empedocles, which he collected in a volume called *Vies imaginaires* (1896). One of them was on Clodia, *matrone impudique*.

For Schwob, biography was above all an art form, and thus quite different from history. Unlike history, 'l'art est à l'opposé des idées générales, ne décrit que l'individuel, ne désire que l'unique. Il ne classe pas: il déclasse.' He admired Plutarch with reservations, but preferred Athenaeus, Aulus Gellius and Diogenes Laertius for the details needed to express the 'uniqueness' of characters from antiquity. Boswell was too all-embracing, lacking the 'aesthetic courage' to choose only the singular detail; John Aubrey, with his wealth of personal minutiae, utterly insignificant on any level but that of the individual's own unique nature, would have been the ideal biographer if only his style had matched his technique.[38] All the same, Aubrey's compilations were some distance from what Schwob proposed:

> L'art du biographe consiste justement dans le choix. Il n'a pas à se préoccuper d'être vrai; il doit créer dans un chaos de traits humains.

---

[35] 'What I *really* want to see is a big Clodius and Clodia *musical* ...' (Brigid Brophy to author, 13 August 1975).

[36] 'Mon cher Schwob, Vous êtes le résurrectioniste le plus merveilleux, le plus illusionnant du passé; vous êtes l'évocateur magique de l'antiquité, de cette antiquité *héliogabalesque* à laquelle vont les imaginations des penseurs et les pinceaux des peintres, de ces decadences et de ces fins de vieux mondes, mystérieusement perverses et macabres' (letter of 1893, quoted by Champion 1927.79).

[37] 'J'ai ici tes admirables *Vies imaginaires*, heureusement, et la perfection irritante de quelques-unes me fait mal dans les cheveux et les picotements dans les mollets ...' (quoted by Champion 1927.283).

[38] Schwob 1896.3, 4-5; this preface was reprinted as 'L'art de la biographie' in Schwob's *Spicilège* (1896) and *La lampe de Psyche* (1903).

Biography chooses what it needs from the details collected by the historians, in order to compose 'une forme qui ne ressemble à aucune autre . . . unique, comme toute autre création'.[39]

If biography is an art form, then as in any other the artist must be free to create – not only by selection and arrangement but by the invention of 'unique' details if they are lacking in the historical record, or by the alteration of that record to achieve a more aesthetically satisfying result. 'Truth need not be his preoccupation.' If the biographer wants to give Petronius a career and a death among the vagabonds and criminals who were always close to Schwob's heart, he does so, and calls Tacitus' narrative a false report.[40] His *Lives* are, as he called them, imaginary lives.

So it is with Clodia, whose love for her effeminate little brother is made the main theme of her life. The sources for her story are Plutarch, Appian, Cicero and Catullus, but several details are altered, no doubt deliberately, and there is one major change, the death of Clodius. He is given a death in the dark: trying to burn down Milo's house one night (apparently in 56, though the chronology is unclear), he is killed by the slave watchmen. Clodia, in her desperation, sinks to the gutter level reached by so many of Schwob's characters.[41] She too dies in the night, and the last few sentences of her story give some hint of the dream-like effect Schwob achieves by his mixture of real and imaginary material, as if the historical characters were seen through frosted glass:[42]

> Elle périt vers le matin d'une nuit étouffante.... Un ouvrier foulon l'avait payee d'un quart d'as; il la guetta au crepuscule de l'aube dans l'allée, pour le lui reprendre, et l'étrangla. Puis il jeta son cadavre, les yeux grands ouverts, dans l'eau jaune de la Tibre.

* * *

The *Vies imaginaires* were translated (with horrendous inaccuracy) in the United States in 1924, and the 'Clodia' also appeared in an American collection of short stories published in 1944,[43] but it does not seem to have influenced any of the English-speaking novelists who wrote about her. However, Schwob's anti-historical technique is very similar to that of

---

[39] Schwob 1896.8–9; cf. Trembley 1969.101–13.   [40] Schwob 1896.30.

[41] Compare his Crates, Petronius and Katherine *la dentellière*. (Clodius' transvestite youth is paralleled by an episode in the life of Gabriel Spencer; his incendiarism recalls that of Herostratus.)

[42] Schwob 1895 = 1896.86–7.

[43] *Imaginary Lives*, trans. Lorimer Hammond (New York: Boni and Liveright); the same translation in Lockridge 1944.87–90.

Thornton Wilder (1897–1975) in *The Ides of March*, which appeared in 1948.

Wilder called his book 'a fantasia on certain events and persons of the last days of the Roman republic', and gave Clodia an important role only by the bold expedient of transferring the Bona Dea sacrilege (and the literary career of Catullus) down to 45–44 BC, to form part of Caesar's reflections on love, religion, government and destiny in the last months of his life.[44] By this means he linked Clodia's story to the profounder theme of Caesarism,[45] but in precisely the opposite way to that employed by his lesser contemporaries, particularly Hardy. Theirs is a tacit anachronism, retrojecting the imperial ambitions of Caesar into the 60s or even 70s BC ('the Destiny of Caesar' is another of Hardy's capitalized abstractions), and linking them with a falsely political Clodia in a way that masquerades as genuine history; Wilder, like Schwob, openly claims the right to alter historical data for the sake of his work of art, and applies it to the less important theme by moving Clodia into the milieu of 'imperial Caesar' rather than vice versa.

Although no closer to the truth than his judicious, patient, even-tempered, puritanical Catullus,[46] Wilder's Clodia is a splendid portrait. Traumatically raped by her uncle at the age of twelve, she wreaks her hatred and vengeance on the world and on herself, fascinating men in order to learn their weaknesses and ruin them the more thoroughly. There is no cheap melodrama – no murder, no incest:

> Not only did I not kill my poor husband, but I got down on my knees and begged him not to kill himself with overeating. I have never felt a tremor of passion for you [Clodius] ... ; in fact, I have too often gazed with astonishment at the starved water-rats that committed themselves to finding you attractive.

But there is horror enough in her character without any such superficial aids. She is a woman, as Caesar is made to put it, 'who has lost intelligible meaning to herself and lives only to impress the chaos of her soul on all that surrounds her'.[47]

The subordination of Clodia to the imperial theme is even more marked in the work of the two other distinguished novelists who have used her as a

---

[44] Ten years later, aware that this summary did not do justice to Wilder's great novel, I tried to provide something more adequate (Wiseman 1985.235–41).

[45] The preface and the dedication show that Italian Fascism was part of the origin of the book.

[46] As incredible as the names of his friends: Ficinius Mela, Lucius Calco, Mamilius Torquatus, Horbatius Cinna. And Clodia is 'Clodia Pulcher' throughout.

[47] Wilder 1948.156, 25.

character. Alfred Duggan (1903–64), writing the story of Lepidus in *Three's Company* (1958), brings her in as a kind of chorus at the end of every chapter, a bored social butterfly with a new young man each time, hoping 'in a few years we shall be gay and smart again'.[48] Rex Warner (1905–86) shows her again through Caesar's eyes, in the superb 'memoirs' of the dictator that he published as *The Young Caesar* (1958) and *Imperial Caesar* (1960; the two were combined as *Julius Caesar* in 1967). Most of Warner's work has been concerned in one way or another with power, but he is also a poet, and one who has himself been influenced by Catullus.[49] So it is not surprising that his magnificent impersonation of Caesar, dry, balanced and detached, should incidentally provide an elegantly economical treatment of Clodia and her lovers in just a few laconic paragraphs where she impinges on Caesar's theme.[50]

Warner's austere account is, no doubt, liable to the complaints Lindsay made of Robert Graves; it does not at all 'body forth the living past' in Hardy's sense; and Tyrrell would certainly have found it an insufficiently imaginative 'romance'. But the historical novelist has obligations to Clio as well as to the unnamed Muse of the novelist's art, and Warner has made his work approximate more closely than most to proper history – not only in its form, narrative without dialogue, but also in its content, dictated solely by the sources. It might reasonably be argued that such severity is the only honest way to deal with characters on whom more or less adequate historical information exists, unless, like Schwob and Wilder, the novelist explicitly announces that for them Clio's rules have been suspended.

'More or less adequate historical information' – there's the rub, so far as Clodia is concerned. All the writers we have looked at – good, less good and downright dire – have taken for granted the historical reconstruction worked out by Ludwig Schwabe in 1862, that Clodia the wife of Metellus was Catullus' 'Lesbia' and that he loved her in the years 62–59 BC, before her husband died. But it is only a hypothesis, and there are strong arguments against it,[51] even though some professional classicists assume an uncritical freedom to accept it that is more appropriate to the historical

[48] At the time of writing I was unaware of the subtle essay in which Duggan emphasized the importance of avoiding hindsight: 'the province of the historical novelist is to investigate the might-have-beens, to show a past where the future is still in the balance' (Duggan 1964.11).

[49] Warner 1945.54: sonnet no. xviii is based on Catullus 8 and 76.

[50] Warner 1958.149 (on her sister, Lucullus' wife), 276–7 (on Catullus' arrival in Rome), 310 (on the death of Metellus Celer); Warner 1960.265–6 (on the death of Caelius Rufus). See now Treggiari 2019.304–5 on Warner.

[51] As I tried to point out in Wiseman 1969.42–60 and 1974.104–14; see now Section 1.1 above.

novelist.[52] Perhaps the next imaginative writer who tries to get behind Clodia's burning eyes (and let it be a woman, for a change) will tackle the more difficult job of being fair to the *evidence*, and not just to Schwabe's seductive theory.

Postscript

When this piece was published in 1975, most of the authors discussed were still alive and some were interested enough to respond to it.[53] Wilder was particularly generous,[54] with an enjoyably brutal view of the genre he had himself adorned:

> Since writing that book I have read the excellent one by György Lukács on *The Historical Novel* [1955] – fine suggestions about how to write a historical novel but making it (unwittingly) clear that the historical novel is a dead horse.

In the meantime, the late republic has provided fertile ground for a variety of novelists, notably Colleen McCullough (1937–2015),[55] Allan Massie (1938–),[56] Steven Saylor (1956–),[57] and Robert Harris (1957–).[58]

The hope expressed in my closing sentence has not, of course, been fulfilled: technical arguments about what the evidence can and cannot tell us are not likely to worry the novelists when they seem not to worry the professionals.[59] Where Clodia Metelli appears, she is still assumed to be Catullus' Lesbia. Allan Massie brings her in as a gratuitous addition to the plot of *Caesar*, and readers who happen to be familiar with Gilbert Highet's *Poets in a Landscape* will know immediately where his description of the trial of Caelius comes from.[60] Stephen Saylor, who devotes the

---

[52] See, for instance, Zarker 1972–3.107: 'For the purposes of this paper the traditional identification of Lesbia with Clodia, sister of Publius Clodius Pulcher and wife of Q. Metellus Celer will be used' (with no reference to any other view). That type of formula became very familiar in the subsequent fifty years (Section 1.2 above).

[53] See above, nn. 13 and 35.

[54] Thornton Wilder to author, 17 October 1975, also quoted in Wiseman 1985.235.

[55] *The First Man in Rome* (1990), *The Grass Crown* (1991), *Fortune's Favourites* (1993), *Caesar's Women* (1996), *Caesar: Let the Dice Fly* (1997), *The October Horse* (2002), *Antony and Cleopatra* (2007); see Treggiari 2019.307–9.

[56] *Augustus* (1986), *Caesar* (1993), *Antony* (1997); see Treggiari 2019.309.

[57] *Roman Blood* (1991), *Arms of Nemesis* (1992), *Catilina's Riddle* (1993), *The Venus Throw* (1995), *A Murder on the Appian Way* (1996), *The House of the Vestals* (1997), *Rubicon* (1999), *Last Seen in Massilia* (2000), *A Mist of Prophecies* (2002), *The Judgment of Caesar* (2004), *A Gladiator Only Dies Once* (2005), *The Triumph of Caesar* (2008), *The Throne of Caesar* (2018).

[58] *Imperium* (2007), *Lustrum* (2010), *Dictator* (2016); see Treggiari 2019.309–10.

[59] See Section 1.2 above.   [60] Massie 1993.41–9, esp. 42–3 from Highet 1957.49–50.

fourth of his Gordianus whodunits to Clodia and the Caelius trial, is much
better informed; but even he uses the traditional Catullus story.[61] So too
do Benita Kane Jaro (*The Key*, 1988), Tom Holland (*Attis*, 1995),
Michelle Lovric (*The Floating Book*, 2003) and Helen Dunmore
(*Counting the Stars*, 2008), four writers who have found spectacularly
varied ways to exploit Catullus and Clodia Metelli in their fiction.[62]

The latest participants in this time-honoured masquerade are Daisy
Dunn (*Catullus' Bedspread*) and Frederic Raphael (*A Thousand Kisses*),[63]
two authors who could hardly be more different from each other, but who
share the same ambition – to recreate Catullus' life and times for a twenty-
first-century readership. Both books offer plenty of scope for pointing out
historical misconceptions, but that would hardly be worth doing. Fiction
has its own priorities,[64] and historical novelists can work only with what
the historians tell them. If the historians come to take a different view –
and in this book it is my urgent recommendation that they should – no
doubt in due course the creative writers will want to use that.

---

[61] Saylor 1995.197 (meets Clodia Metelli in Verona in 62 BC), 367 (dies in 54).

[62] For Jaro, Lovric and Dunmore, see Theodorakopoulos 2013.

[63] Dunn 2016, hyped by Paul Cartledge as well as Boris Johnson; Raphael 2019, developed from a
BBC radio play broadcast in 2010.

[64] As Raphael's Calvus observes, having just made up a quote from Archilochus, 'Nothing shines like
pristine counterfeit. All literature is second cousin to a swindle' (Raphael 2019.26).

Bibliography

Agnesini, Alex. 2007. *Il carme 62 di Catullo: edizione critica e commento* (Quaderni di 'Paideia' 5). Cesena.

2011. 'Catull. 67, 1s: *incipit* della *ianua* o *explicit* della *coma*?', *Paideia* 66: 521–40.

Azzarello, Giuseppina. 2008. 'Sprecherhinweise in homerischen Papyri', in Sandra Lippert and Maren Schentuleit (eds.), *Graeco-Roman Fayum: Texts and Archaeology* (Wiesbaden): 27–44.

Baehrens, Aemilius. 1878. *Miscellanea critica*. Groningen.

Baker, Ernest A. 1914. *A Guide to Historical Fiction*. London.

Bandelli, Gino. 1990. 'Colonie e municipi delle regioni transpadane in età repubblicana', in *La città nell'Italia settentrionale in età romana* (CEFR 130, Rome): 251–77.

Barchiesi, Alessandro. 1997. *The Poet and the Prince: Ovid and Augustan Discourse*. Berkeley, CA.

2005. 'The Search for the Perfect Book: A PS to the New Posidippus', in Kathryn Gutwiller (ed.), *The New Posidippus: A Hellenistic Poetry Book* (Oxford): 320–42.

Battaglia, Gabriella Bordenache and Emiliozzi, Adriana. 1990. *Le ciste prenestine*, I Corpus: 1.2. Rome.

Baumbach, Manuel and Bär, Silvio (eds). 2012. *Brill's Companion to Greek and Latin Epyllion and Its Reception*. Leiden.

Beard, Mary. 2002. 'Ciceronian Correspondences: Making a Book out of Letters', in T. P. Wiseman (ed.), *Classics in Progress: Essays on Ancient Greece and Rome* (Oxford): 103–44.

Beesly, E. S. 1865. 'Catiline as a Party Leader', *Fortnightly Review* 1.2: 167–84. 1866. 'Cicero and Clodius', *Fortnightly Review* 5.4: 421–44.

Beesly, Edward Spencer. 1878. *Catiline, Clodius, and Tiberius*. London.

Bellandi, Franco. 2007. *Lepos e pathos: Studi su Catullo*. Bologna.

Benton, Kenneth. 1974. *Death on the Appian Way*. London.

Berlin, Isaiah. 1954. *Historical Inevitability*. Oxford.

Bernstein, Frank. 1998. *Ludi publici: Untersuchungen zur Entstehung und Entwicklung der öffentlichen Spiele im republikanischen Rom* (Historia Einzelschriften 119). Stuttgart.

Biffi, Nicola. 1988. *L'Italia di Strabone: Testo, traduzione e commento dei libri V e VI della Geografia*. Genoa.

Bispham, Edward. 2007. *From Asculum to Actium: The Municipalization of Italy from the Social War to Augustus*. Oxford.

Bonaria, Marius (ed.). 1965. *Romani mimi*. Rome.

Bremmer, Jan N. 2005. 'Attis: A Greek God in Anatolian Pessinous and Catullan Rome', in Nauta and Harder 2005: 25–64.

Brommer, Frank. 1978. *Hephaistos: Der Schmiedegott in der antiken Kunst*. Mainz.

Brophy, Brigid. 1969. 'The Beautiful People', *Sunday Times Magazine*, 9 March: 32–37.

Broughton, T. Robert S. 1952. *The Magistrates of the Roman Republic*, vol. 2. New York.

  1986. *The Magistrates of the Roman Republic*, vol. 3 Supplement. Atlanta, GA.

Brunt, P. A. 1988. *The Fall of the Roman Republic and Related Essays*. Oxford.

Butterfield, David. 2021. 'Catullus and Metre', in Du Quesnay and Woodman 2021: 143–66.

Cameron, Alan. 2011. *The Last Pagans of Rome*. New York.

Carandini, Andrea and Cappelli, Rosanna (eds). 2000. *Roma: Romolo, Remo e la fondazione della città*. Milan.

Champion, Pierre. 1927. *Marcel Schwob et son temps*. Paris.

Clausen, Wendell. 1976. '*Catulli Veronensis liber*', *Classical Philology* 71: 37–43.

Coarelli, Filippo. 2019. *Statio: I luoghi di amministrazione nell'antica Roma*. Rome.

Coleman, Kathleen M. (ed.). 2006. *M. Valerii Martialis liber spectaculorum*. Oxford.

Colin, Jean. 1954. 'Les sénateurs et la Mère des dieux aux Megalesia: Lucrèce, IV, 79 (d'après les MSS de Leyde)', *Athenaeum* 32: 346–55.

Cooper, Diana. 1958. *The Rainbow Comes and Goes*. London.

Copley, Frank O. 1957. 'The Unity of Catullus 68: A Further View', *Classical Philology* 52: 29–32.

  1958. 'Catullus *c.* 4: The World of the Poem', *Transactions of the American Philological Association* 89: 9–13.

Cornell, T. J. 1995. *The Beginnings of Rome: Italy and Rome from the Bronze Age to the Punic Wars (c. 1000–264 BC)*. London.

Courtney, E. 1996. 'Catullus' Yacht (Or Was It?)', *Classical Journal* 92: 113–22.

Crawford, Michael H. 1985. *Coinage and Money under the Roman Republic: Italy and the Mediterranean Economy*. London.

Crump, M. Marjorie. 1931. *The Epyllion from Theocritus to Ovid*. Oxford.

Damon, Cynthia. 2021. 'Situating Catullus', in Du Quesnay and Woodman 2021: 7–25.

Degrassi, Atilius (ed.). 1963. *Inscriptiones Italiae*, XIII *Fasti et elogia*, fasc. 2 *Fasti anni Numani et Iuliani*. Rome.

De Maria, Robert. 1965. *Clodia*. New York.

De Melo, Wolfgang David Cirillo (ed.). 2019. *Varro: De lingua Latina*. Oxford.

Devereux, G. 1973. 'The Self-Blinding of Oidipous in Sophokles: *Oidipous Tyrannos*', *Journal of Hellenic Studies* 93: 36–49.

Duff, J. Wight and Duff, Arnold J. (eds). 1934. *Minor Latin Poets* (Loeb Classical Library). Cambridge, MA.

Duggan, Alfred. 1964. 'An Historical Novelist's Approach to History', *Transactions of the Woolhope Naturalists' Field Club, Herefordshire* 38: 5–15.

Dunn, Daisy. 2016. *Catullus' Bedspread: The Life of Rome's Most Erotic Poet*. London.

Du Quesnay, Ian. 2012. 'Three Problems in Poem 66', in Du Quesnay and Woodman 2012: 153–83.

2021. '*Catulli carmina*', in Du Quesnay and Woodman 2021: 167–218.

Du Quesnay, Ian and Woodman, Tony (eds). 2012. *Catullus: Poems, Books, Readers*. Cambridge.

(eds). 2021. *The Cambridge Companion to Catullus*. Cambridge.

Dyck, Andrew R. 2004. *A Commentary on Cicero, De Legibus*. Ann Arbor, MI.

Dyson, Julia T. 2007. 'The Lesbia Poems', in Skinner 2007: 254–75.

Ellis, Robinson. 1889. *A Commentary on Catullus*. Oxford.

Fantuzzi, Marco and Hunter, Richard (eds). 2004. *Tradition and Innovation in Hellenistic Poetry*. Cambridge.

Feeney, Denis. 2012. 'Representation and the Materiality of the Book in the Polymetrics', in Du Quesnay and Woodman 2012: 29–47.

Flower, Harriet I. 2017. *The Dancing Lares and the Serpent in the Garden: Religion at the Roman Street Corner*. Princeton, NJ.

Fo, Alessandro (ed.). 2018. *Catullo: le poesie*. Turin.

Fordyce, C. J. (ed.). 1961. *Catullus*. Oxford.

Fowler, D. P. 1986. Review of Wiseman 1985, *Greece and Rome* 33: 89.

Fraccaro, Plinio. 1957. *Opuscula III: Scritti di topografia e di epigrafia*. Pavia.

Gabba, Emilio (ed.). 1958. *Appiani Bellorum civilium liber primus*. Florence.

Gaisser, Julia Haig. 1993. *Catullus and His Renaissance Readers*. Oxford.

(ed.). 2007. *Oxford Readings in Classical Studies: Catullus*. Oxford.

2009. *Catullus*. Malden, MA.

Gale, Monica R. 2012. 'Putting on the Yoke of Necessity: Myth, Intertextuality and Moral Agency in Catullus 68', in Du Quesnay and Woodman 2012: 184–211.

2021. 'Catullus and Augustan Poetry: *lasciuus Catullus* and the Formation of Latin Love Elegy', in Du Quesnay and Woodman 2021: 219–41.

Gantz, Timothy. 1993. *Early Greek Myth: A Guide to Literary and Artistic Sources*. Baltimore, MD.

Garrod, H. W. (ed.). 1912. *The Oxford Book of Latin Verse*. Oxford.

Giancotti, Francesco. 1967. *Mimo e gnome: studio su Decimo Laberio e Publilio Siro* (Biblioteca di cultura contemporanea 98). Messina.

Gibson, Bruce. 2021. 'Catullan Themes', in Du Quesnay and Woodman 2021: 89–115.

Giuliani, C. F. and Verduchi, P. 1993. 'Basilica Iulia', in Eva Margareta Steinby (ed.), *Lexicon Topographicum Urbis Romae*, vol. 1, A–C (Rome): 177–9.

Goldberg, Sander. 1998. 'Plautus on the Palatine', *Journal of Roman Studies* 88: 1–20.

2011. 'Roman Comedy Gets Back to Basics', *Journal of Roman Studies* 101: 206–21.

Gordon, Arthur E. 1983. *Illustrated Introduction to Latin Epigraphy*. Berkeley, CA.

Gorski, Gilbert J. and Packer, James E. 2015. *The Roman Forum: A Reconstruction and Architectural Guide*. New York.

Gowers, Emily. 2016. 'Performance Art: Were Roman Texts Designed to Be Read Out Loud?', *Times Literary Supplement*, 28 October: 14.

Green, Peter. 2005. *The Poems of Catullus: A Bilingual Edition*. Berkeley, CA.

Greene, Ellen. 1999. *The Erotics of Domination: Male Desire and the Mistress in Latin Love Poetry*. Baltimore, MD.

Haeussler, Ralph. 2007. 'At the Margins of Italy: Celts and Ligurians in North-West Italy', in Guy Bradley, Elena Isayev and Corinna Riva (eds), *Ancient Italy: Regions without Boundaries* (Exeter): 45–78.

2013a. 'De-constructing Ethnic Identities: Becoming Roman in Western Cisalpine Gaul?', in Andrew Gardner, Edward Herring and Kathryn Lomas (eds), *Creating Ethnicities and Identities in the Roman World* (BICS Supplement 120, London): 35–70.

2013b. *Becoming Roman? Diverging Identities and Experiences in Ancient Northwest Italy*. Walnut Creek, CA.

2015. 'The Galli', in Gary D. Farney and Guy Bradley (eds), *The Peoples of Ancient Italy* (Berlin): 719–54.

Hanson, John A. 1959. *Roman Theater-Temples* (Princeton Monographs in Art and Archaeology 33). Princeton, NJ.

Harder, Annette. 2005. 'Catullus 63: A "Hellenistic Poem"?', in Nauta and Harder 2005: 65–86.

Hardy, W. G. 1938. *Turn Back the River*. Toronto.

1957. *The City of Libertines: A Novel of Rome*. Toronto.

Harris, William V. 1991. 'Why Did the Codex Supplant the Book-Roll?', in John Monfasani and Ronald G. Musto (eds), *Renaissance Society and Culture: Essays in Honor of Eugene F. Rice, Jr.* (New York): 71–85.

2007. 'Quando e come l'Italia divenne per la prima volta Italia? Un saggio sulla politica dell'identità', *Studi storici* 48: 301–22.

Harrison, Stephen. 2005. 'Altering Attis: Ethnicity, Gender and Genre in Catullus 63', in Nauta and Harder 2005: 11–24.

2021. 'Catullus and Poetry in English since 1750', in Du Quesnay and Woodman 2021: 343–62.

Hartnett, Jeremy. 2017. *The Roman Street: Urban Life and Society in Pompeii, Herculaneum, and Rome*. New York.

Hejduk, Julia Dyson. 2008. *Clodia: A Sourcebook*. Norman, OK.

Highet, Gilbert. 1957. *Poets in a Landscape*. London.

Hollis, Adrian S. (ed.). 2007. *Fragments of Roman Poetry c. 60 BC–AD 20*. Oxford.

Hölscher, Tonio. 1988. 'Historische Reliefs', in *Kaiser Augustus und die verlorene Republik* (Berlin): 351–400.

Holzberg, Niklas. 2002. *Catull: Der Dichter und sein erotisches Werk*. Munich.

Horsfall, Nicholas. 1985. 'CIL VI 37965 = CLE 1988 (Epitaph of Allia Potestas): A Commentary', *Zeitschrift für Papyrologie und Epigraphik* 61: 251–72.

Howell, Peter. 1980. *A Commentary on Book One of the Epigrams of Martial*. London.

Hubbard, Thomas K. 1983. 'The Catullan *libellus*', *Philologus* 127: 218–37.

2005. 'The Catullan *libelli* Revisited', *Philologus* 149: 253–77.

Hutchinson, G. O. 2003. 'The Catullan Corpus, Greek Epigram, and the Poetry of Objects', *Classical Quarterly* 53: 206–21.

2012. 'Booking Lovers: Desire and Design in Catullus', in Du Quesnay and Woodman 2012: 48–78.

Isayev, Elena. 2007. 'Why Italy?', in Guy Bradley, Elena Isayev and Corinna Riva (eds), *Ancient Italy: Regions without Boundaries* (Exeter): 1–20.

Janko, Richard. 2000. *Philodemus On Poems Book I*. Oxford.

Johnson, William A. 2009. 'The Ancient Book', in Roger S. Bagnall (ed.), *The Oxford Handbook of Papyrology* (Oxford): 256–81.

Kaibel, Georgius (ed.). 1899. *Comicorum Graecorum fragmenta*, I fasc. 1. Berlin.

Kassel, Rudolf and Austin, Colin (eds). 2001. *Poetae comici Graeci (PCG), vol. 1: Comoedia Dorica mimi phlyaces*. Berlin.

Kaster, Robert A. (ed.) 1995. *C. Suetonius Tranquillus: De Grammaticis et Rhetoribus*. Oxford.

Kay, N. M. 1985. *Martial Book XI: A Commentary*. London.

Kenyon, Frederic G. 1951. *Books and Readers in Ancient Greece and Rome*, 2nd ed. Oxford.

Keppie, Lawrence. 1983. *Colonisation and Veteran Settlement in Italy 47–41 B.C.* London.

Kiss, Dániel. 2021. 'Editions and Commentaries', in Du Quesnay and Woodman 2021: 291–317.

Koch, Guntram. 1975. *Die mythologischen Sarkophage 6: Meleager*. Berlin.

Konstan, David. 2007. 'The Contemporary Political Context', in Skinner 2007: 72–91.

Kragelund, Patrick. 2016. Roman Historical Drama: The *Octavia* in Antiquity and Beyond. Oxford.

Kritz, Friedrich (ed.). 1840. *Vellei Paterculi quae supersunt ex historiae Romanae*. Leipzig.

Krostenko, Brian A. 2001. *Cicero, Catullus, and the Language of Social Performance*. Chicago.

Lada-Richards, Ismene. 2008. 'Was Pantomime "good to think with" in the Ancient World?', in Edith Hall and Rosie Wyles (eds), *New Directions in Ancient Pantomime* (Oxford): 285–313.

2013. '*Mutata corpora*: Ovid's Changing Forms and the Metamorphic Bodies of Pantomime Dancing', *Transactions of the American Philological Association* 143: 105–52.

Lindsay, Jack. 1934. *Rome for Sale*. London.

1935. *Last Days with Cleopatra*. London.

1939. *Brief Light: A Novel of Catullus*. London.

1962. *Fanfrolico and After*. London.

Lintott, Andrew. 1968. *Violence in Republican Rome*. Oxford.

Lockridge, Norman (ed.). 1944. *Bachelor's Quarters: Stories from Two Worlds*. New York.

Lomas, Kathryn. 2007. 'The Ancient Veneti: Community and State in Northern Italy', in Guy Bradley, Elena Isayev and Corinna Riva (eds), *Ancient Italy: Regions without Boundaries* (Exeter): 21–44.

2015. 'The Veneti', in Gary D. Farney and Guy Bradley (eds), *The Peoples of Ancient Italy* (Berlin): 701–17.

Lowrie, Michèle. 2010. 'Performance', in Alessandro Barchiesi and Walter Scheidel (eds), *The Oxford Handbook of Roman Studies* (Oxford): 281–94.

Lyne, R. O. A. M. 1978. 'The Neoteric Poets', *Classical Quarterly* 28: 167–87.

Manuwald, Gesine. 2001. *Fabulae praetextae: Spuren einer literarischen Gattung der Römer* (Zetemata 108). Munich.

Maschek, Dominik. 2018. 'Not *Census* but *Deductio*: Reconsidering the '*Ara* of Domitius Ahenobarbus', *Journal of Roman Studies* 108: 27–52.

Massie, Allan. 1993. *Caesar*. London.

McCarthy, Kathleen. 2019. *I, the Poet: First-Person Form in Horace, Catullus, and Propertius*. Ithaca, NY.

Mitchell, Jane F. 1966. 'The Torquati', *Historia* 15: 23–31.

Mueller, L. 1869. 'Der Mimograph Catullus', *Rheinisches Museum* 24: 621–2.

Mulroy, David. 2002. *The Complete Poetry of Catullus*. Madison, WI.

Munro, H. A. J. 1878. *Criticisms and Elucidations of Catullus*. London.

Nauta, Ruurd R. 2005. 'Catullus 63 in a Roman Context', in Nauta and Harder 2005: 87–119.

Nauta, Ruurd R. and Harder, Annette (eds). 2005. *Catullus' Poem on Attis: Text and Contexts*. Leiden.

Neudling, C. L. 1955. *A Prosopography to Catullus*. Oxford.

Newlands, Carole. 2021. 'Rewriting Catullus in the Flavian Age', in Du Quesnay and Woodman 2021: 242–62.

Nield, Jonathan. 1929. *A Guide to the Best Historical Novels and Tales*, 5th ed. London.

Nisbet, R. G. M. (ed.). 1961. *M. Tulli Ciceronis in L. Calpurnium Pisonem oratio*. Oxford.

North, J. A. 2008. 'Caesar at the Lupercalia', *Journal of Roman Studies* 98: 144–60.

Oakley, S. P. 2021. 'The Manuscripts and Transmission of the Texts', in Du Quesnay and Woodman 2021: 263–90.

Olson, S. Douglas. 2007. *Broken Laughter: Select Fragments of Greek Comedy.* Oxford.

O'Neill, Peter. 2003. 'Going Round in Circles: Popular Speech in Ancient Rome', *Classical Antiquity* 22: 135–76.

Osgood, Josiah. 2006. *Caesar's Legacy: Civil War and the Emergence of the Roman Empire.* Cambridge.

Panayotakis, Costas (ed.). 2010. *Decimus Laberius: The Fragments* (Cambridge Classical Texts and Commentaries 46). Cambridge.

Papi, E. 1999. 'Tabernae argentariae', 'Tabernae circa forum', in Eva Margareta Steinby (ed.), *Lexicon Topographicum Urbis Romae*, vol. 5, T–Z (Rome): 10–13.

Paris, Rita, Bruni, Silvia and Roghi, Miria (eds). 2014. *Rivoluzione Augusto: L'imperatore che riscrisse il tempo e la città.* Milan.

Purcell, Nicholas 1990. 'The Creation of a Provincial Landscape: The Roman Impact on Cisalpine Gaul', in T. F. C. Blagg and Martin Millett (eds), *The Early Roman Empire in the West* (Oxford): 6–29.

Quinn, Kenneth (ed.) 1970. *Catullus: The Poems.* London.
   1972. *Catullus: An Interpretation.* London.

Raphael, Frederic. 2019. *A Thousand Kisses.* Newbury.

Rawson, Elizabeth. 1991. *Roman Culture and Society: Collected Papers.* Oxford.

Roffia, Elisabetta. 2018. *Le 'Grotte di Catullo' a Sirmione: Guida alla visita della villa romana e del museo.* Brescia.

Roller, Duane W. 2018. *A Historical and Topographical Guide to the Geography of Strabo.* Cambridge.

Rosen, Ralph M. and Farrell, Joseph. 1986. 'Acontius, Milanion, and Gallus: Vergil, *Ecl.* 10.52–61', *Transactions of the American Philological Association* 116: 241–54.

Rudd, Niall. 1966. *The Satires of Horace.* Cambridge.

Sauron, Gilles. 1987. 'Le complexe pompéien du Champ de Mars: nouveauté urbanistique à finalité idéologique', in *L'Urbs: Espace urbain et histoire (Iᵉʳ siècle av. J.C. – IIIᵉ siècle ap. J.C.)* (Collection de l'École française de Rome 98, Rome): 457–73.

Saylor, Steven. 1995. *The Venus Throw.* New York.

Schafer, John K. 2020. *Catullus through His Books: Dramas of Composition.* Cambridge.

Schmidt, Eva Maria. 1997. 'Venus', *Lexicon Iconographicum Mythologiae Classicae* 8.1: 192–230.

Schröder, Bianca-Jeanette. 1999. *Titel und Text: Zur Entwicklung lateinischer Gedichtüberschriften* (Untersuchungen zur antiken Literatur und Geschichte 54). Berlin.

Schwabe, Ludwig. 1862. *Quaestiones Catullianae.* Giessen.
   1870. 'Zu Varro', *Jahrbücher für classische Philologie* 101: 350–2.

Schwob, Marcel. 1895. 'Clodia, matrone impudique', *Le Journal* (Paris), 11 November: 1.
   1896. *Vies imaginaires.* Paris.

Sear, Frank. 2006. *Roman Theatres: An Architectural Study*. Oxford.

Shackleton Bailey, D. R. 1960. *Towards a Text of Cicero, Ad Atticum*. Cambridge.

 (ed.). 1977. *Cicero: Epistulae ad familiares*, vol. 1 (Cambridge Classical Texts and Commentaries 16). Cambridge.

 1991. *Two Studies in Roman Nomenclature* (American Classical Studies 3). Atlanta, GA.

 (ed.). 1993. *Martial: Epigrams* (Loeb Classical Library 480). Cambridge, MA.

Shaw, Brent D. 1987. 'The Age of Roman Girls at Marriage: Some Reconsiderations', *Journal of Roman Studies* 77: 30–46.

Sheets, George A. 2007. 'Elements of Style in Catullus', in Skinner 2007: 190–211.

Skinner, Marilyn B. 1981. *Catullus' Passer: The Arrangement of the Book of Polymetric Poems*. New York.

 (ed.). 2007. *A Companion to Catullus*. Malden, MA.

 2011. *Clodia Metelli: The Tribune's Sister*. New York.

 2015. 'A Review of Scholarship on Catullus, 1985–2015', *Lustrum* 57: 91–360.

Skutsch, O. 1969. 'Metrical Variations and Some Textual Problems in Catullus', *Bulletin of the Institute of Classical Studies* 16: 38–43.

Stegmann, Helena. 2003. 'Clodia [1]', *Brill's New Pauly: Antiquity* 3 (Leiden): 463–4.

Sutherland, C. H. V. 1984. *The Roman Imperial Coinage*, 2nd ed., vol. 1. London.

Syme, Ronald. 1968. 'People in Pliny', *Journal of Roman Studies* 58: 135–51.

 1979. *Roman Papers*, vols. 1–3. Oxford.

 1988. *Roman Papers*, vol. 4. Oxford.

 1991. *Roman Papers*, vol. 6. Oxford.

Syndikus, Hans Peter. 1987. Review of Wiseman 1985, *Journal of Roman Studies* 77: 247–50.

 1990. *Catull: Eine Interpretation. Zweiter Teil: Die grossen Gedichte (61–68)* (Impulse der Forschung 48). Darmstadt.

Taplin, Oliver. 1993. *Comic Angels and Other Approaches to Greek Drama through Vase-Paintings*. Oxford.

Tatum, W. Jeffrey. 1991. 'The Marriage of Pompey's Son to the Daughter of Ap. Claudius Pulcher', *Klio* 73: 122–9.

Theodorakopoulos, Elena. 2007. 'Poem 68: Love and Death, and the Gifts of Venus and the Muses', in Skinner 2007: 314–32.

 2013. 'Catullus and Lesbia Translated in Women's Historical Novels', in Lorna Hardwick and Stephen Harrison (eds), *Classics in the Modern World: A Democratic Turn?* (Oxford): 275–86.

Thomas, Richard F. (ed.). 2011. *Horace Odes Book IV and Carmen Saeculare*. Cambridge.

Thomson, D. F. S. 1997. *Catullus Edited with a Textual and Interpretative Commentary* (*Phoenix* Supplementary Volume 34). Toronto.

Torelli, Mario. 1982. *Typology and Structure of Roman Historical Reliefs* (Jerome Lectures 14). Ann Arbor, MI.

Tortorella, Stefano. 2000. 'L'adolescenza dei gemelli, la festa dei *Lupercalia* e l'uccisione di Amulio', in Andrea Carandini and Rosanna Capelli (eds), *Roma: Romolo, Remo e la fondazione della città* (Milan): 244–55.

Townend, G. B. 1987. Review of Wiseman 1985, *Classical Review* 37: 13–15.

Tozzi, Pierluigi. 1988. 'L'Italia settentrionale di Strabone', in Gianfranco Maddoli (ed.), *Strabone e l'Italia antica* (Naples): 23–43.

Treggiari, Susan. 1969. *Roman Freedmen during the Late Republic*. Oxford.

2019. *Servilia and Her Family*. Oxford.

Trembley, George. 1969. *Marcel Schwob: faussaire de la nature*. Geneva.

Trendall, A. D. 1967. *The Red-Figured Vases of Lucania, Campania and Sicily*. Oxford.

Trimble, Gail. 2012. 'Catullus 64: The Perfect Epyllion?', in Baumbach and Bär 2012: 55–79.

Tyrrell, R. Y. and Purser, L. C.. 1890. *The Correspondence of M. Tullius Cicero, Arranged According to Its Chronological Order*, vol. 3. Dublin.

Ullman, B. L. 1917. 'Horace on the Nature of Satire', *Transactions of the American Philological Association* 48: 111–32.

Usener, Hermann. 1892. 'Ein altes Lehregebäude der Philologie', *Sitzungsber. k. bayr. Ak. d. Wiss.* 4: 582–648.

1913. *Kleine Schriften*, vol. 2. Leipzig.

Vermaseren, Maarten J. 1977. *Cybele and Attis: The Myth and the Cult*. London.

Vermeule, Cornelius C. and Comstock, Mary. 1988. *Sculpture in Stone and Bronze in the Museum of Fine Arts, Boston: Additions to the Collections of Greek, Etruscan and Roman Art, 1971–1988*. Boston.

Vinson, James. 1972. *Contemporary Novelists*. London.

Viscogliosi, A. 1996. 'Neptunus: aedes in Circo', in Eva Margareta Steinby (ed.), *Lexicon Topographicum Urbis Romae*, vol. 3, H–O (Rome): 341–2.

Von Rohden, H. and Winnefeld, H. 1911. *Architektonische römische Tonreliefs der Kaiserzeit*. Berlin.

Vretska, Karl. 1966. 'Das Problem der Einheit von Catull c. 68', *Wiener Studien* 79: 313–30.

Wallace-Hadrill, Andrew. 1983. *Suetonius: The Scholar and His Caesars*. London.

2011. *Herculaneum: Past and Future*. London.

Warner, Rex. 1945. *Poems and Contradictions*. London.

1958. *The Young Caesar*. London.

1960. *Imperial Caesar*. London.

White, Peter. 2009. 'Bookshops in the Literary Culture of Rome', in William A. Johnson and Holt N. Parker (eds), *Ancient Literacies: The Culture of Reading in Greece and Rome* (New York): 268–87.

Wilamowitz-Moellendorf, Ulrich von. 1913. *Sappho und Simonides*. Berlin.

1921. *Griechische Verskunst*. Berlin.

Wilder, Thornton. 1948. *The Ides of March*. New York.

Williams, Gordon. 1968. *Tradition and Originality in Roman Poetry*. Oxford.

Williams, J. H. C. 2001. *Beyond the Rubicon: Romans and Gauls in Republican Italy*. Oxford.

Wilson, Edmund. 1952. *Shores of Light: A Literary Chronicle of the Twenties and Thirties*. New York.

Wiseman, T. P. 1969. *Catullan Questions*. Leicester.

1970. 'Pulcher Claudius', *Harvard Studies in Classical Philology* 74: 207–21.

1974. *Cinna the Poet and Other Roman Essays*. Leicester.

1979. *Clio's Cosmetics: Three Studies in Greco-Roman Literature*. Leicester.

1980. 'Looking for Camerius: The Topography of Catullus 55', *Papers of the British School at Rome* 48: 6–16.

1982. '*Pete nobiles amicos*: Poets and Patrons in Late-Republican Rome', in Barbara K. Gold (ed.), *Literary and Artistic Patronage in Ancient Rome* (Austin, TX): 28–49.

1985. *Catullus and His World: A Reappraisal*. Cambridge.

1987. *Roman Studies Literary and Historical*. Liverpool.

1988. 'Satyrs in Rome? The Background to Horace's *Ars poetica*', *Journal of Roman Studies* 78: 1–13.

1992. 'Erridge's Answer: Response to James Zetzel', in Karl Galinsky (ed.), *The Interpretation of Roman Poetry: Empiricism or Hermeneutics?* (Studien zur klassischen Philologie 67, Frankfurt): 58–64.

1995. *Remus: A Roman Myth*. Cambridge.

1998. *Roman Drama and Roman History*. Exeter.

2004. *The Myths of Rome*. Exeter.

2007. 'The Valerii Catulli of Verona', in Skinner 2007: 57–71.

2008. *Unwritten Rome*. Exeter.

2009. *Remembering the Roman People: Essays on Late Republican Politics and Literature*. Oxford.

2014. 'Suetonius and the Origin of Pantomime', in T. J. Power and R. K. Gibson (eds), *Suetonius the Biographer* (Oxford): 256–72.

2015. *The Roman Audience: Classical Literature as Social History*. Oxford.

2017. 'Life in the Street, or Why Historians Should Read the Poets', *Syllecta Classica* 28: 81–110.

2019. *The House of Augustus: A Historical Detective Story*. Princeton, NJ.

Wohlberg, Joseph. 1955. 'The Structure of the Laodamia-Simile in Catullus 68b', *Classical Philology* 50: 42–6.

Woodman, Tony. 2012. 'A Covering Letter: Poem 65', in Du Quesnay and Woodman 2012: 130–52.

Woolf, Greg. 1998. *Becoming Roman: The Origins of Provincial Civilization in Gaul*. Cambridge.

Wray, David. 2001. *Catullus and the Poetics of Roman Manhood*. Cambridge.

Wrede, Henning. 1995. 'Der Venus Felix peinvolles Schicksal im Lupercal', *Römische Mitteilungen* 102: 345–8.

Zahlhaas, Gisela. 1975. *Römische Reliefspiegel* (Kataloge der Prähistorischen Staatssammlung München 17). Munich.

Zanker, Paul and Ewald, Björn C. 2012. *Living with Myths: The Imagery of Roman Sarcophagi.* Oxford.

Zarker, John W. 1972–3. 'Lesbia's Charms', *Classical Journal* 68.2: 107–15.

Zetzel, James E. G. 1988. Review of Wiseman 1985, *Classical Philology* 83: 80–4.

1992. 'Roman Romanticism and Other Fables', in Karl Galinsky (ed.), *The Interpretation of Roman Poetry: Empiricism or Hermeneutics?* (Studien zur klassischen Philologie 67, Frankfurt): 41–57.

Zwierlein, Otto. 1966. *Die Rezitationsdramen Senecas* (Beiträge zur klassischen Philologie 20). Meisenheim am Glan.

Index

Index Locorum

CPSIA information can be obtained
at www.ICGtesting.com
Printed in the USA
LVHW010459181022
730943LV00006B/334

9 781009 235747